SICILIAN ESCAPADE

SICILIAN ESCAPADE

A Devil in Eden

MILTON PASHCOW

Library of Congress Control Number:		2013911541
ISBN:	Hardcover	978-1-4836-5971-8
	Softcover	978-1-4836-5970-1
	Ebook	978-1-4836-5972-5

This book was printed in the United States of America.

Rev. date: 07/13/2013

To order additional copies of this book, contact:
Xlibris LLC
1-888-795-4274
www.Xlibris.com
Orders@Xlibris.com
131028

Acknowledgments

No man is a world unto himself. As man must have his mate, so must he seek encouragement and the help of others to consummate the goal of his personal inner drive.

As a literary trespasser amongst titans, I tiptoed lightly. Under the circumstances, my humility grew more quickly than my conflicting ego.

The memory of my dear departed Sicilian war bride, who knew nothing of my present literary effort but was an integral part, created the real love interest in the diaries I kept.

First, my perceptive and gracious editor, and author in her own right, Marjorie Gillette Jones, was my horizontal balancing pole that kept me on the tightrope of acceptable taste and publication criteria. For her input I am most grateful.

My critical and quick-witted son, Allan, and his beautiful wife, Louise, more daughter than daughter-in-law, had the saintly patience to attend to this very aged widower's comfort and his antipathy toward computers and provided the necessary means of modern communication that is necessary for manuscript publication. They provided an initial proving ground for some of my new phraseology.

Briana and Shannon, my dearest and attractive granddaughters, kept me abreast of present young adult morals that allowed me to expand on some of my original more conservative phrasing. My typists and computer experts, Malinda R. Pater and Lillian Katz, amazed me with dexterity by solving logistic problems I thought were at times insurmountable. My wise-cracking secretary and off-the-record editor Joann Malec also had her worthwhile comments and support, never to be held back: "You need more love interest, boss."

Grateful advice and support from friends who are already experienced in the writing initiation process Dan Barbiero and literary writer Geoff Robson always caught my ear. To **New York Times best-selling author,** Nelson DeMille, a family friend, who graciously offered his support—who could find a greater source of inspiration? Many thanks, Nelson.

Whatever success I may achieve will certainly be through these good friends. To any person I may have overlooked, my regrets and my sincerest appreciation.

Preface

WW I was called the war to end all wars. That optimistic review was proved false all too soon.

December 7, 1941, was the date the Japanese Air Force chose to shatter the peaceful atmosphere of Hawaii, sending countless Americans to their death with their bombs.

President Roosevelt declared war, and the lives of countless Americans changed quickly. Young men and older disappeared from the home scene as they were conscripted to serve in the armed forces.

With so few men in the state, women went to work in jobs that were traditionally men's. For instance, on assembly lines producing planes, tanks, etc. Many necessities that had always been available to the public were in short supply. The government issued special ration stamps permitting limited purchases for sugar, shoes, meat, and other staples.

I was a college grad when war began and worked in a war defense plant that was considered essential. My induction into the armed forces was therefore deferred temporarily. It was two years later when they took me.

The army was notorious for moving people. This Brooklyn boy was sent to Camp Upton, Long Island, for basic indoctrination. That's where you're taught to obey orders, make a tight bed, and wake up at an ungodly hour.

After that, the moving began: Mississippi, North Carolina, North Africa, Sicily, Germany, and France.

In the foreign countries, I felt my name was changed from Milton to Joe. From Casablanca through Italy came the incessant "Hey, Joe, ya got a cigarette, gum, chocolate?" from kids everywhere.

In Casablanca as we disembarked, the ruffians welcomed us with "Hey, Joe, ya want my sister?"

We saw the hollow eyes of hungry children and war-weary adults, human degradation demanding great sacrifice and humiliation from the survivors—a few with surprising resiliency.

To this day, these first impressions have hardly dimmed. For many veterans, it was a life-shattering nightmare. For the lucky ones, it was a great adventure that changed our lives forever.

This is not meant to be a tale of blood and guts, already well chronicled by others and in no way is meant to blunt the sacrifices others have made. I apologize for any such inference made.

I was a draftsman, trained in printing, technical drawing, map reading, etc. We fought the war from behind a desk and faced reality in different ways. Our ingenuity worked overtime in converting our former lifestyle into various schemes that we firmly believed were necessary for our well-being.

From a "Repple Depple" (replacement depot) in Casablanca to the Fifty-First Troop Carrier Wing Headquarters of the Twelfth Air Corps, I was brought eventually close behind front lines to a large city, Catania, Sicily. The important railroad junction, already damaged in that important city, drew occasional air raids by the retreating enemy. Our military appropriated and converted a four-story, unscathed condominium in town as our headquarters. It rarely came under fire.

We lived and worked with the civilians. I marveled at the equanimity and acceptance of the disastrous destruction to property and life. I picked up the basic language quickly and earned their respect for my empathy.

Into this arena as a young Brooklynite, I was unceremoniously dumped. I had the idea that a diary for friends and family should interest them someday.

A common kid rivaling the travels of Marco Polo would put a feather in my cap, my last hurrah. I was wrong. At home everybody was wrapped up in peacetime recovery from shortages and getting back to prewar life. We were happy to see and hug each other, and I was grateful to be home. Mother cried and smiled happily at the same time.

My twelve handwritten pads gathered dust until recently. In my nineties, a hidden desire to spread the facts of the bizarre events experienced on the other side sprouted like a weed. Almost seventy years have elapsed since my last entry. A review of the contents stoked smoldering flames into sad and happy memories—I hope it will bring a lighter side to a conflagration that we must never forget. We played a lot, but we never forgot why we were there.

Three blasts of the ship's horn alerted us to board ship. I was soberly on my way up the gangplank, heavily laden, on the good ship that was to be our home and redoubt for the next twelve days. With no close friends to see me off, I wish myself "Bon voyage."

Chapter I

NEWS HEADLINE: ***September 8, 1943*****—Italians' Surrender to Allies Is Announced**

November 15, 1943

Now our shipping group, number AC-633A, departed at Seymour Johnson Field, North Carolina for parts unknown. Stuffed into large open trucks, we rode through two miles of green, grassy meadows, knowing only we were bound for a train ride. The station was only a dusty shack in a deserted, flat land, sliced only by a double track that led through the boundless landscape straight to the horizon—no Station Master visible.

The lengthy train puffed into the station on time, and we quickly boarded the dilapidated, wooden seated cars. Finally ensconced in our bone-banging, wooden seats, the question arose as it had for the past few hours. "Where in hell are we going?" my nervous buddy asked. "Just relax," I said. Across the aisle a few rows down, I was fortunate in spotting the unofficial clairvoyant of the outfit. "Hey, Charlie!" I bellowed across the rickety clatter as we pulled out. Charlie was revered for his uncanny ability to outguess anybody when it came to secret army movements, and he loved it. Officials were silent on the matter of our destination, which bothered me.

All eyes were turned to the wooden throne on which Charlie sat, his subjects lying prostrate before him. "Where are we headed?" I asked with proper reverence. I was surprised when he didn't answer immediately. "This is a tough one. Considering the strange clothing issued," he hedged but did not explain. Finally, "New York or New Jersey, I would bet."

Our hopes were high until we switched out in Richmond, Virginia, and headed for Camp Patrick Henry for our embarkation, which, finally revealed, was North Africa. Charlie slumped lower in his seat, deflated, and remained silent. We were now restricted to camp. Censorship began: no telephone or letters permitted.

November 22, 1943

There was a short train trip to Hampton Roads, the point of our embarkation. A welcoming brass band greeted us with some coffee warmly dispensed by the lovely Red Cross ladies. Our ship, the *SS Glen Anderson*, was a comparatively large one of heavy tonnage and speed sufficient to outrun a submarine, with four five-inch guns and many 20 mm machine gun turrets. Thus, she was qualified to travel alone without convoy. This also was to be her maiden voyage, hopefully not her last. We were impressed, but not convinced that the trade-off with a convoy was a good idea. Sleeping quarters were tight and crowded. Luggage hung from pipes, beds, and girders. With seven thousand souls aboard, we'd never make it topside, up those narrow stairs, should a torpedo strike.

Anybody without an assigned duty on deck was mainly restricted below. I felt privileged to be on deck and assigned to a 20 mm gun tub for eight hours a day. All our air corps men were advanced detail and were given gunmen and crew lookout assignments. A naval officer welcomed us and hopefully asked, "Anybody here with 20 mm gun training?" Silence. "Well," he sighed. "We'll have to start at the bottom." He then proceeded patiently to demonstrate. The infantry got the KP and other dirty work, and that burned them up. "Hey, butterflies," they razzed us jealously. I was gunner, and another was a loader and one guy a trunnion operator. A telephone operator stayed in touch with the bridge. We strained our eyes for ships, subs, and passed one friendly ship. Our route zigzagged through choppy seas, and we saw nothing else as we neared Casablanca. The ship heaved and tossed, sometimes to a frightening degree. I was seasick for a day or so, but my friend Larry Gittleson, who slept beneath me, was chronically sick all the way. "You'll feel better topside," I suggested. "Maybe they will make an exception." He was too sick to answer.

Leisure time was usually spent sleeping, washing, eating, waiting for ice cream, or crap shooting. I was the unofficial gambling banker with strict orders not to return any winnings during any losing streaks, regardless of their pleadings. I must have had an honest face. The PX, our military goodie shop, had loads of chocolate bars; and we stocked up just in case supplies ran low in Africa. Food was quite good; but in order to save space, we ate standing up, off high shelves instead of at tables. The men on details never had to sweat out the chow line but were led directly up front. We also had three meals while others had only two. Approaching Casablanca Harbor, the ship snaked its way through well-marked routes to avoid any possible undetected mines. We docked before noon, and I had my first look at the bedraggled Arabs standing on the docks.

I was shocked. The poorest men on the New York soup kitchen lines of the Great Depression days were elegantly clad compared to the sight I beheld. Somehow the great majority were "dressed" in illegal white U.S. mattress covers and were used with head and arm holes cut at the closed end. The "uniforms" almost suggested cult gatherings of more peaceful times. They milled about aimlessly.

The original white crisp color had long since been replaced by random streaks of filth, probably as old as the "garment" itself, not one being without holes, tears, and stains. Footwear varied from old, worn ill-fitting rejects to bare feet. They would buy soldiers' goodies with profits on the black market. They had no hesitancy in selling their sisters whom they loudly hawked. The girls were slightly better dressed but didn't seem willing to cooperate. I preferred to think it was not their choice but that they were miserable victims of the fortunes of war. We stood, observing these poor women. "See anything you like, Morty?" I quipped to my friend, who was standing next to me.

He laughed at my question. "Are you nuts? I will never be at sea long enough to need that." We moved on, and I thought how glad I was that the letter *A* stood for American for us and not for Arab.

With no incoming brass band to accompany our debarkation, we piled into trucks and departed to Camp Don B. Passage (named after the first American to die in Morocco). The impoverished Arabs pitifully rode on their bare-backed and over-burdened burros while their wives trudged alongside, barefooted. Numerous beatings to the head and neck were administered to urge the poor animals on.

The immediate approach to camp was drab and flowerless adorned by a weather-beaten wooden arch with the camp name. Morty Rosen gaped at everything and sidled over to me. "This looks more like a cemetery," he joked. "And just as welcome," I added. Camp was a mess of large tents. Beds were something we had to find ourselves. We scavenged unused tents to fill our needs, but *bed* was hardly the word for what we found. There were four-legged wooden frames covered with chicken wire. Supporting metal straps helped. I found a new one, but the great majority were badly torn and almost useless. The first night was torturous, and the next day was spent in repair work. Daytime weather was fair, but night chill required blankets and overcoats to keep warm. We had no electricity. An occasional candle lit the way. On the bright side, Italian prisoners excelled in handling the kitchen and serving work, and were cheerful cooks.

December 9, 1943

Today was our first ride into Casablanca. The original ancient Medina section was off-limits to us and consisted of narrow cobblestone pathways and tunnels. It seemed highly possible to get lost and never find the way out. We did enter but dared only as far as we could find our way back. We shopped for, but only found, low-quality souvenirs in their shallow alcove stores recessed into stone walls. A buggy ride out to the Sultan's beautifully jeweled palace was well worth it. Restaurants were few and open only at mealtime. Lines of people waited. Meat was scarce, and our dinner was poor. However, there was plenty of wine and champagne to compensate.

The city was quite modern looking in sections; but upon close inspection, the cheap, shoddy construction and decorations gave rise to a feeling that they were not quite complete. People seemed engrossed mainly in surviving. Feisty trading took place for every conceivable article of wear, food, or furnishings. An occasional smile followed a good deal. War refugees were present in great numbers and were well dressed compared to the unkempt, languorous Arabs. Few nightlife bistros spotted the empty streets, but a few Arabs were in groups and rolled or attacked drunks in secluded areas. The ARC (American Red Cross) operated a very comfortable snack bar and a theater for just a few francs.

December 10, 1943

In town again, and we've met two teenage boys who spoke Yiddish, which I partly understood (being similar to German) and who led us to their father's nearby upholstery shop. This humble man would have graciously invited us to dinner were it not for the extreme shortage of meat. We would never have imposed on him in any case. We appreciated his gesture and left him with a few packs of cigarettes for which he blessed us.

December 12, 1943

Payroll day! In exchange for our helping out with the payroll paperwork, Morty, Larry Gittleson, and I earned a pass into town. A tropical cloud burst drenched us during a long wait for our pickup truck. Although dripping wet, we stayed in town and bought a few souvenirs and had a fifty-cent meal at the Seaman's Club. According to our in-house clairvoyant, Charlie, this was to be our last visit into town since we would be shipping out. This time he was correct.

Chapter II

NEWS HEADLINE: ***October 14, 1943*****—Italy Declares War on Germany**

December 14, 1943

Tuesday, at about 2:00 p.m., we loaded ourselves into trucks and left for Casablanca station about two miles away. Each truck was loaded with twenty-eight men and a lieutenant—meant for a twenty-foot car. These cars consisted of the old covered "forty and eights" used in World War I (*forty men or eight horses*). It was crowded, and the smell of horses was still discernible.

We arranged to sleep fourteen men on each side of the car, our legs intermeshing. For additional discomfort, a water-filled twenty-gallon water bag hung in the middle of the car. It began to rain about the time that we got aboard, so we immediately issued ourselves cold food rations and made ready for bed. We had no lights except for the candle one of the men brought with him. I had worn-out batteries in my flashlight, recharged with salt water for about a week, but I wanted to save them. The trip was to last eight to ten days, and we expected to be miserable all the way. Wisecracking in the face of adversity was a palliative when there were no other choices. I scoured my brain for good jokes and felt relieved.

Our beds consisted of blankets, instead of mattresses. However, we made the best of it; and amidst typical American wisecracks about living it up at the Waldorf, we settled down to our floor for a night's rest. The two wheeled couplings on the car bumped the hell out of us.

In our arrangement for sleeping, there was not an inch of space for walking. This oversight was quite apparent when several of the fellows had to heed nature's call during the night. Many faces, necks, and legs were stepped on; and many were the groans, grunts and curses that ensued. I distinctly remember standing on a fellow's face for a few seconds before realizing it. He must have been exhausted because he merely snorted and turned over.

December 15, 1943

Countless short stops were made during the night, which made our progress exceedingly slow. At best, we never exceeded twenty-five miles an hour. We arose early in the morning when our rations were issued, and we ate a cold breakfast. There were also a few biscuits enclosed with our rations, which tasted much like dog biscuits. We soaked them in our beverage to make them tolerable.

About 2:00 p.m. in the afternoon, we stopped at Tarza, 250 miles east of Casablanca. During the hour we stayed there, we were once more beset by many villagers, mostly five-year-old children. These kids were a pathetic sight even in this poverty-stricken country where one is not shocked by much. The universal cry, as it was at every stop, was "Hey, Joe! Gimmee bonbon. Hey, Joe! Hey, Joe!" With the train in motion, they would run alongside the cars over sharp broken stones and tin cans with their bare feet. Little girls were quite bashful and would lag behind a little; but their pitiful, wistful expressions would get them more than their fair share of the crackers, candy, and sugar we would toss out of the cars. Helping them lifted our spirits. The boys, on the other hand, were quite bold and persistent, and would follow the train far out of the station, even picking up half-empty ration cans for something to eat. Most of the men couldn't believe the sights before them, but they gradually began to callously shoo them off like flies. Most kids had some kind of injury or sore infestations. All of them had the traditional red-dyed fingernails of their Islam religion. We threw as many bonbons as we could spare, which were immediately tucked away in their ragged clothing for safekeeping. When we rode through open country, children would run along the tracks shouting, "Hey, Joe! Gimmee bonbon!" For them, that was all the English they had to know.

December 16, 1943

We decided on some improvements for sleeping this night by suspending four hammocks, thus alleviating the crowded floor space. At 10:00 a.m. we entered Telemcen, a rather large city. There was a French Red Cross at the station, but we were somewhat afraid to try the native food. At the center of the station was a water pump worked by a revolving wheel and turned by a native boy who was given candy from unknown benefactors. It was here I washed, brushed my teeth, and felt greatly relieved. The latrines available were some filthy outhouses that were quite overfilled, and so we used any semiconcealed place to relieve ourselves. I became interested in a small-stake craps game where I promptly lost sixty cents. It was fun anyway.

When we left Telemcen, we gained altitude quickly and rode through some beautiful mountains and long, sprawling green valleys. Here and there a few Arab mud and straw huts dotted the hillsides. Some of the Arabs close by waved friendly greetings. The train climbed to Sidi Bel Abbès, a comparatively large railroad center.

I think our elevation at this point was at least a few thousand feet because it was very chilly, and occasionally snowcapped mountains came into sight. At one point during a short stop, we jumped off and threw a few snowballs. In spite of having both rear and front engines, the train traveled so slowly uphill that we ran alongside sometimes just for the exercise.

December 17, 1943

Sleeping during the night was only slightly more roomy, but anything helped. At 4:15 p.m. we reached tiny Boufarik. The French Red Cross was nothing like the American Red Cross. It was far simpler, not as clean, and would not be taken for a place to relax. We appreciated it nonetheless. Usually one man and a woman served.

Next stop was when our train entered Maison Carrée. It was the first bombed city seen on the entire trip. Along both sides of the right-of-way lay rows of smashed buildings. Other parts of the city were untouched. Here again we were beset by hordes of running children, but they were not allowed in the station. We remained for an hour or so while another train pulled in. It was very crowded with Arabs, French soldiers, French WACs, and others. They hung on, standing on the running boards outside the doors. When it stopped, a bedlam of people got on and off. In the meantime, also on the platform, one or two heavy craps games were going on; and they stopped for nothing. Arabs were climbing out of the windows with their baskets and their wives, while crowded seated passengers cursed at their disturbance. The craps games were trampled on but never extinguished, and the crap shooters hardly noticed the chaos around the station.

En route again. The cars had an added two-by-four beam across each opening. Four men could lean on each side at a time, while a few others could stand behind. In normal altitudes, there were extensive orange groves, and much of the land was plowed up and not yet cultivated. The soil was rocky, and piles of stones lay near the tracks. Trees were much like ours, yet the bark seemed to be much softer like cork and the trunks dwarfed. There were many fields of grapevines, but to our dismay no grapes. Throughout the countryside, big drainage pathways of stone ran down the slopes of the hills and alongside or under the tracks. They seemed to be the only improvements other than a few bridges and the roads.

December 18, 1943

We were still up in the mountains, at Sétif, another large railroad center. Here we met trainloads of British and French soldiers. In the evening, five or six of us sat around on the blankets. We played ghost, which was a popular word game at that time. Ghost was a very convenient game since it required no props, lights, or space. Each player must add a letter to the continuous formation of a word supplied by the previous player in rotation. He must avoid adding a letter that forms a completed word. For instance *mechani* can go to *mechanization* instead of simply adding a *c* and losing.

December 19, 1943

At 10:30 a.m. we arrived at Guelma where I washed again. Washing was important because we became filthy quickly. Ration cans became covered with soot when heated in an open gasoline fire. Our hands always picked it up, and we would rub our eyes that usually teared as the smoky fire carried it up into our faces. It was quite messy, and that was why many of us looked forward to such a simple benefit as washing. When we did have the chance, we usually filled our helmets at the pump or a leaky pipe on the locomotive. Then we could have water and take it along on the car so as not to be caught washing when the train pulled out of the station—no conductor shouted "All aboard." There were rumors during the day that we might reach our destination, Tunis, tomorrow or the next day for sure. We were quite weary of this hobo's life.

We were awakened by cries of "Tunis! Tunis!" as we slowly entered the once-embattled city outskirts. Most of the shouts were only guesses, but by the boxcar grapevine, the rumor was substantiated in fact. We stopped at seven fifteen with a newsboy running alongside selling a British *Union Jack* newspaper and the *Stars and Stripes*. I read my first news in more than a week. Overhead there were endless formations of all types of friendly planes, and I am certain I was not the only GI who felt reassured. Soon we were off the train with bag and baggage, pulling ourselves and our equipment together.

Tunis had a large station, twelve tracks in width. We noted bomb craters, and many buildings were blown right down to the foundation. Others had their walls leaning at precarious angles while the floors and windows were gone. Morty was now shaving on top of a pile of our clothing while an Arab approached with a horse cart filled with garbage and dumped it into a nearby hole. His interest and attention was on us, however. He was engrossed in the American custom of washing. It was a warm, cloudless day. We hoped for and deserved better new lodgings. An officer quickly dispelled our fears with an announcement that we were going to a nearby camp, and we were all smiles again.

For several hours we did nothing but sit around the tracks, talk, or have a snack of tea and cookies at the Salvation Army canteen. At one, we left for the camp located about fifteen miles from Tunis. The Germans had occupied it before we did. Big red crosses were on the tile roofs but were fast fading and peeling away. We were warned that possible booby traps might still be around and not to mess around with junk piles. I think I vowed to stay still and indoors when I heard that.

These new barracks were a great relief from the boxcar life. We had canvas cots and finally electric lights at night. The light system failed occasionally due to faulty wiring resulting from former bombings and strafing. After arriving we plopped ourselves onto the beds and sometime later arranged our barracks, bags, and clothing. Showers were soon allowed, and Gittleson and myself made sure that we were first on line. The water was cold and the room crowded, but it didn't matter. The one thing we wanted most was to get clean.

The chow was very tolerable, and here at least we had benches and tables whereas in Casablanca we ate standing up. In the evening, Gittleson and I went to the Idle Hour Club, which was mainly a saloon on the post. Glasses consisted of Coca-Cola bottles cut in half. We had some vermouth. Water here tastes much like hydrogen peroxide, which must be the reason that drinking liquor is encouraged. There is no whiskey. I played some poker later with Gittleson and another fellow and lost a few cents. I think I had better give up gambling altogether, not because of the money, but I become depressed.

December 21, 1943

Breakfast at six thirty—hot coffee and cold oatmeal. It was depressing. Wallpaper paste would taste better than cold oatmeal. Luckily I had a can of C rations with me, which saved the meal. We all had plenty of laundry to do, and one Italian prisoner recommended a woman in a small town close by. He smiled. "She's a *bella signorina.*" I knew he had more business with her than just plain laundry. I spoke to her, and everything was arranged. It seemed that the whole village was occupied with washing. We had to supply our own soap. We hoped there were no scabies infestations. Movies here were shown only once a week, and everybody attended. Four or five breakdowns were expected during any performance.

December 22, 1943

We attended an interesting lecture on the history of French North Africa this morning. In the afternoon, a short hike up the nearby hills gave us a good view of the lush countryside. Upon returning, we rested awhile and had supper.

A Christmas program was being arranged. One of the fellows was practicing on his clarinet on the bed next to me. Another had a little too much to drink and was continually jumping out of the bed and running outside to barf.

December 23, 1943

Breakfast came and with it a near mutiny: Today we had cold oatmeal for the second time. We all left the mess hall hungry. Our chef, Sergeant Pesce, said that most of the food was going to Italy.

"Well," I said sarcastically, "let's get to Italy as fast as we can." I had Pesce on the carpet, and he didn't see the humor or like the ridicule. We were all steamed up. "I only cook what they give me," retorted Pesce angrily. "And besides, both stoves broke down. Sorry about the cold oatmeal." "Can't you find some eggs or bacon over here if you look hard enough." I asked. Pesce sympathized, "The brass doesn't always allow shopping. They don't want to leave the civilians short." Fortunately, today we were to get our PX rations for the week, and some of the candy came in very handy. We laughed to think how most of the folks back home thought of the fairly decent meals we boys must be getting over here.

Chapter III

Hot showers this afternoon, and in connection with the upcoming Christmas program, I was approached by the director on the matter of piano playing. I was doubtful. "Am I your last choice?" I asked. "Don't sell yourself short. I've heard you before. You'll be okay, Milt." I needed that. We'd have some sort of rehearsal tomorrow afternoon to see what's what. Seems they think I can do it.

Gee, I wish cigarettes were edible. I managed to get plenty of them. "If they can ship cigarettes, they can ship food and chocolate," I said rhetorically. "What's the matter with the Hershey lobby in Washington anyway?" Well, I still have one can of C rations that I'm hoarding for a real rainy day. I wonder what they'll have for Christmas? Should be good—and so to bed.

December 24, 1943

Breakfast came like a bolt from the blue. Two pieces of French toast, cereal, syrup, and coffee! It seems that a few complaints reached the headquarters, and they are starting bigger rations now. At 1:00 p.m. rehearsal started for the evening show. We only had an hour or so of time, and I was to accompany three singers and a tap dancer. I played songs from old operettas, "Student Prince," and "Naughty Marietta," etc. I was better than I expected. I got myself shaved and dressed in olive drabs, had supper and returned at about six for another hour of practice. I was enjoying the welcome change from routine and had a great time.

There was a large decorated Christmas tree and several bouquets placed about in empty food cans. We had no footlights, only temporary electric lights hung along the entire ceiling of the building. What we really needed was a spotlight. The show is scheduled to start at 8:00 p.m. At seven forty-five, the incoming crowd was pretty noisy and restless, so in response, Lieutenant Jones in charge asked me, "Can you play a couple of songs to keep them amused?" I said, "Okay, if somebody would sing," so one of the older men in the cast with a brusque throaty baritone voice came up willingly and definitely stewed. I later confirmed this when he bent over close to ask me if I knew "No Biz Like Show Biz?" I did, plus several others. Pretty soon his lyrics got slightly off-color, and the lieutenant hopped onto the stage. "Hey, fellas. The chaplain is coming in at any minute, and since it was Christmas, would you please be a little careful?" The singer apologized profusely in true drunken style almost holding himself up by the lieutenant's lapels. Then the lieutenant tried to get me to play alone by telling the singer, who was to come on later in the program, that perhaps he shouldn't strain his voice too much. "My voice is in top shape," he boasted, breathing profusely and exterminating every bug in site, and told the lieutenant that "It's a pleasure and no trouble at all." I looked at the lieutenant, the lieutenant looked at me, and we both shrugged our shoulders helplessly, and the man sang on.

Finally, the stage was cleared, and the show began. Everything went off fine, and my stage poise surprised me. It was only after I came off that I started to feel shaky. This happened every time I went on and off. However, I did enjoy it a great deal, and I was glad that I tried it. It was a musical debut for me. Other acts consisted of hillbilly singers, guitars, violins, harmonicas, and accordions. Then came the Christmas carols played by a fellow on a portable organ followed by Protestant and Catholic services. We had no military schedule for the weekend, or so we thought, but guard duty came up, and most of my barracks was on it. However, prospects of a turkey dinner were enticing, and so this temporary inconvenience was no obstacle at all. We had nothing in particular to do anyway.

It had been a few weeks since we had had a man-sized meal. Dinner surpassed our greatest expectations. There was deboned turkey, mashed potatoes, dressing, gravy, cranberry sauce, salad, bread and butter, orangeade, and a piece of fruitcake. There was also the traditional Christmas candy. It was too good to be true really, and we had vague fears that this extravaganza was to be dearly paid for out of our future meals. Nevertheless, we forgave the mess sergeant, silently of course, for his past sins and hoped for the best.

Speaking of guard duty, there is nothing special to say about guard duty, if anything can be said of it at all. It is just another uneventful duty. However, Morty and I had the main gate, and we were equipped with loaded .45 caliber automatics. That was the only armed post in the camp. The time passed very quickly in conversation, and it was hardly a job at all except for inspecting the occasional incoming and outgoing vehicles and personnel. Morty was nineteen and, in spite of his young years, has had several romantic affairs of which the full content he boasted to me in some detail. I don't know if he would approve of my making the last note, so I will say no more about it as he was a good pal. We always joked about how we'll meet in Dubrow's Cafeteria when the war is over. Everybody from Brooklyn knows Dubrow's on Eastern Parkway and Utica Avenue. I gave him my cousin Mary's address, and he has already written to her. (Nothing ever came of it.)

In the evening in our free time, Morty and I tried to play some chess and went to the Idle Hour Club to borrow a set. That club was appropriately named. About the only things that weren't idle were the patrons' elbows. The place smelled dankly of lime and smoke, and the walls were covered with works of art ranging from pinups to Sad Sack cartoons. We found that too many of the chess pieces were missing and so gave up the idea. There was a GI phonograph in one corner, but there were no needles, and it didn't work well even after we tried a toothpick. Besides, there was only one worn-out record.

They changed my guard post to one that had the colonel's house on it. I had to walk up a hill to his house then walk down on a straight piece of road to a small bridge and then repeat the whole thing. His house had an old, faded French sign on it that read "Le Perchon" (The Rooster). Many French homes named their houses in such a manner. I saw the colonel only once during the two hours, and we gave each other a snappy salute as we passed. With guard duty done, we walked over to a bakery in a tiny village immediately outside of the camp and bought a loaf of bread. It was not bad and the best we tasted in all of North Africa. The bakery shop was in a building adjoining the baker's living quarters and smelled pleasantly of fresh warm dough. The baker himself was a handsome young Frenchman, whose clothes and blonde hair were covered in a fine dusting of flour. He spoke some

English but preferred speaking in French. Bread was rationed to the civilians there, and our supply was necessarily curtailed. Therefore, his position entailed certain responsibilities to the village and which, from my observations, were assuredly done most efficiently and honestly. He was a sort of benevolent and friendly tycoon with the bread market cornered. Children who came to buy loved him and clung to his apron.

I learned that wine had been given out free in any quantity (usually a canteen cup) at the Idle Hour Club. However, no one had to be told because that fact was plainly evident everywhere. There was the loud sighing, the guffawing, and the tipsy drunks. Several fully dressed carcasses were lying facedown on cots in a drunken stupor. Occasionally one leapt to his feet, bolted for the door in a gastric emergency. One sat up in bed and in a yodeling voice offered a local ditty warning, “Jack of diamonds. Jack of diamonds. I know you of old. You have robbed all my pockets of silver and gold.” I found it amusing. Then he resumed in a plaintive voice, “Rye whiskey, rye whiskey, I cry! If I don’t get rye whiskey, I surely will die. If the oceans were whiskey and I was a duck, I’d swim to the bottom and never come up.” Then he plunked down in bed again and was quiet.

December 27, 1943

Today was an especially quiet day. We got our PX rations, took hot showers, and just lay around most of the day. In the evening, several of us, including Gittleson, went to a piano concert in Tunis sponsored by a British entertainment committee. We had no chance to see the other parts of town, but it looked better than Casablanca. We’ll be back in town on Thursday.

December 28, 1943

We had a slight drizzle this morning, and our training program was cancelled. I decided to mail the camel skin belts and cigarette cases to sisters-in-law Helen and Hannah while I have the time. That being done, I had them approved at the post office and returned to find that I was on a water-carrying detail. All water in camp is brought in by tank trucks. Drinking water is put in canvas Lister bags and wash water is put in fifty-gallon drums with faucets attached. We had to carry a few five-gallon containers of water from the tank truck to the drums, requiring only about a half hour. On the way back, I noticed two Arab peddlers on a wagon selling eggs, which were a rare commodity here. I bought four then ran over to the bakery, got a loaf of bread, and returned to my barracks. We never got fresh eggs here, so I decided to boil them and make myself a meal. A couple of other guys did the same thing. I'd cook them tomorrow night because fires were only allowed at night. In preparation for the meal, I got some sugar and a small tin can. The sugar was for C ration coffee I still had with me, and the tin can was procured from one of the mess halls to boil the eggs. If the eggs didn't break or disappear before tomorrow, all would be well.

December 29, 1943

A cloudy morning and somewhat chilly. Our poison gas equipment was inspected in the morning, and we tested it in a gas tent in the afternoon with real gas. A gas attack, although always possible, was never used on the battlefields. It was lethal, and it was advisable that we be familiar with the briefest whiff of the various types. I bought another loaf of bread in readiness for tonight. Supper was C rations and lima beans mostly, so I thought the eggs would be a treat. I made the coffee and boiled the eggs on the stove and then went out with a couple of other fellows to get firewood. We chopped a tree down and dragged it back to the barracks. Many of the villagers will probably blink twice in bewilderment when they see it gone in the morning.

December 30, 1943

Morty and I dressed in our suntanned shirts and got the camp truck into town at 8:15 a.m. Here, as in Casablanca, there were modern and ancient parts of the city. The Casbah, as the ancient part is known, was forbidden to us except for the opportunity to go in on Red Cross tours. The Casbah has narrow winding streets and is dangerous. It is also a hot bed of illegal prostitutes. Many of our boys who come to town did so just for the hot beds. Here they call it "ziggy-zig." Every child in the street knows what is meant by the term, and half of them are pimping. Not only them, but also barbers, storekeepers and waiters, etc., are part and parcel of the trade.

During our wanderings, we ran into a young fellow, Andre, nineteen who had been born in England. Casually we asked him about the business jokingly, and he just came out point-blank and said that if we wanted to go, he would take us to "his" place. About this time we were joined by two comrades who, upon hearing the news, became decidedly interested. We decided, however, that we'd go along and wait for them since the English fellow was a pretty good guide and knew many interesting things about Tunis. When we arrived, Morty and I waited about a block away for fear of attracting the MPs. The others returned soon after, empty-handed and slightly frustrated, because the old bags were scared of MPs and not worth the three or four bucks they may have asked. Andre, unabashed, turned around and brought us to another place. They didn't even have to go upstairs. There she was standing in a dirty doorway involved in low head-to-head conversation with a soldier. She was dressed in black flimsy pajamas and looked old enough to be our mothers. We were pretty tired by now, and so were our still-eager friends. Everybody was tired except Andre. We wanted to sit down badly. A kid, not more than seven, saw us watching and, gathering the facts, told us that there was "another one" across the street. The two boys left us but soon returned saying that nobody had answered the door. We figured it was about time for a rest.

After giving Andre some cigarettes and bidding him adieu, we went for a snack. A few kids stuck to us like Band-Aids. Resistant to our calloused responses, they gave us sexy propositions until we finally shed them.

We walked around town, approaching the Casbah. As we did, we saw no "Off-limits" signs, so we believed that we were still outside of it. The streets quickly narrowed to an aisle's width. Twilight was falling fast. Streets rarely crossed each other but twisted like a path between closely set buildings. Occasional tunnels came beneath overhanging buildings. We soon hopelessly lost our way and stopped the only two kids we saw on the deserted street and tried to make them understand that we wanted to get out. It was now almost dark, and we hoped that nothing would cause us to miss the truck back to camp. They led us for a while, and to our surprise, to a house that they wanted us to enter. We refused. They lived there and promised to take us out after they went upstairs for "something." We had heard many stories of the Casbah, mostly bad, and so it was with a leery eye that we decided to go up with them. We felt that they might not come down again after they left us. After one of the kids called out "Ici avec ami!"[1] a light flashed on

1 Translates to "We are here with friends!"

in the dark upper hallway, and we went up the flight of rickety stairs and immediately into an apartment. The scene of a lovely-looking family sitting around a living or dining room presented itself. The man spoke English, and we learned that he had lived on Monroe Street on Manhattan's East Side many years ago in New York City. What a welcome surprise. All of our fears dissipated . . . but not for long.

We learned that the family income consisted mainly of the earnings of two has-been prostitutes that they supported like cows in a stable. Our two "harmless escorts" brought us here thinking that we might be interested. Apartment life went on as usual, and the little children took it all as very natural. The man began to speak hurriedly to the little boys in Arabic, apparently scolding them for bringing us here at this hour, and we gathered from his gestures that if any Arabs found us on the streets now, our lives wouldn't be worth very much. The particular gestures that impressed us were the quick passing of his right finger across his throat and then an imaginary blow to his head with a fist. Both gestures were accompanied by the proper facial contortions. Then he turned to us and smiled, but our uneasiness mounted by leaps and bounds. To make matters worse, the two cows came out of their room. In our presence, one gave the other a shot in the arm with a hypodermic needle. We never expected to stumble into anything like this. Their haggardness and chalky makeup together with their bedraggled bedclothes were so appalling as to defy description. Our host smiled again reassuringly, noticing our popping eyes. He assured us that we would be safely led and helped by the kids. We felt relieved, and noticing a piano in the corner of the room, I asked him, "Who plays it?" "I don't know" is what he answered, but he asked me if I could play him something appropriate. I remembered the song "As Time Goes By" from the movie *Casablanca*. With the music we became a little bit more relaxed and friendly as the minutes passed and talk of New York continued.

When we left, we needed guidance. Morty grabbed one of the kids' arms to guarantee their continued attachment. It was dark now. Everything seemed unreal to us as we scurried through a mystical "Casbah" in North Africa while in danger of our lives. We removed our hats so that our silhouettes would not resemble the military and proceeded at a brisk pace. My heart was pounding. One of the kids asked for fifty francs for his work, and Morty lied, "Okay," but held on just the same. "I was really worried," I said, "How about you?" "Nah, other guys have made it." Morty snorted. If my life ended in this alley, I wondered if my family would ever know of my fate. I shivered with cold, never usually associated with North Africa. My imagination ran rampant, and I was ready for the worst—someone to pounce on us. People were sitting in holes in the walls amidst unbelievable filth, continuous house frontage, without alleys for ventilation or light. It was walking dreamlike in a bewildering labyrinth without any sense of direction.

Emerging frightened but unscathed, we gave the kids a few francs and a couple of cigarettes for their trouble. We were roundly cursed for doing them out of the fifty francs we had promised, but we shook them off and left, very much relieved. That finished that, and except for the purchase of some cake and a few bingo games at the Red Cross. (No, I didn't win at bingo either.) One other thing, we learned that our old PX ration cards from Casablanca were good here, so we bought two weeks' supply of candy, towels, soap, etc. As soon as we came out of the PX, we were again besieged by the native boys and men trying to buy our supplies. We left for camp at 9:00 p.m. carrying our cake, raincoats, and PX stuff. The ride back was about half an hour. About the only thing we passed worth noticing was the Sultan of Tunis' palace, which was large and artfully decorated with lustrous tile.

CHAPTER IV

NEWS HEADLINE: ***January 22, 1944*—Allies Land at Anzio, South of Rome, Italy**

December 31, 1943

Today we planned on going into town on a special trip for Jewish services. There is a large synagogue there. However, the weather suddenly changed from a warm sunny day to cold rain and blustering winds. Besides, Special Services wanted to put on a show Wednesday night and asked some of us to start rehearsing. We didn't have much material to work with. We needed a drum. I'd have been surprised if we got it though because there weren't any in camp. This show would be taking place tonight, and we didn't have any notice. New Year's Eve was celebrated quietly for some unknown reason. Some wine was consumed, and Morty got a little tight. At twelve he awakened me just to shake my hand.

January 1, 1944

Here it was New Year's Day, again in a place I never expected to be. I hereby resolved to wish harder than ever that I was home again and not in this mess. I also hereby resolved that when such a day comes, and thereafter, I would gripe at a minimum concerning civilian difficulties and hope that people will be more content with their lot in the future—avoid fascist fakers like Hitler and Mussolini in the United States. That was quite a lot to hope for. Sergeant Gittleson fought in the volunteer Abraham Lincoln Brigade in Spain for a year and a half in 1936, and received shrapnel wounds in the face and leg, which were still visible. He had a profound hate for fascists naturally and knew their tactics very well. Oddly enough, before he was sent overseas, he was investigated time and again by the FBI. He lived in my barracks at Seymour Johnson Field in North Carolina, and even I was questioned once concerning his character before granting him permission to leave for Spain.

Today's notes began somberly because I forgot to mention that yesterday I met a few fellows in Tunis whom I last saw in my barracks at Seymour Johnson Field. They survived a torpedoing at which many drafting students I knew well were lost. It happened when they were leaving North Africa for India. A German torpedo plane fired a new type of rocket torpedo and blew a hole in the center of the ship that spanned about fifty feet, setting it afire. Out of twenty-one hundred men, only nine hundred lived. It was hard to believe they were gone. Names passed through my mind, and I pictured the faces that went with them. I teared up. They were so young. No one should die that young, or so violently. The terrible price demanded by war. We were told that we would probably fly out of here to our next post. It's safer in the sky.

Dinner today was turkey and altogether very similar to Christmas dinner. A few thoughts at random. Morty was flat broke as he lost all his money in a craps game the day we were paid. The boys were singing along with "Chic," the composer, accompanied by our clarinetist and drinking wine out of a five-gallon can. It was very cold, rainy, and blustery out; and we were keeping warm with a roaring woodstove.

January 2, 1944

The sergeant, our NCO[2] in charge, now blew an annoying whistle at the revelry that was fast leading to an estranged relationship. Prankishly and with disturbing nudges, he would say almost in a mock pleading voice, "Come on, fellows. Let's get up." Yes, he was quite a guy up until the time that the whistle reared its ugly head. Now that he had assumed a more expected interpretation of his role as sergeant, we were once more becoming our grumpy selves, and everything was proceeding along more credulous lines.

[2] Non-commissioned officer.

Today is Sunday, but we were awakened at six thirty in the morning nevertheless. The weather had settled down to being windy with an occasional drizzle and sunshine. This afternoon in Tunis, a piano concert was given that Gittleson and I attended. It was played by Niedzielsky, who was quite well known in Europe and Africa. He was about to play in the United States for NBC when the war broke out. The concert was enjoyable. At 5:00 p.m. we left the hall and looked for something to do until 9:30 p.m. when our camp's truck would pick us up. We had a few drinks of Moscato wine and looked around the neighborhood for a movie. A macaroni peddler was selling cookies for an inflated price. I bought one just for a sample and was disappointed. Prices everywhere are high just because they knew that Americans were the highest paid.

Gittleson and I finally came upon a French review that looked fairly good from the outside, but inside it was a muddied disillusion. The place was small, and the stage was no more than seven feet high and ten feet wide. Oddly enough, the star of the show was also the master of ceremonies. I don't know if they were shorthanded or short monied, but it was very amateurish. He wore a tight-fitting blue serge suit with a short jacket and somewhat baggy pants. As he sang his snappy French song, his head jerked and eyes popped so much so that he got a good dose of heckling, screeching, and guffawing from the American soldiers in the audience. He never flinched once, however, and was saved from further humiliation by his timely introduction of other numbers in the program. Every time he made an announcement in French, his counterpart on the opposite side of the stage would repeat it in such broken English that he would never fail to receive a laugh as a good comic. The remainder of the program consisted of dancers, acrobatic skits, etc., that was all-in-all corny. We nevertheless enjoyed it as a new experience.

January 3, 1944

Our regular training program was cancelled in order that we might clean up several buildings that until yesterday were occupied by previous outfits. As this was a remote part of camp, there was still the possibility of coming upon booby traps or unexplained hand grenades. We were told to push a stick into the ground next to anything that looked suspicious. While this area had been occupied by other friendly outfits, it was possible that they missed something. We did not particularly like the assignment. We moved in slow motion, did a lot of breath holding. My nerves were raw. I expected any moment to be blown to bits arms and legs going upward, my head into the clouds. When the job was finally done and we found ourselves intact, we both pretended nonchalance.

While looking around, Morty and I found a small battery and connected it to some headlight bulbs we had taken out of a small Italian jeep. There were quite a few wrecks of trucks and plane parts already stripped down. I made a reflector out of a tin can. It worked quite well, and I expected to use it until I could get a flashlight from home. The light I had until recently had fallen into a latrine pit one night in Casablanca.

A peddler was selling eggs and oranges just outside of the camp. He wouldn't take money, however, and would only trade for goods. One pack of cigarettes was worth three or four eggs. So was a pack of gum. A new deck of cards was worth ten eggs. I bought six eggs and boiled them hard so that I could eat them at any time. In the evening we attended a movie, and there were no breakdowns for a change, which was much appreciated.

January 5, 1944

This morning the NCO in charge awakened us and punished the last four guys out for roll call with KP duty. The four didn't gripe because they thought they would get a crack at some food, but they didn't. They were closely watched as they gave out the toast, coffee, and sugar for breakfast. We were put on a woodcutting detail today. Tree trunks are brought here from Bizerti seventy miles away and had to be cut up by handsaws every day. Morty and I didn't feel up to it, so with two other fellows, we headed for the open hills just behind camp. At only one hundred yards, I noticed a figure about two hundred yards ahead watching us. He was a lieutenant, I think, put there just for the purpose of catching those in our slippery category. We weren't sure until we stopped a moment and started to walk back and he started chasing after us. We hotfooted it out and back to the "woodchopper's ball." He couldn't see our faces because of the distance, and we were fortunate for that. It really wasn't bad, and the exercise was needed. I bought five more eggs and bread. Everybody did it because with the small rations we usually got, it was necessary to supplement the meals with something else.

The weather was still windy and drizzly but not cold, although we did have a hailstorm. Since my flight jacket along with some other laundry was at a nearby washwoman, Gittleson loaned me his woolen sweater for the interim. Today the air corps was dealt a crushing blow, but to our prestige only. A large shipment of men was expected in a few days, and among the many things being constructed for them, digging latrines was at the bottom of the list. We were given that choice detail. The soil was almost solid rock, and progress was very slow. We still had a day or two more of it. Although firewood was rationed out to us, we in our barracks had a plentiful supply due to the great resourcefulness on the part of its occupants who come walking in at all times of the day with the forbidden fruit pilfered from various sources. I wouldn't exactly say "pilfered," perhaps "borrowed" is a prudent substitute. As of now several of the wooden training platforms had become very well ventilated and appeared to have sustained major "termite" attacks. As I said before, our barracks knew of no wood shortages, and I will just leave it at that. We were getting quite used to this place now, and wouldn't mind staying in spite of the poor food. The barracks were very good compared to other places we could be. However, three or four are shipped out every day, and I suppose my turn would come soon.

January 7, 1944

Nobody has gone to town the last few days because the trucks were being used to carry supplies for the new incoming troops. I hoped to go in once more at least, before shipping out. Today I was put on a high level and dangerous mission. Toilet paper is very scarce here and rolls of it had been disappearing out of a latrine a few minutes after being placed into that sanctuary of relief. This called for action on the part of the NCO who promptly countered the threat by appointing latrine guards to keep an eye open for bulging overcoats or back pockets on the emerging patrons. That was my position of responsibility today, and I must say I did my best, but no one had the gumption to make off with the goods. The paper and the day were both saved.

In the evening I called for my laundry that I had left in another new place, which was also Italian. The Italians here are very agreeable, and many women do washing because most of their husbands are prisoners somewhere else. We were detailed to erect tents for the incoming men, and this took all day. Today our NCO, Sergeant Wood, was transferred to a new job; and we acquired a new NCO in charge. Wood was really quite bright compared to Hall, the new man. Hall has neither the diplomatic touch nor the ability to scare us into cooperation. However, he is more typical of the screen version of the thickheaded sergeant. His facial expression is very grouchy, and his voice has a strong drawl. In fact he barely opens his mouth while speaking. The food is getting quite bad again, and bread is now giving way to brittle biscuits. Another poison-gas-sniffing exercise is scheduled tomorrow morning. Dinner is strangely overloaded with gassy beans. Is it a coincidence that the night before a sample sniffing, a heavily bean-laden dinner is served as a precursor of the real thing to come?

I got my first letter from home today. It was from Mike, my brother, and it was most welcome. Letters close the gap across the ocean; nobody misses "mail call." A shipment of seven men has come in this morning, mostly from Seymour Johnson Field. I met Doug Harmon and Schumaker from my Boston engineering school and my barracks at Seymour Johnson field. It was good seeing them, and we talked over our school days.

We had turkey for dinner, which I guess was a reception for the new boys. I'm optimistic that better food is on the horizon. So many men have been shipping out that one NCO is now enough for two barracks. Luckily we lost Hall, our "Melon Head" sergeant in the ensuing consolidation.

January 10, 1944

Guard duty over at noon. The day is beautiful and sunny, and the broad flat plain below us basks in vegetation and sleepy farmhouses. To our rear, the abrupt green hills are dotted here and there with languorous sheep. The hooded sheep herders, staff in hand, have a slouching dog following just as languorously always with an eye for strays. The air is still. In front of the barracks, I wrote a letter or two and try to realize that it is the middle of January and freezing back home. I also wonder what is going on back home as well. Have brothers Arthur and Mike been inducted yet? Are both Mother and Father okay? My "three sisters"? I prefer to think of them as sisters rather than sisters-in-law, for that is just how they have been to me. Their babies will probably be quite different when I see them again, and who knows, there may be more. I miss them very much. Such thoughts keep us going. In the evening, another movie. Shall I say any more?

January 11, 1944

PX rations were issued this morning. The afternoon was for washing, or rather I should say five minutes of the afternoon was for showers. Apparently there is a scarcity of hot water because we were allowed only five minutes from the time we entered the shower room fully clothed until the hot water was shut off. It must be the snappiest shower on record. Three days ago I was surprised to run into a gambling casino on the post. There was a regular craps concession going on in one of the barracks with a regular craps table set up. One of the guys who run it keeps the game going with a line of patter better than a Coney Island barker at a side show. The windows are covered, and there is the customary low-hanging shade light. Some influential bigshots here must be involved, to put it nicely. The same thing goes on with our food. Fellows who work at an airport twenty-five miles from here get good every day while we usually get some camouflaged C rations.

In the evening, passes were announced for the following day for three out of nine men. We divvied ourselves into groups of three and cut the cards for it. I cut a queen and won. So Morty, Gittleson, and I are scheduled to go to town on the morrow.

Chapter V

NEWS HEADLINE: ***March 4, 1944*****—First Major Daylight Bombing Raid on Berlin**

January 12, 1944

We headed off to town early, and having a seat next to the back of the truck, I had a good chance to observe the route we traveled over. We were on the main highway that traverses northeastern Africa. It turns at Tunis to go south and Tripoli in the east, as one of their road signs directed. Road conditions were improved and were equal to something like a second rate U.S. road. We followed the mountain curves almost all the way. The scenery was empty except for a few towns and some passing trucks and motorcycles. These mountains are solid rock, and an occasional quarry is seen in operation providing stone for the road-widening project that is now under construction. The Arabs split the stones by hand. A drizzle has been in the air all morning, and several of the mountain tops are wreathed in mist. The vegetation is generally spotted, and the hills appear as great mounds of potato salad covered with parsley. I must admit that the simile was prompted by some very wishful thinking.

An occasional child or an adult would be chasing or beating a burro or cow whose front legs were tied together with enough rope to allow only short steps. I have never yet seen an Arab treat an animal in any humane manner whatsoever. He is addicted to buying, selling, bargaining, and hardly ever washing. About halfway to Tunis there is a huge junkyard of wrecked cars, trucks, tanks, and airplanes, which are being dismantled for salvage. A few miles farther, an airport is situated and some B-17 bombers are on the ground. In town, we immediately descend on a Red Cross station for a haircut and a snack. That done, Morty, broke from his New Year's Day losses, decides to sell anything he has to dig up a little cash. My friend Gittleson meanders around the jewelry shops in town. He is searching for a gift for his wife. I purchased a broach that I thought my mother would like. We return but can't find Morty, so we proceed alone for the remainder of the day.

There is a movie playing. I saw *Footlight Serenade* when we were in Boston, but two doses of Betty Grable wouldn't harm anybody, so we buy a ticket for the two o'clock show. Then we head for the Allied troop canteen in the rear of the Mono Prix department store. Believe it or not, we found a hot roast beef sandwich there! There was plenty of cake, but we wanted a box to carry it in as we contemplated buying about five dollars' worth for us and the boys back at camp. We decided to wait until later and returned to the show. The picture went off without a hitch. Back at the Red Cross for another snack. These periodic snacks very effectively took the place of eating. Gittleson had the address of a young native fellow of Tunis who had asked him to call at his home if he ever had the opportunity. We decided to try it. The boy Claude spoke some English and said that his sister, about twenty years old, spoke English very well.

The home was situated on the Rue de Provence near the waterfront. We had to knock twice at different times before someone answered. The man who answered was Claude's father, Mr. Raymond Kern, a most affable fellow. Although Jewish he spoke no Yiddish. I got along pretty well with him in French, and he surprised me by complimenting me on my French, which I thought was quite poor. Claude was probably at the movies he said, but about his daughter, he said nothing as he was probably suspicious. We drank some very fine wine that he had offered us, and I was glad I remembered "La bonne santé" ("To your health"). He said that if we needed anything, he would be glad to help us out with pleasure. His home was furnished quite well, and he was probably some sort of importer because he mentioned that he had imported shoe polish from Boston at one time. We left some cigarettes for him and some candy for Claude and also left a note letting him know that we would be at the Red Cross. Back there we reunited with Morty. He had sold an old ring for three dollars and immediately paid off a small sum due to me. About half an hour after we had returned there, Claude showed up, and we chatted a few minutes after Gittleson had introduced him to me. He then left for supper, but we told him that we might see him on Sunday if possible. After a snooze, we left for the truck, together with a cake we purchased, and returned to the comfortable confines of our camp.

January 13, 1944

I must have performed a very admirable job as latrine guard sometime ago because company headquarters was clamoring for my services a second time. However, there was no flattery attached to it, so I took my post dutifully, and at twelve noon I was relieved. In the afternoon, we took our three-minute soft-boiled showers and did nothing the rest of the day except write letters home. It was becoming increasingly difficult to write home for lack of new material, but I do anyway. I had now received a total of one letter in two months.

January 14, 1944

This morning I sent the broach off in the mail to mom. The censoring was done quickly with mere glances cast at the contents. On the way back from the post office, I passed a ditch-digging detail that I probably should have been on. "Hi, fellas!" I yelled as I waved cheerily. "Fuck off!" yelled one from down deep. I felt no guilt. They would do the same thing if circumstances permitted. This particular morning circumstances were especially permitting for me; and I, not being one to pass up an opportunity, naturally made the most of it.

Our new NCO sergeant (the Enforcer) is not one who understands the more common faults that permeate human nature, so I naturally avoid him. Avoiding a sergeant anytime is always the best policy. No matter how good your excuses may be, they are bound to ask some personal questions like "Where are you supposed to be, soldier?" or else they may look you up and down coldly as if to say, "Why the hell haven't you a pick or shovel or rake in your hand?" That is, he may ask you this question if you do not throw him off guard first. The best way is to try a greeting of "Hello, Sarge!" When a sergeant hears the word *hello*, he'll turn to look over his shoulder not believing it is he you address. Once he realizes that, he will create a wall of defense. He wonders where he has seen you before and refrains from any caustic remarks based on the theory that you may be that rarity, an old friend.

Friend and *drill sergeant* are two words that don't go together very well.

The true military sergeant is a strange character who usually comes down from the hills of some yet undiscovered territory to harass his resentful wards. This task must fall on somebody's shoulders; it is true. He becomes imbued with a sense of glorified eagerness and cheerfulness in contemplation of the task at hand. His eye twinkles as he shakes your bed at revelry. His voice is inspired during close ordered drill, and as KP pusher, he is sadistic with excitement. Needless to say, and unfortunately true perhaps, he is in a world of his own.

I have sometimes wondered whether I ever caught the slightest sign of a misty eye as he watched the men turn away from him at "ten minute" break times, for a spot of relief. If I did, it was only for an instant and no more. At such times I am almost foolishly prompted to run to his solitary side with comforting words. The picture that is most difficult to bring to mind is the sergeant once more in civilian life. Aside from the obvious danger of running into some of his old "problem children," there is the incongruity of his formerly giving orders to taking orders from anyone. The sergeant is quite "shout happy" and can stand very few voices outside of his own. I don't doubt that quite a few men will be lost outside the army and will probably remain in it. I probably exaggerate, but only to make the point that war requires teachers, leaders, and reluctant dogface GI followers, the latter making us the vast majority, the former by necessity; exercising stringent means to follow a syllabus to victory.

Chapter VI

January 15, 1944

This morning's circumstances were just as permitting as yesterday's, but since some of my friends had decided to join the work detail, I had no desire to be a lone wolf. So for purely social reasons I joined it. As it later turned out, there was not much to it. We just carried a few rocks from a pile to a spot where a walk was being built. We were free after lunch; so Morty, Chic, and I walked over to the Idle Hour Club, which was recently moved to a new location and contained more ping-pong tables, magazines, and less wine. A phonograph still without needles and new pile of old records were lying around. We made a needle from a pin, which worked well, but wore down too quickly. We gave that up and walked next door to the armory that had a piano in it. Chic is a clarinet player and has written some good songs and lyrics, even during a stint in the guardhouse—just proves that art may flourish anywhere. We have suggested that he copyright his material. They are really fine works. I hope that my predictions for his success are substantiated. Time will tell. There are movies tonight, but the sound broke down, so the whole thing was a washout.

January 16, 1944

We had our first formal inspection this morning in spite of our annoyance that it was such a useless formality. Most of the day we were left to ourselves. I have some film with me, just right to get pictures of us in our dressed-up olive drabs. Then a few in Fonduke, a tiny nearby village—plenty of native background and obliging people who are glad to pose for a few bonbons. Photography has been my absorbing hobby since my elementary school days. Had my own darkroom too. It is a beautiful sunny day. In the evening we sit around the burning stove, which removes the slight chill in the air. Gittleson tells us a few of his Spanish experiences. He was an American representative of the Abraham Lincoln Brigade[3] in Spain in 1936 and met many celebrities in that country. His stories are most interesting about the well-fought but futile revolt against the dictator Francisco Franco.

January 17, 1944

This morning the men who came in two Sundays ago got ready to pull out. Harmon and Showmaker were in it, and they were heading back to Oran for a boat to India. The boys were in for a four—or five-day grimy boxcar trip back and had our sympathies. PX rations came in the afternoon, and I also received twelve letters today and now have plenty of interesting material to read. It was nice to be sure, through my prearranged coded letters, that my family knew where I was. I don't think I gave away any military secrets or caused any risk to lives or property.

I gave the film for developing to a fellow going into Tunis. Stores in Tunis close from 11:30 a.m. to 2:30 p.m. for lunch. With the scarcity of food I guess they just siesta a great deal. Morty and I went down to the armory and played around with the piano. While there I printed up some music and made a melody arrangement for Chic's song, called "All Alone." He asked me to write out the melody later when I saw him, so he thanked me and said he would send it in for copyright. I returned to the barracks to find that I'm alerted for a shipment. Morty too, but not Gittleson. Perhaps Morty and I will go together. I received three more letters today from family. I have become an uncle once more.

---

[3] During the Spanish Civil War (from 1936 to 1939), 2,800 Americans were among almost forty thousand men and women from fifty-two countries who traveled to Spain to join the International Brigades to help fight fascism. The American volunteers served in various units and came to be known as the Abraham Lincoln Brigade.

January 20, 1944

Being alerted for shipment is no excuse from detail, so consequently at about 9:00 a.m., I found myself with a pitchfork in hand watching a few other guys chopping away at the grass around our barracks. I followed up by pushing it all aside. It is amazing how our first sergeant thinks up these pleasantries when he could have been lying around in bed. No matter how many times we promised ourselves not to be around when our NCO comes to get us, we are caught flat-footed in our barracks. When you really get down to it, goofing off requires careful strategic planning.

The army is a wonderful prelude to a WPA project.[4] I refer at this time to the work effort that Franklin D. Roosevelt put out with the greatest sincerity. Tools also break and wear away from our leaning on them. During one of these leaning sessions, conversations on various topics abound and crept up. This morning's topic flitted about from the condition of the poor permanent party men back in the States to the fleecing of the Arabs. One of the fellows had emptied packages of cigarettes and refilled them with toilet paper and stale bread for which the Arabs fell hook, line, and sinker. He was careful to fill them from the bottom so to not break the wax wrapper which is used for overseas shipping. Any night now we expect to find a dead guard with a dagger in his back, dramatically piercing a package of phony cigarettes. Then the conversation switched to horse racing. Chic was a prewar bookie, and he explained the intricacies of handicapping and the power of the betting machine. He has no sympathy for the suckers and says "It's an in-the-bag business." In the afternoon, we don't take any chances and go right down to the armory right after dinner and play around there. Chic was there, and I wrote out the entire song for him. In the evening, we throw the bull around the stove as usual.

January 21, 1944

Because there are so few men in camp now, we have no detail this morning. After lunch we dress in our ODs and get ready to march

4 The Works Progress Administration, created by President Franklin D. Roosevelt in 1935, was among the largest and most ambitious New Deal agency. It employed millions of unskilled workers to carry out various public works projects.

off to the guardhouse. At that moment a messenger runs up and pulls eleven of us out for a shipment. We are glad to get out of guard duty and look forward to the trip, which is by airplane, and it will be my first flight. After packing quickly, I say good-bye to friends and especially to Gittleson and wish him well. Morty is going with me, but probably not to the same place. Nevertheless, we are happy to be together. El Aouina is the airport north of Tunis. No planes were ready, so we had to be put up at the Hotel De Gink. This is the name given to a few collective battered buildings that serves to house transients who are awaiting planes. Suddenly the lieutenant announces twelve names that will fly out on a plane that has just come in. Destination? Catania,[5] Sicily. I am on it, but not Morty. He helps me carry my barracks bags out of the hotel and reload them onto the truck. I wave good-bye to all the fellows I knew and settle down to making new friends among the eleven strangers who are to travel with me. It is really a tough break being split up from them because the other eleven passengers are all friends. However, it can't be helped. The airport is a half mile away, and upon arriving, we back up to the plane and load ourselves and our baggage onto it.

The time is 5:00 p.m. The doors shut, and the engines start and zoom. The noise is deafening for the moment. At the end of the runway, we pause for a few moments. I await the great moment of my first takeoff. Here it is! Slowly over the fabricated steel runway, nose high, we begin to race. The tail wheel squeals, and I know that when it stops, we will be off the ground. It has stopped, and the ground rapidly falls away and appears in miniature. Higher and higher, we circle once and head for the east coast. It is thrilling and fearless. We seem to be floating lazily over the terrain like a goldfish in a bowl. Another "fish" darts by beneath us. By now we do not mind the noise, but we begin to feel chilly. The electric heating system begins to function, and the temperature becomes quite comfortable. Over the Mediterranean, I fall asleep for a while. The air is very smooth, and we travel along with hardly a bump. At 7:00 p.m. a few lights appeared below, and our plane flashes its lights in response. In a few minutes we land. I learn that we are more than a hundred miles from Catania and have landed because

---

[5] Catania is an Italian city on the east coast of Sicily located near Mount Etna.

of approaching bad weather. We will continue in the morning. At the field, we get a bite to eat and then are driven to a town two miles away for sleeping quarters. In the darkness, the curfew is 6:00 p.m. It is difficult to make out any details. At one or two “flop houses,” inquiries are made; and a dorm is secured in a building with many rooms and, as far as I can tell, no windows. Six of us are in a room with beds of a sort, and my mattress is stuffed with straw. I remember Gittleson warning me that lice are prevalent in straw. I seriously doubted that I would have a good night’s sleep. There are only eleven of us now in the hotel because one is sleeping with a “friend” he had just met a few minutes ago in a nearby house. He later told me that the gal’s fiancé was sleeping in the same room and wasn’t in the least disturbed. Four packs of cigarettes had eased the situation. Cigarettes here are worth a dollar per pack. The fiancé probably got half.

Before going to bed, I met one of the occupants of the house who was an old, short, stocky, gray-haired Italian man who surprised me with a good deal of English. Where did he learn it? In Brooklyn twelve years ago where he worked as a laborer in a shipyard, he told me proudly. He returned in 1934 to Sicily and later was refused permission to return to the States by Il Duce.[6] He scowled profusely as he mentioned the latter character. He had a daughter, quite old, who I later found out did a lot of hand needlework and to whom he conducted several of us in the hopes that we would make a purchase. She lived in another part of the cavernous building, her prices were reasonable, so I bought ten bucks worth of some silk place mats made from parachutes to send home as soon as I get stationed. Sleeping was not as bad as I expected, and there was only a slight itchiness—probably scabies.

[6] Il Duce (The Leader) is the nickname used to reference the fascist dictator Benito Mussolini.

Chapter VII

January 22, 1944

At 6:30 a.m. somebody awakened us. After a quick wash, I dressed and got back on the truck to return to the field. Now more than ever, I look forward to the second half of our plane hop to Catania. We had a breakfast of bacon, flapjacks, and coffee and boarded the plane. One of the pilots had slept on the plane all night on a stretcher. We awakened him at seven thirty. We were ready once more, and we shot off the runway toward Catania, twenty-five minutes away. The scenery was lighted by a bright, sunny, cloudless sky; and the mountains below were dotted with farms, bomb craters, and plane wrecks. Most of the mountains were plowed steplike along the sides similar to Chinese rice fields. Elsewhere there are no scenic eyesores. Everything is welded into a smooth, unruffled tapestry. Filth and squalor disappear, and there is nothing but design. I now see snowcapped Mount Etna, and I know now that we have arrived at the Catania airport. After a safe landing, we unload, most of us rather unwillingly, and await further orders at the base operations building. We are now part of the ATC,[7] which is said to be the best branch of the air corps. Its purpose is the transportation of men and materials by air, using those wonderful C-47 cargo planes.

A sergeant steps out of the base operations building calling my name from a sheet of paper. "Here!" I respond. He says, "Take the next bus into town and go up to the Fifty-first Wing headquarters building and see Mr. Dorgan the warrant officer."

---

7 Air Transport Command.

I ask, “Should I take my barracks bags along?” “You’ll be back later,” he says. “The other boys will look out for them.” That’s okay with me. I scribble down the information, and in the meantime, I can’t help wondering if it means an assignment in the city. I certainly hope so. I had about a half-hour wait for the next bus, and in the meantime, another C-47 has landed. I see some of my friends whom I left last night. Morty is there, and this time I help him carry his bags. In a few minutes, he learns that he has been assigned to the Sixtieth squadron TC, about a ten-minute flight from here. We can probably see each other often because of daily courier plane service between all the fields. That’s great, but I regret that he is not assigned with me. The bus arrives, and I am the only passenger going into Catania. I show the Italian driver the written address, and his gestures indicate that he understands. The ride is bumpy, and the bus seems to be held together by wires and the grace of God. We travel along a short, vacant stretch of road and then into the crowded, dirty streets of the city. The absence of Arabs is welcome. There is more semblance of modernity here.

At 11:30 a.m. the shoppers are busy. Here and there is a bombed or gutted building. Its rubble reaches the gutter, and the throngs walk into the gutter to avoid it. Horse carts block the way; and the lame, deaf, and aged hobble across the streets into our path unconcerned. The architecture takes on an increased ornamental and flowery aspect. The colors are bright, and brightly decorated horse saddles are everywhere. The words “Il Duce” painted on the side of a few buildings catch my eye. At the wing headquarters building, I get off and find my way to Warrant Officer Dorgan. He is friendly, but to the point. His inquiries concern my army specialization, namely drafting. I think he is satisfied because he tells one of the fellows to get me dinner. After picking up the other boys, we drive back to town to our sleeping quarters in a school building pockmarked by bombs. Snowcapped Mount Etna rises majestically a few miles away. There are excursions up that famous volcano, which I will take on my day off. The floors of the school are tiled, the corridor is long and ceiling high, but most of the corridor’s windows are blown out. Windows in rooms have been repaired. We sleep on stretchers tonight because of a temporary cot shortage.

For the last day or two, I have been bothered by itching bug bites on the legs, back, and wrists. If it gets any worse, I will probably go on sick call. First Sergeant Guzi tells me to report to wing headquarters nine tomorrow morning to get indoctrinated and to be back at one. Later that afternoon, I walk back from the headquarters office up to our sleeping quarters. Children beset me. "Arancie, Joe?" they plead and try to sell me some "Belle grosse aranchie." "Okay, carusi," (kids) I give in affectionately. Six or seven of them are ten lire. I had no money, so simply said in Italian "Trust me till tomorrow?" "Si si capitano." Their eagerness is delightful, and my debt was repaid as promised. I was concerned about the events soon to unfold—Officer Dorgan who informed me that I was to be attached to wing headquarters in town. I hardly believed my good fortune. Only four others were to join me, and none of them were draftsmen. I was to be a new addition to the Wing. They had not had a draftsman for a year or so and had been anxious for one. My particular office is the S-2 section (intelligence and statistics), but I will probably be useful to others as well. I go back to the airport to tell Morty the good news. At supper, which was tasty beef, I met up with Chic Indivari who shipped out the day after I left Tunis. He is in a small outlying airport, still on his clarinet.

January 23, 1944

At 6:00 a.m., after a few minutes of calisthenics, I shave and dress in ODs before proceeding to headquarters. I am introduced to the officers of our department. Colonel Gardiner, former governor of Maine and Italian treaty negotiator, is head of intelligence. He is a very congenial man and even brings oranges to his staff every day. He asks my previous background, etc., etc. Brigadier General Beverly is head of the Wing, but I haven't seen him yet. The room I am to work in is curtained off. Its contents are secret. Suffice it to say that it is interesting work; and I work alone, that is, with no other draftsmen. There is a large shipping case full of drafting supplies and equipment that was left to my investigation. Two drafting tables were available. By the afternoon, I turned out my first piece of work, which was merely a line drawing assignment for a statistical chart. They were pleased with it, and I was happy. At 4:30 p.m. we quit and went back for supper. Our room is about twenty feet by twenty feet, and we have plenty of room in these former classrooms. All the bunks are at the walls, and there is a large open space in the center under a central light. Italian prisoners keep it clean. We have our own theater about eight blocks away, and there are new movies almost every night.

January 24, 1944

This morning I had to go on sick call. Scabies itch again. I had to swab myself from head to foot daily with a sulfur solution and have all the recent clothes I had been wearing cleaned. I returned to the barracks and gave two kids four cigarettes each for cleaning my trousers, flight jacket, and three blankets in gasoline. While doing this, they enlightened me as to what it was like when the Germans were here with many intelligible gestures and much unintelligible talk. They were cleaner and better dressed than the Arabian kids, but they were still ragged. Their ill-fitting shoes were anything they could find, and some wore German boots. This job done, I ate and then had a canvas bed repaired at the parachute repair shop. After that, I showed up at the office and began work at about 2:00 p.m. on a diagrammatic chart of the intelligence office setup. There is no rush and no ordering about. I am treated like a professional. Oh, happy change! Catania is blacked out after 6:00 p.m., so there isn't much in the way of nightlife.

January 25, 1944

After seeing the doctor again, I returned and shaved in a helmet of hot water, then up to my office. After dinner, I bring one of the little *orange* girls outside of headquarters a stick of chewing gum. She is really surprised as she never believed the promise I had made when I had seen her in the morning. She is so surprised that she didn't insist on my daily purchase of oranges; instead she smiled "Domani, domani" (Tomorrow, tomorrow). In the afternoon, I did a special job for the colonel Gardiner who is taking a plane trip somewhere and asked me to draw up a route. This required the remainder of the afternoon.

I forgot to mention that the gasoline-soaked blankets I used last night smelled to high heaven. Therefore, I left them airing out all day on a railing that ran along one side of a terrace looking down on a courtyard. When I returned, two were gone.

January 26, 1944

Two letters came in today that were quite old but welcome nonetheless. Went down to sick call again, but this time it was just for the checkup. The doc told me to come back if I had any more trouble. I washed the blankets in gasoline again, but this time I watched them dry up until lunchtime. One of the neighborhood boys has worked for the army here and knows English. We spoke while I guarded my blankets. He told me much of what had happened here before the Unites States had moved in. As a student, he had been attending the University of Catania and specializing in chemistry when Germany invaded in 1942 and we were bombed out. He had been bayoneted by a German in a street encounter. "I didn't have my identity papers in order," the boy explained. "They took you for a dangerous spy, of course," I joked, "unbelievable." Germans made good soldiers but were unusually callous in the consideration of civilians. Our consideration for others, he said, has made the American soldier most liked of all Allied troops. I couldn't help but give him a few cigarettes before I left.

January 27, 1944

Up at 6:00 a.m. to the strains of a bugle blown out in the hall. After a few minutes of calisthenics, breakfast, and down to the office by 8:00 a.m. Mount Etna is very beautiful in the early morning light during calisthenics time. The top is snowcapped and is in fleecy racing clouds. It appears very close but is actually several miles away. Around the streets in empty lots, there are outcroppings of hardened black lava, the remains of many eruptions. Going to work in the afternoon, a camera is offered for sale by an Italian civilian on a bicycle. "How much?" I asked.

"Twenty-five packs of cigarettes," he says.

"Sorry, too much," I said. Anyway, I expect my own camera soon.

January 29, 1944

All of the wing headquarters squadron have one day off a week. Mine is today, and it is a real day off because I don't have to answer revelry. In fact, I can stay in bed all day. I chance a shower at 9:30 a.m. then shave back in my room in a helmet full of hot water from the sink. Italian prisoners come in to sweep up and put things in place. One salutes me awkwardly and smiles while bowing and says, "Good morning." Without waiting for my jumbled answer, he goes to work. These men are honest and dependable. I told one that I lost a towel the other day and not only did he find it on the bathroom floor, but he cleaned it before returning it. I always give him a cigarette when he comes in. At 1:00 p.m. I go down to a small carpenter shop two blocks away to see about a chest that will substitute for a footlocker.

The other boys have them, and they are well made with a lock and cost about four bucks. I order one of them. Walking back, those hardy kids demand chewing gum and everything else. I throw some hard candy over their heads and watch them jump for it.

In the afternoon, I sit on the low granite steplike fence on the sloping street at the front of our school barracks. There was an iron fence once, but now only stubby posts remain. The sun is hot on a cloudless day. Little children are playing, whooping and hollering. Some of them are clitter-clattering in their wooden shoes. All but the tops of their heads are hidden behind the stone fence around an open lot. Some of the men are having a catch with them, and others are just sitting like myself. I will stop now to write a few letters.

A scrumptious nurse-lieutenant in dress military clothes hops out of a newly arrived jeep and leaves a major waiting in the backseat. The chauffer chats a moment with him, and a minute later the nurse comes bouncing out, and after a few words, the jeep drives off without her. She has dropped her gloves. Without calling out, I pick them up and return them to her. "Thank you," she says, looking into my eyes. What a lead in!—but, no soap. She's a lieutenant; and I, as a lowly private first class, would have had to be screwy to think I could compete with a major. I accept retreat sadly but graciously.

I finish two letters to my brothers and go back inside to learn I'm on guard duty again. For the past few nights, leather from the seats of several of the command cars has been cut out. We have orders to fire away on the slightest provocation. With two guards, the time goes by fast while we throw the bull up and back all night. Then at 6:00 a.m., down to the mess hall for a bite and then to bed.

January 30, 1944

Up at 11:00 a.m., shave, eat, and then to the office. At 2:00 p.m. there is a movie of the "Articles of Warfare" at our theater. By 3:00 p.m. we are back. This will be my first opportunity to see the town in daylight. There are no cars on the street, and our jeep attracts some attention. It is Sunday and a little quieter than usual. People are better dressed than on weekdays, and a large group of them is waiting for the double streetcars near the theater entrance. We are not allowed to ride the streetcars for fear of bringing lice back to the sleeping quarters. Conductors close an eye when we hitch a ride.

There is not much to do at work except study the map, reading codes and grids. In the evening, we have boxing matches, but I'm not interested. I hang around the dayroom. There is a big game of blackjack going on at ten dollars or more a card.

The box I ordered from the carpenter was ready, and I was about to pay him eight packs of cigarettes instead of four dollars when some black marketing guy offered me five dollars, and I readily accepted. The highlights of a deal can change in a split second!

Chapter VIII

The Bellini Opera House ignored the war completely. A friend, Herman Baker, and I went to see *Madam Butterfly* by Puccini and found it very enjoyable. During the second act intermission, we met some girls chaperoned by two aunts. We must have made a good impression because, after a short character inquest, they invited us over to their house Saturday night. I was happy and ready. After the show, we walked them part of the way back to their house. On the way, we talked—or tried to. Sign language is not much use in the blackout, and only the younger girl knew a slight amount of English, so we slaughtered the conversation up and back.

February 3, 1944

Our date to get to the girls' house was for 6:30 p.m. I would have taken a jeep there, but given the location, we felt that it was not necessary. At night the streets are blacked out, and you have to know your way around before you attempt to go anywhere. At 6:20 p.m. my friend and I arrived without any mishap. The girls were waiting at the door of their apartment. We walked through a darkened hall at the end of which came a living room. The girls and a married sister, Graziella, and her baby were all there to meet us. We shook hands. The salutations were lengthy and cordial. The married girl, about twenty-three, was a private teacher. The younger, at eighteen, was in college. The married sister's husband was an Italian army captain and now a prisoner in North Africa. An album showed many snapshots taken during the Italian-Ethiopian campaign in the early 1930s. She herself had been a prisoner there because wives could join their husbands there.

After a while, we were led to a dining room and sat down around the round table where we continued conversation. A little wine was brought out, and they apologized for the absence of vermouth. The younger girl, Maria, sat next to me. The father, an elderly man who had joined us, acted suspiciously. I felt he was serving in the capacity of a sentinel rather than a host. Nevertheless he was quite cordial, but cool.

In Sicily I thought it quite possible, that American cigarettes, being a high-premium item could make friends even of enemies. Nevertheless, we had nothing to lose by offering the open pack on the table under the father's hungry eyes. He took only one. They were well-mannered people. The mother sat with a granddaughter on her lap, and I felt she was glad to have us, and she said so. I also felt that she was amused at our poor Italian. She was typical of the black mourning-garbed, reserved Italians we knew back home. What did we speak about? Anything and everything that entered our heads. Of course, discussion was held to a bare outline of any topic. The shades and undertones of speech familiar to us were completely lacking, but our facial expressions, hand and body motions helped. Maria had a small Italian to English dictionary, which she used occasionally. Nevertheless, a typical sentence meaning "When are you coming over to my house again?" ran like "When come my house you more?" I couldn't even form Italian sentences. Just a word here and there.

We talked about the coming opera *Barber of Saville*, and I invited the two girls to go with us. They were slightly embarrassed and asked, "You mean alone?" Then we learned that many Sicilian girls don't go anywhere without chaperones, so we had to include the parents in the deal. "I guess I'll never get my hands on Maria," I said salaciously to myself. That meant six of us in one box, which was the maximum. They were really surprised and unhappy when told that chaperones were more or less passé in America. The time passed quickly, and at 9:30 p.m. we bid them adieu. The old man was smiling a little now, and we were invited over for Monday night. Since we liked their company and had nothing else to do, we readily accepted.

February 7, 1944

The weather grew cold, and suddenly Mount Etna was covered with snow one morning, but none at our altitude. At 6:00 p.m. we started to our appointed place and made a similar entrance as the day before. This time the old man was there to meet us. We had left the unfinished pack of cigarettes there the night before. I had brought two dictionaries with me at their request, and I thought I was ready for anything. The dictionaries were small and incomplete and only served to exasperate me. We finally boiled down to comparing any English word with its Italian counterpart. That lasted a little while. The older sister, Graziella, had baked some cookies hoping for a compliment. If we stopped chewing for a few seconds, then, apologetically "No, like?" whereupon we had to resume rather than explain. They were very pleased with a few gumdrops we offered and asked us when we might like to come again. I thought that they would like to go out somewhere some evening, but they did not go out at night alone since the war because it is dangerous. Besides that, they seemed to really want to have us over. We were hesitant but finally accepted a dinner invitation for Thursday night. Their kindness was exceptional.

Maria asked quietly, "When part you Catania?"

Matching her grammar, "Me not know," I said in Tarzan talk.

She said she would be sad to see me go. I really liked her because she was very clean-cut, sincere, and ladylike and incidentally had a figure that would make a nonagenarian pop his cork. I asked her if she would like to go to the cinema. She was willing but would not chance walking with me for fear of being seen by the family or a neighbor. She agreed to meet me inside. I didn't want to be the cause of any family squabbles and let her know that I understood. I was rather flattered that she would take such a chance for me, so what could I say, but yes. Herman, my friend, concerned himself mostly with Graziella, which wasn't a bad one to be concerned with either. We left with a promise to return on the morrow.

February 8, 1944

I changed my mind about seeing the Grimaldis for no particular reason. This evening I had a note written by an interpreter telling Maria not to expect us tonight. I shoved it under the door and left. Krotec, the darkroom man, has a lab a few doors away from my office; and I go in there occasionally to talk photography. I was asked to print up a sign to be photographed for a title to a movie trailer for the Signal Corps. In the evening, I developed two rolls, and they came out quite good. The smell of dark room chemicals brought fond memories of days spent in my own darkroom.

February 10, 1944

At six thirty we found ourselves at #7 Toselli Place, the Grimaldis. I see the father's scrutinizing eyes are in fine focus, and we are calling him "Old Eagle Eye." He frowned when he saw me move my chair closer to Maria. I had to leave the room to get something from my overcoat pocket. One of the girls was nice enough to turn on the light for me, and the old boy broke all speed records getting there ahead of me. This practice is becoming annoying. I could readily sympathize with the lives that the girls must be leading. They don't visibly object but surely rumble within, like Mt. Etna. Perhaps, like WWI, this war will bring a radical lifestyle. Maria presented me with an Italian grammar; on the inside was inscribed a charming little note: "In remembrance of days passed together." I brought her a pack of gum. She was very delighted and shared it with the family after dinner. The dining table was immediately set, and my hopes began to rise although I could not imagine what they would serve for dinner. There was a fish-pasta dish, which I did not like at all. There was also an artichoke, which made them laugh when they saw how I fumbled with it. There was plenty of vino and aqua. The payoff came when they begin to insist that I eat another plateful. I gently declined, referring to a slight headache. The next course was another artichoke, and I tried to appear very pleased as I ate it to make up for some of the wry faces I made during the first course. The next course consisted of pancakes, which was a tasty relief. They asked to be excused for the lack of meat, but that was okay with us. We didn't want any part of a horse.

After the table was cleared, we talked awhile. Maria told me not to forget about the movies on Saturday. I assured her I would not, and she told me not to show the folks that I was taking the grammar book with me because only engaged couples exchanged gifts. (More hogwash.)

February 11, 1944

Tonight was our meeting for the *Barber of Seville*. From the Grimaldis, we all walked together. We walked in the gutter mostly because the sidewalks are very narrow in many places. In some places, buildings come right down to the sidewalk. There is no such thing as gardens or setbacks from the sidewalk line. There is perhaps one alley on a block breaking the solid front of stone masonry. These buildings depend totally on courtyards for lighting and ventilation. In fact, as you walk along and pass an open door, the bedrooms, kitchens, and dining rooms adjacent to the sidewalk and on the street level are visible just as if we were inside—all intermingled with noisy, smelly, commercial business. Balconies are their predominant architectural delight. To see a second-story window without one is rare.

At the opera, an enjoyable performance of the *Barber of Seville*. The mother and two daughters sat up in front, and we and old Eagle Eye sat just behind them. We are all "cawn-tent" (happy) as the older girl says. There are many *masimo* Italians in the Bellini opera house. It is run by the English and fortunately is without damage. It is beautiful and compares well to the Met[8] in New York. The Italians are proud of this monument to their native-born opera composer. The walk back is uneventful, and after bidding them good night at their house door, we return to the barracks at about 11:00 p.m.

February 12, 1944

My day off today, but a new regulation requires us to arise just the same in the morning. I am to meet Maria in the movies at 10:00 a.m. It is a sunny day, but slightly brisk. Nevertheless, I do not wear a coat over my shirt. On the walk through town, I see people busy and everything humming. Sala Roman is what we would call a dump, but it's an average movie house for Catania. I got there first, and a few minutes later she arrived. An Italian picture is on. She gave me a hand-painted handkerchief. I thanked her very much, and she was quite happy. There was no smooching. When it was over, she left the theater first and I after her. We would smile at each other occasionally—I, on one side of the street, and she on the other. After a while, we chanced a good-bye gesture, and both went our separate ways—how romantic!

February 13, 1944

Pretty busy in the office these days. Now that all the departments know there is a draftsman attached to the organization they bring quite a steady stream of work. I make a couple of perspective drawings

[8] Metropolitan Opera House.

once in a while as special jobs. It is nice to have captains, majors, and colonels thanking me for a piece of work. It is quite different from the nondescript previous army life. There should be a sergeant's rating in it eventually.

February 14, 1944

They are building a road about half a block from headquarters. It is to cover part of the lava-buried section of the old city. Continuity of connecting streets sometimes run over some deep gullies requiring several thousand cartloads of bomb rubble to fill in. Each cart holds a small amount, and carts are decorated with bright paintings and elaborate harnesses. The burro has to be backed up to the end of the unfinished road, and it is not without difficulty forcing a contentious burro to back up. A continuous uproar of swearing and pushing results.

This evening Herman and I are at Grimaldis again, dictionary in hand. The old man and the mother are somewhat lenient and, in their place, have substituted an aunt temporarily. After a while, she casts a knowing wink at us, signifying that as far as she was concerned we would not have to suffer the surveillance of the old man. Our visits here have become quite taken for granted as part of the family routine. Our language has improved slightly, and so has our familiarity, but not as far as Maria is concerned.

February 16, 1944

We visited the girls with chaperones attached. I may see them in the movies on Friday, my day off. At the office, everything is running smoothly. A package arrived with everything intact. The flashlight is unbroken and works fine. A salami is hanging on the wall next to my bed but is camouflaged to keep the predators away.

February 18, 1944

A day off, but up at 6:00 a.m. nevertheless. I wrote some letters. Herman and I walked downtown to see the sights. It was chilly, and we wore our overcoats. We regretted taking them at first, but on the way back, it began to rain, and we were glad we had them. On Via Etna we stopped at a bookstore, and I bought an English-Italian dictionary. The store was loaded with all sorts of language guides for us foreigners. Via Etna was the Fifth Avenue for smart-set shoppers and is bouncing back slowly. Some of the shopkeepers, mostly women, look at us through glass doors. There are few Americans in Catania, but many English. The latter are disliked for some reason. That isn't my opinion but is the opinion of almost every Italian I speak to. I suppose our difference in pay or our sense of humor has much to do with it. They seem okay to me.

The quality of merchandise in the shops must be closely scrutinized. Staples are of mixed low quality. A poorly made pair of shoes costs about twenty dollars. Their needlework is fine. The English send limes and lemons home, where there are none. Bellini Park, a verdant jewel in the center of the city on a sloping hill, spotted with marbled Greek statuary, stands out. At the center is a white statue to Bellini, the famous Catania-born opera composer. The main center of attraction, however, is a vast multitude of men waiting to be discovered as black marketeers. They mill about, but upon closer inspection, can be seen deftly exchanging money and packages. Without any interference from any police, they rush through their transactions, paying behind shrubbery or in horse carriages. Once I saw ten or fifteen men chase another man up the street. Evidently, he had something everyone else wanted. Like a pack of bleating hounds, they beat and tugged at him. He ran into a hallway ignoring all offers and standing firmly on his monopolistic advantage. We never saw the final act on the deal because we moved on up the street to the theater where we were to meet the Grimaldi girls, without chaperones we hoped. They never showed up. We returned through a different area, some of which was off-limits. A wagon parked along the curb was hawking a dissected animal carcass that didn't appear to be beef.

I whipped out the dictionary I had just bought and inquired of a stranger "Cavallo?" (Horse?). "Si," he responded as parts were being carried into a building. A couple of kids were running down the street, saw the cart and running up to it, bit at the horse meat, and scampered off. Another tot reached up and splashed his fingers in one corner of the cart where a small puddle of blood and dirty water had collected then licked his fingers. I was repulsed at the sight and left quickly. We completed our round trip back to our school dorm, ate a steak supper, and were unusually thankful for it as we remembered there were hungry people and horse meat close by.

Chapter IX

February 19, 1944

We go to see the Grimaldis, but that is beginning to be old hat and going nowhere. We danced awhile to some German music, and it was very cramped. The old man seems to have lost track of us for five or ten minutes. The house is a sort of railroad flat they had to move into when the English occupied the town and forced them to evacuate. The master bedroom is elaborately decorated with every conceivable painting, statuette, and lighted candle to the savior. They are dissatisfied with the place and told us of the much larger home they once had. They dance just about the same as we do. It was the first time that I had danced since I left the States.

February 20, 1944

Getting up at 7:15 a.m. on a Sunday by order of the commanding officer, I go right down to eat and get to work by 8:30 a.m. You could go to church if you wished. I haven't seen any synagogues around town as of yet. It was good to see new proclamations pasted up on many buildings stating that the rights of Jews were to be restored to prewar days. I'd like to see that same poster in Berlin one day.

February 22, 1944

Washington's birthday today. Roast chicken for dinner. Some of the boys complained "Air corps chicken. All wings and no legs." Strack, a comical, feisty friend and roommate who is short, cranky, and in his late thirties, is in an especially lamentable mood. As a leg man, he was the leader of the "Air corps chicken" theme. "Christ! You'd think chickens over here are born without legs!" he wailed as he came up from the mess hall dangling his mess kit. "Air corps chicken never seems to fail." He threw the mess kit on his cot and lay down alongside of it, still wailing. He was probably correct, but even after I explained that a chicken had only two legs and that they were outnumbered by the other organs and appendages, he still muttered on, lamenting the state of affairs that existed concerning chickens attached to the air corps. He was the same about coffee. If there was none at a meal, the meal itself was hardly worth eating. He was particularly comical with a day's growth of beard on his face, heavy and Bowery bum style. "Tea, tea, tea! What do they think we are anyway, English? Christ!" "Soup, soup, soup! It's too damn fat to drink. See what I mean?" he says as he wags his head sadly. However, over a canteen cup of coffee, he could relax the entire afternoon in perfect contentment.

Washington's birthday, in the evening we visited the Grimaldi family again. I explained to Maria about Washington. They had never heard of him!

February 24, 1944

Busy day at the office. Plane wreck today and twenty-two were killed. The cause was unknown. Nettuno Beach up north is a pretty tough spot. There are about three of our divisions up there against nine German divisions that are surrounding them on two sides. Air support is what's keeping them going. Some of our men fly in every day in unarmed planes, bringing supplies and blood plasma. I shivered every time I thought of the dead and the ordeals experienced.

February 25, 1944

Today I have off, and together with Herman I walked into town this afternoon. In the morning it was rainy, and as I was sick the night before with an upset stomach, I slept all morning. I took a camera with us but brought the wrong-size spool. Just our luck. Better luck next time. I picked up a bracelet for a couple of bucks and a pair of small scissors, walked up a steep hill on a steplike sidewalk. Here was a residential section, but everywhere were the French doors opening directly onto the sidewalk. Everywhere behind these glass doors were old women and young girls sewing on all types of articles. The younger ones looked up and smiled at us as we walked by. The old ones squinted quizzically and somewhat bewilderedly as if to say, "Oh, another uniform. I have seen so many," and waved us off. We caught the truck coming from the airport with the line boys. We hopped on and were back in the barracks just before it began to rain heavily.

We visited the girlfriends again. I don't understand why they keep asking us back as we talk about the same things every time. Maria is teaching me some Italian, and I am teaching her some English. We don't dare invite them anywhere as we don't want the entire family trailing along. A squadron dance is coming up, and our commanding officer said that no parents or relatives will be allowed in with the girls. He further stated, "If parents won't take our word about the girls' safety, especially after they continually praise the Americans, they can go plum to hell." He was referring to the previous dance when the place was overrun with food-grabbing parents, nephews, nieces. I've already asked the girls if they would like to go, but it looks hopeless.

February 26, 1944

Nothing much during the day. In the evening at about 8:00 p.m. there was an air raid alert and complete blackout. We heard some terrific explosions that came from Augusta, which was about thirty miles north of us. A few minutes later, we heard the drone of some planes circling about overhead. They proved to be our own. Strack and I were the only ones in the room, so we just lay down on our bunks away from the windows with our helmets on. Pretty soon the whole thing was over, and we fell asleep. I am surprised at the laxity with blackouts. They are not enforced. There were several lights on in the neighboring houses that didn't go out during the duration of the raid. Our own headquarters building is probably the only one in town that doesn't use blackout shades. The last raid on Catania was New Year's Day when a lone plane dropped a stack of bombs on an apartment house killing about fifteen people. These lone raiders almost always get away.

February 27, 1944

Today the Red Cross building opened officially, and free doughnuts and coffee were dispensed. I took off for an hour, with the permission of Lieutenant Jones. General Beverly was to make an informal tour of inspection at the main entrance. Photographer Krotec waited with his

Graflex camera to catch his entrance. I waited with him. The general came and gave his blessing. I think I got myself in the background of the picture.

I visited Maria and Graziella tonight with Herman. I showed Maria the pictures I recently developed that had been taken in Tunis. I gave her one of me. She asked for an inscription, which I gave. It was somewhat idiomatic, and she got all tangled up trying to translate it from the dictionary. I expected that. "*Dearest, we could have made beautiful music together*." She won't find that in the dictionary.

February 28, 1944

Started to help with our news reports at 7:00 a.m. We prepare items for broadcast by the English. News is collected and mimeographed by our department for distribution throughout the military points in Catania. It is compiled the day before by the lieutenant, and the next morning, late flashes and corrections are put in by me for a 7:00 a.m. broadcast. The broadcasts are from BBC stencils and are typed at 8:00 a.m. and mimeographed at 9:00 a.m. before being distributed.

February 29, 1944

Looks like it's a leap year. Payday. Enough said for today. Went to the opera with Herman and saw *Rigoletto*. We went alone this time. My brother Mike's package came today and was full of goodies. The toilet paper shortage is at an end, it's safe to say, but you never can tell. Eternal vigilance is the key word.

March 1, 1944

Haven't received mail from home for about ten days. At guard duty, we previously were allowed to build fires in a large iron cooking pot near the gate, but too much gasoline was being wasted, so we switched to wood for a while. A few scarce packing cases were chopped up for the purpose. That cancelled all fires permanently. As I was saying, when we had fire, we cook cans of C rations to pass the time. No fires, so I took the salted crackers and American cheese that Mike and Bee sent, and they really filled the bill. This new morning news job is very handy. I wake early with the others but are allowed to miss roll call and calisthenics so I can start work at 7:00 a.m. We have a new boss now, Major Salomon. This a.m. I finished a few medical charts for the wing surgeon. Major McKee just got back from a spree at the Isle of Capri and asked me to bring two bottles of hair tonic over to a British general as a gift from our wing. He was out, so I left it with a servant.

March 3, 1944

Today starts my second year in the army. That isn't much cause for rejoicing although it has gone by most rapidly. A year is a long time in the army. The ocean crossing to Casablanca and the train to Tunis stand out as the most forgettable episodes. I would certainly dislike going through that again. Yet I shouldn't complain. Some of the good friends I had at Seymour Johnson Field are now dead.

March 5, 1944

Sunday again, but I had to get up early anyway to get the 7:00 a.m. broadcast. Otherwise, I'd have slept another hour. At the Red Cross, there's a dance at 3:00 p.m. The relatives will not be allowed in, but the ARC provides a few chaperones.

The weather here has been unpredictable as it is at home. The Italians have a saying "Marzo pazzo" (crazy March). I probably failed to mention our laundry system here. We give it to private women who live nearby and are almost always at our main entrance or at the sidewalk below the steps sitting on the low stone fence. They are friendly rivals and no double-crossing tactics have ever come to my attention. Of course, there may be a short fracas over a new customer as he comes walking down the steps soiled clothing in hand, but it is always short-lived. On the way up from chow, we sometimes bring the children some bread and meat, which they immediately tuck away to take home.

This evening we visited the Grimaldi sisters and learned that the older one, Graziella, was leaving the next day for a town called Bronte. She is to go to school there and will be gone about four months. She doesn't want to go because it is a rough town and cold this time of year. Herman will not join me in my visits to the home for quite some time since Graziella will be gone. I am rather reluctant to visit alone naturally, but the other sister Maria will be all alone now, and she seemed so downhearted at her sister's leaving and the probable discontinuance of our visits that I will probably be around just the same. Herman promises to come down once in a while too.

March 7, 1944

Got mail from my old friend Ely Brody today. Brother Mike saw him in New York. Lucky guy. The weather is sunny, and Mount Etna is very beautiful in the morning when the orange morning light reflects off the snow. The days are getting noticeably longer. In the evening, the USO show came to Catania. It was very good and was a welcome change.

Scabies again! A slight case has come on again, which makes it the third one in six weeks. Many in Sicily have them continually. It is especially noticeable on the legs of young kids and women.

I saw the photographs taken at the grand opening of the ARC, and sorry to say, I did not manage to squeeze into the picture with the general. He came out okay though. The Red Cross building is okay too. They have a pet monkey tied on a string, and she is very friendly. She climbs all over anyone who allows it. I always give her Life Savers with the paper on them and watch her peel it off. Then she jams about seven of them into her little mouth and sucks away like the devil while looking fretfully out of the corner of her eye at our laughing faces.

March 10, 1944

At lunchtime we happened to be near the officer's hotel and living quarters, so we dropped in there to eat. It's a very nice place, and the meals are naturally better prepared than in our place. We ate out of real plates. While walking up Via Etna, we stopped in at a store or, rather, as the young woman who was the storekeeper called us inside. After chatting a few minutes in some English, she laid her cards on the table and told us about a camera she had for sale. I had lost mine. It was a dandy, and all she wanted was three hundred dollars. Without our hardly trying, she came down to two hundred fifty. I asked her to get it and I'd take a look at it. The camera is in nearby Syracuse, but her husband taught there, and he'd bring it back and will visit me at the headquarters.

This evening I went alone for the first time to the Grimaldis house. Because Graziella was not expected, Herman didn't come. However, she was there much to my surprise. The weather was too cold up in Bronte for her, so she came back for a couple of days. Otherwise, the evening passed routinely.

March 11, 1944

Sergeant Klibee is back from Capri, and he has taken over my news job. He brought me the two souvenirs I requested before he left. Small Bells is a good luck legend on the island of Capri. It concerns a little girl finding a small bell on the beach and the sudden following up of good fortune for her.

About the camera, at 6:00 p.m., Herman and I went down to see it, and the price had come down to two hundred and thirty dollars. We offered the husband a hundred bucks. "It's out of the question," he fumed. Nevertheless I told him to think it over. He stormed out.

It was raining on the next day with occasional sun. I was thinking about the Grimaldis, so I asked Lieutenant Jones if I could go over to the dance at the Red Cross. Lieutenant Jones was a pretty nice fellow, but rather cautious. He thought a moment at my request and then seeing that Major Salomon was busy said, "Okay. Go." In two seconds, I was in the rain-soaked street wearing only my field jacket. Maria had said she'd try to come down without anyone knowing, but she couldn't promise. Weekdays there was always school or studying at a friend's house that she might use as a pretext. As it was, the chances were pretty slim, so I waited downstairs in the archway for a few minutes expecting to see her across the street as we had arranged. No luck, so I thought I'd go back and see how the dance was going. There were only a very few girls there. I went downstairs looking for Maria, but she never came. At about four, after a few dances I left and returned to the school. I was still very anxious about the outcome of the camera deal. My hopes for getting it were short-lived however. They had sold it the night before. I was highly disappointed. Herman and I sat in a small park up on a hill gazing out over the rooftops of the surrounding homes.

Chapter X

March 14, 1944

Thompson, the corporal who was in our office, was no longer with us due to his ill health. His replacement now had the job of standing around in front of the school chasing the kids away with a big club. This was sad because in the past all of the children knew and liked Thompson a great deal. He would spend a lot of time with them and acted sympathetically to their needs and always controlled them. In a way, I think he had better results than the tough guys before him. The new man employed harsh words and false swings of his club.

In the evening, a friend and I went to a free English entertainment that had a successful run in London. It was very amusing and well done. We are to have a squadron dance tomorrow night. I bought some oranges from one of the little girls. They often wait around for a sale and sometimes are not lucky. Today I didn't have the correct change to give her, but she trusted me. My credit in Sicily has been firmly established as you can plainly see. I saw Maria tonight at home. Her kid sister and baby niece both had colds and had to endure nose drops being forced down with the willingness of a steer to be branded. Such screeching and hollering! A couple of spankings calmed the situation until the operation was completed. Maria came up with a choice bit of news that she had gone and got herself engaged on the sly. That is, her fiancé's parents did not know. I was surprised when she asked me to continue my visits just the same! He wouldn't have to know she told me. She was leaving the next day to go with her sister who had again temporarily returned. She'd call me when she got back. I figured it was time to call it quits, but I couldn't say so then.

Tonight the squadron held a big blowout. We obtained the use of an English hall, which suited the purpose admirably. It was all decorated with crepe paper and flowers for the dance. Refreshments consisted of sandwiches, cake, and champagne. The girls were invited by ticket only. A few of their parents tagged along. An orchestra from the Sixtieth troop carrier group played well. It was as crowded as Macy's on a sale day. The food started to disappear so fast they had to close up for a few minutes for a breather. When the smoke and dust cleared away, the champagne was at a considerable low level. That was mostly our own doing though. The party lasted until 11:30 p.m., and when it broke up, we were all pretty well plastered.

During that afternoon, I bought a .38 caliber revolver from one of the civilians. It was handy to have around sometimes when walking the streets at night. There were plenty of people in this town with grudges against Americans for our bombings. Some had relatives who were killed. Others were just fanatics. I would probably never use it outside of a little target practice. It might be needed only once, but I hope never.

Wrote a few long letters early while Strack continually interrupted with plenty of amusing dribble comparing army life in the States to army life over here. He laughed himself almost sick as he traipsed around in his long woolen underwear, mechanic's cap, and army shoes. He joked about our always carrying gas masks back home and never even seeing them over here. He went into hysterics over the fact that we had such good rifle coaching at home and now after travelling five thousand miles never had a rifle issued to us. "Take it out of your A-bag and out it in your B-bag," he satirized about useless army training and orders we sometimes followed. "Take it easy," I said, looking up on one occasion when I could not help laughing. "I'd like to get a shot of you in that outfit with your shirttails down to your knees and your socks coming up over your underwear." With that he pranced about some more, showing himself off to better advantage. He almost always wore his locomotive engineer cap, and for that we sometimes called him "Ninety-nine" after a historically famous early locomotive. He was in rare form poking fun at military topics ranging from generals to cigarettes.

Chapter XI

March 17, 1944

Tonight, alone, I'd gone to the opera. During the intermission at the Bellini opera house, the patrons darted about the lobby smoking, ordering drinks, and discussing the opera. Suddenly, above the cacophony, I couldn't help overhearing a well-dressed young lady speaking English to her aged father. Why was this obviously Italian girl speaking English? After a few sentences, it became clear. She was criticizing some of the patrons for their lack of proper dress and was inoffensive in English. She was attractive, and I could not resist the golden opportunity to present myself in English with the appropriate savoir faire.

"Pardon me, miss. You are perfectly right," I threw at her as if I too were offended.

She turned to face me, and I was mesmerized by her startling good looks. "Sorry," she threw back, ignoring my surprise, "this is a private conversation."

Wariness of soldiers was understandable. I ignored the rejection and quipped, "Where did you learn to speak so well? I'm really surprised!"

She fell for the compliment but didn't exactly relent. "Thank you." She smiled coolly. "It's a long story, and a private matter."

"Frankly, I'd like to hear the rest of the story," I continued with false bravado, pulling the line a little tighter. The quivering voice of her father finally interjected, also in good English. "Gina, is he bothering you?"

Drawing up her fine, lithe figure and casting a suspicious eye at me, she assured him, "No, Father, I can handle it."

"I'm sorry," I quipped, but before I could say another word, her father lost his balance and uncontrollably fell. I ran to lift his frail body and then went to find a chair before he could fall again. "Hold on to him!" I shouted. That done, the old man was relieved and thankful. Gina gave me a cautious but genuine smile. Hollywood could not have written a better script. At that moment, a soft warning bell signaled intermission's final seconds. Without further words, we separated and returned to our seats. Puccini's *La Traviata* was delightful. On the way out, she signaled to me and approached. "My father is very grateful for your help, and besides there are very few people with whom he can use his English." That reassured me further. "He would be pleased to have you visit us at your convenience." Then pausing and smiling, she gave me her address. Was I too anxious? Time would tell.

March 18, 1944

Back at work, all the department heads wanted me to make signs for them to pretty up their offices for the incoming General Ecker. They always wait till the last minute, so I'm busier than the proverbial one-armed paper hanger with the hives. Besides, I have scabies again. In the afternoon, I printed up dinner place cards for the general's welcoming reception dinner. Some of the boys would like to get an orchestra organized here, and a piano was recently installed in the Red Cross building. We have drums and a bass fiddle. Nobody else plays the piano but me, so we decided to try the three instruments together this evening. It worked out quite well. We did have a little trouble carrying the bass fiddle and the drums around in a jeep, but otherwise our efforts were encouraged, and we hope with practice and prayer we can make something good out of it.

March 19, 1944

A note from Gina invited me to dinner. Naturally, I lost no time rearranging my work schedule and answering her invitation. A short walk and her directions led me to a well-appointed marble-faced home on the Viale Venti Septembre, Catania's equivalent to New York's Park Avenue. A ring of the bell brought Gina, who personally opened a pair of large, carved Italian doors leading to a high-ceilinged rotunda area ringed with small Greek statuary. "Please come in, Milton," she beckoned, leading me to a large living room off to the right. This room was artfully furnished and, in my humble opinion, included some worthwhile collectible artworks. Her father who was ensconced in an overstuffed club chair seemed in better health than at our first meeting. "Happy to see you here," he said and then apologized. "I really didn't have much of a chance to show my appreciation for your help."

My eyes were on Gina who seemed well aware of my glances. "I'll have a brandy," I responded to her offer of a libation. She and her father joined in, and we sipped in silence for a few moments while I wondered why all this cordiality to a relative stranger? Evidently these were people of means, surely with connections that would preclude me from their circle of friends. "We'll have dinner in a little while," the old man joined in.

"Tell me, Milton," Gina asked, "how do you like army life, and what is your work?" I couldn't help feeling she already knew. "You appear, if I may say, to be more than a dirt soldier and capable of greater responsibility." She paused before continuing, changing the subject. "I also assume you are an opera lover just as we are."

"You are right on both counts," I answered and then cleverly added, "Opera lovers are some of my best friends. My work, I'm a draftsman in Catania. I like my work very much but can't discuss it." Gina's offer of a refill was graciously accepted.

A minute later, we sat down to a dinner table set with fine Irish linen and classical silver cutlery. The meal was nicely served by Gina. "How do you come by this fine English capability?" I couldn't wait to ask. Gina's father took the floor and in the King's English, he seemed eager to explain.

"Many years ago," he slowly recounted, "my wife and I immigrated to the United States. Separated from most Italians, we learned English quickly as a matter of survival and pride. Tragically, my wife died suddenly after giving birth to Gina in 1921." Then wistfully and slowly he added, "It seems as if one life is meant to replace another, and I accept it that way." He had my undivided attention. "I was torn between returning to Sicily or emigrating to England where employment and living were easier. I chose the latter. I worked as a librarian, but even after all those years, I still yearned for my native Sicily." Tired, he stopped and took a breath before he continued. “Before returning permanently in 1935, we had vacationed there twice to convince ourselves that we would be happier there. Gina loved Sicily.” The old-timer stopped for a sip of water.

“Now you know the rest of the story,” Gina added, “English is really my native language, and I put it to good use as an official translator for military and legal work. Our meeting was one of the rare times I used it socially. I’m happy I did.” She smiled. Progress, Milton.

Through all this, I could see Gina reflecting my glances, which were even more inviting than the conversation. When dinner finished, I was offered a return engagement in the near future, which I readily accepted. On the way out, I took her hand. “I’m really looking forward to seeing you again real soon, Gina.”

“You’re sweet, Milton. Good night.” Her happy smile reassured me. “Let’s not wait for the next opera.” I laughed, bouncing down the steps.

March 23, 1944

I can’t get Gina out of my mind. I risked going AWOL (absent without leave) and placed a desperate phone call. “Gina, I have to see you again. Can you meet me at the Hotel Excelsior at about noon for lunch?”

A short pause and then she responded, “It’s short notice, but I’ll break a previous appointment. I’m so glad you called.”

The lilt in her voice excited me. The Excelsior is the largest and finest hotel in central Catania. It is a mecca for newly developing commercial clientele and high-level social affairs. It was expensive, but it was worth it. I waited at a café inside and could see Gina drive up. A valet took her car. She was dressed impeccably in a snug pink skirt and blouse and sported a fur-collared white cape.

“Hi, Milt,” she brimmed. Before she could say another word, I planted a swift kiss on her lips, which she willingly returned. “My, you’re impetuous today.” She laughed while ignoring a few catty onlookers. By her expression, I felt that she might be more aggressive than I was. I was about to order cocktails when Gina leaned over brushing my cheek and whispered, “Wouldn’t it be more comfortable in a private room upstairs?” With that look in her beautiful eyes, I didn’t mind her stealing my lines. In fact, I couldn’t have done better myself. While trying to maintain my male ego, I joked, “Look who’s impetuous now.” She pinched me.

In the interest of propriety, I approached the registry desk alone and chose a room. Returning to the table, I gave Gina the room number, left, and turned to the elevator. Almost ten minutes later, there was a soft knock on the door. I threw it open; and there, like a Da Vinci portrait framed before me, was the apparition I had dreamed about, schemed about, and fantasized about. Her supple body flew into my arms, and while balancing on one leg, I kicked the door shut with the other. We fell back onto the bed in a torrid embrace. I don't think it is necessary to describe the details of two souls in ecstasy. I forgot the cocktails, but they certainly would have added nothing. We left with plans for a future tryst, arm in arm to our cars.

March 24, 1944

Day off. Slept until 11:00 a.m. when Strack woke me up and asked me if I wanted to go to chow. I lay there until about eleven thirty and then got up, ate, and came back. We had gotten our PX rations this morning, and Strack and I decided to go down to Bellini Park to sell some cigarettes. We figured we would do away with the middleman by this operation and perhaps get a better price. He stuffed three cartons into his flight jacket, and I took one along. Bellini Park was busy and thriving at this hour of 1:00 p.m., so we thought we would have little trouble. However, wherever we mingled and mentioned cigarettes, a small crowd would gather. This attracted too much attention, so we wandered off with one persistent dealer in our wake. He started out by offering six dollars a carton, but we were out to get seven fifty. He refused to raise his offer so we ignored him, but he kept along with us. He was young and tenacious.

Along the way some kids met us and agreed to pay eight and one-half dollars. We should have known something was amiss in spite of the warnings from veteran operators. Nevertheless, we followed them around the corner and into a large doorway that led to a courtyard. Pretty soon there were fifteen kids around us waving money and yelling loudly. As it was, they never intended paying anything like eight and a half dollars for it. They folded the money in such a way as to be able to withdraw part of it as it was handed over. This had actually happened to a friend of mine sometime back, and I recognized it immediately. They wouldn't let go of the money until they had a grip on the cigarettes, which we would not allow. We finally had to shake them off and leave before the military police came around to see what the commotion was all about. Our friend was now up to six dollars and fifty cents a carton and mixing in a little social conversation on the side. If nothing else happened today, I certainly was learning to fluently count in Italian. Walking back to Via Septembre along Via Etna, we got a lift in one of our trucks going back to the school. Just as we were getting in, the offer went up to twenty-seven dollars for four cartons. As we closed the door, it was twenty-seven dollars, but we wanted twenty-eight dollars or nothing. What we got was nothing.

March 25, 1944

Cleaned up for our weekly inspection before going to work. The weather is very windy and rainy. A note from Gina invited me for dinner tonight. “My father likes you,” she said. “It runs in the family.”

“Of course,” I rejoined. A few cocktails after arriving, he really looked happy. I gave him a couple of packs of cigarettes, and while eating, we spoke all about changes in the United States since he left. “It’s still a great country,” I said, “but we never wanted to get into the war. President Roosevelt knew it was inevitable.”

After coffee, Gina cutely asked, “Dad, are you all right? It’s really your bedtime, you know.” I followed Gina’s line of attack. “You go to bed, and I’ll keep Milton company for a while.” I was really ready for her company. The old man probably knew the score. We bid him goodnight as he tottered to his bedroom. In a moment we were in each other’s arms. Gina had prepared a small, unused maid’s room and lost no time reaching it. In less time, we were both as naked as two jaybirds. We really enjoyed each other’s company. Immodestly I must admit, she praised my performance. She didn’t do too badly herself, feeling she was no ingenue.

March 27, 1944

A few minutes after I got to work, Captain Mckee called me into his office. “Sit down,” he said grimly and paternally. He had never offered a chair before. “I want you to know,” he began, “that I have very little heart in what I have to say. If I didn’t have the greatest faith and confidence in you, I wouldn’t be saying it at all, but instead would leave you in the hands of others less interested in your welfare.”

What on earth was he talking about? I thought to myself. He continued, "Your security clearance gives you access to classified information here. The FBI constantly monitors all of us." He stopped to light a cigarette. "I'll get to the point. Gina, your friend, has been under surveillance because of you. They know all her movements, and with her contacts, she is highly capable of undercover work, even though without any suspicion at present. Any classified leak from this A-2 section would bring suspicion on you because of your close association with her. I know this sounds like guilt without a trial, but this is war, and no such risks are acceptable. I think you know what I'm going to advise you to do. For your own good, consider it carefully. A possible dishonorable discharge is a blight forever, Milton. In short, break it off. I know it will hurt for a while. Take whatever time off you need to straighten yourself out."

I left in a terrible quandary. How could I take his advice? How could I cast off the one thing that gave us so much delight? I will be shipped out someday, and we will sadly part—but why now?

Without wasting anytime, I telephoned Gina. "I must see you immediately, but only to talk," I emphasized. "Do you understand?"

"What's wrong, Milton? What's wrong?" she asked with alarm in her voice.

"I can't explain. If you are going to be home, I can come right over." I was on my way, rehearsing for a terrible act, but could not find any words that would suffice. She flung open the door at my approach, and I brushed by her with barely a hug. I winced, searching for an opening. I sat her down. "Gina," I began and then more subdued, "you know how much you mean to me, and I would never hurt you." I began to relate my conversation with Captain McKee. While I spoke, my mind did flash back to our first dinner meeting when her pronounced cordiality surprised me. Was Gina a latter-day copy of Matta Hari, that infamous spy of World War I? Smarter soldiers than I have been duped. Yet there was never an invasive question that I could remember. Perhaps it was too early in the game. I tried to dismiss such sickening thoughts from my mind.

"Milton! How can you believe such possible accusations?" she cried, "I have never cared for anyone as I do you! You must believe that! I do have close contacts with the Italian authorities, and honestly, the enemy has attempted subverting me, but I swear that I love my country and could never double-cross it or you." Tears swelled up in her eyes. I could not help but believe her, and so I reassured her.

"But the facts are," I continued sadly, "that any leak of classified information of which I have knowledge would certainly backfire to you, Gina, guilty or not. I cannot let that happen. Better that we separate for a while and be patient." She tearfully agreed.

Little did I know that this would be the last time that I would ever see her alive.

March 29, 1944

Two days later, I couldn't resist calling. Her father answered in a terribly dejected monotone. "Little Gina was killed yesterday in an automobile accident." He could hardly get the words out. I was so shocked that I could not speak, and I mentally replayed his awful words in my head. "I can't believe it. I'm coming right over," I told him. I couldn't believe the monstrous bad luck that had befallen the two of us. This was my first indescribable experience with the death of someone close to me. He filled me in on the gruesome details, which hardly mattered. She was gone, and although I commiserated with the poor man, I was hardly prepared for a disrupted future. I attended her funeral and extended my condolences to her small family and said a heartfelt good-bye to them, a good-bye forever. It was a closed chapter that would be, if ever, hard to forget.

Chapter XII

March 30, 1944

A very blue Monday—still in shock over Gina's death—makes one wonder what it's all about. A drizzly day, which is the most and best I can say for it. Work is becoming something like any job, and one would hardly know this is the army. When I think back to sterile army life back home, I am struck by the percolating lifelike experience over here—an explosive change in new lands, customs, and most of all the suffering but hopeful humanity. Discipline is not as strictly enforced here, but we are expected to remember our duties. Our commanding officer maintains good discipline with one eye closed.

This evening I saw a movie named *Coney Island.* You should have heard the cheering that went up when a picture of some sauerkraut and frankfurters appeared. They looked absolutely three dimensional!

March 31, 1944

Walked around town with Herman and stopped at the park for a while. We found ourselves with a group of military hospital patients talking and writing letters. Some patients were dressed in their bright blue civilian type suits with a loud red tie. We were all taking in the sun. A couple of kids followed us all the while pestering for a cigarette and orange trade. Nut vendors were there to greet us, and there were others to collect the cellophane bags that contained the nuts. Nothing is expendable. While basking awhile, who should come up with profuse greetings in accented English but a Sicilian who had known the luxury of several years in Brooklyn. *Coney Island* had made the biggest impression on him, and Mussolini definitely had to go. He appeared to hold himself in a different category from his surrounding compatriots because of his period abroad, and he confessed a definite kinship to Americans. He smoked a stubby clenched cigar in a nonchalant American manner as a token of proof. We felt sorry for him because there must have been good reasons indeed to bring this man back here after having tasted Brooklyn.

Wow, what was this? Suddenly a silver pocket watch dangled in our faces from the end of a chain. I was about to utter the involuntary question of "How much?" when I thought better of it and checked myself. Its owner smiled down at us in the manner of an experienced collector who has recently come upon a rare curio and is now presenting it to a selected few, prior to a public unveiling. Herman always made it somewhat unpleasant for these boys by examining everything they had to offer. Taking things apart, listening to them, tapping them, rubbing them, and in general treating the items as rough as possible without damaging them. In this case, he opened the watch with no intentions whatsoever of buying it and proceeded with his routine inspection. "How much?" The inevitable question popped up. The other answered in Italian. "Five dollars and five packs of cigarettes." Herman bargained with him just to kill time; and pretty soon, when the news got around that we had some cigarettes, all the local dealers gathered around and started bidding. They came up to sixty-five cents, but we wanted seventy cents a pack. Two of them retreated in a football huddle while making a few calculations on a newspaper and then burst forth a few seconds later with an offer of two dollars and sixty cents for four packs, which was still sixty-five cents a pack! We stood firm. "Settantacinque" ("Seventy-five"). They retreated again and maybe this time to shorten their lines of communication because they never came back. After shooing away a few of the five-minute face sketchers—artists who will cut your silhouette from a piece of black paper, we made our way back toward the school. We examined a few cameras that were for sale on our way and then called it an afternoon. Right after chow we did sell our cigarettes.

The entertainment this evening was somewhat different. It was in a large unused room in the dispensary as a "smoker." We all wondered whether it would be a regular smoker. It was different. "Drinker" would have been closer to the truth. Rosario is our chief unofficial headquarters interpreter, and it was he who secured the female attractions. There were to be five, but only two appeared. Rosario felt somewhat at fault and was determined to make sure the two did "all right" as compensation. Their program consisted of a series of consecutive dances, each being accompanied with a lesser degree of clothing. One got cold feet and refused to go all the way. The other was fairly well lit up and did right by her profession. After which a couple of drunk guys began to think they were in a different kind of a house and had to be subdued. I don't think she would have objected anyway. It finally ended up with several of the more enthusiastic onlookers pouring champagne over her. During the entire sequence of dances, Rosario, on several occasions, had to see to it that different articles of apparel were removed more quickly than the girls had anticipated. In fact, if it were not for his untiring efforts, the show would have been a flop. He was a real trooper. He swore, and he scolded at their unprofessional shyness until he went in and did the job himself. Such was the man Rosario. The girls were paid to the extent that they undressed. One got five dollars; the bashful one got three dollars.

April 1, 1944

April Fool's Day, but no pranks. No roll call this morning. Probably too many hangovers anyway. Quiet day in general.

April 2, 1944

I met a new friend, Private Abbe Sussman. Abbe was somewhat different from my other friends. He knew what he wanted and was determined to use his half-baked friendships with officers as a stepping stone to personal benefits on the road ahead. Being egregious myself, we got along. This was Palm Sunday. Everyone was carrying his palm and dressed in the finest for the occasion. Even so, it was rare to see a pair of stockings that didn't have two or three unrepaired runs in them. Most of them wore no stockings. We returned to the Red Cross for the regular Sunday afternoon dance, and it was relaxing.

April 3, 1944

Forgot to mention that on Friday afternoon I got permission to go out and test my submachine gun, which I had just taken apart and cleaned. I shot about fifteen hard-kicking slugs into a stone wall, and I was satisfied that it worked. Today we rearranged our large wall maps in the office so that the England/France area was highlighted for the coming invasion of the continent.

April 4, 1944

The Russians sure are plowing ahead toward Berlin. I reset the censored news map out in the hall every morning together with the news sheet as explanation. My coworkers watch eagerly as I move pins about and adjust the string boundary of the front lines. I like my responsibility in this respect. "Where is such and such a place?" asks one. I point without any hesitation toward the spot. "Where do you think they'll go next?" queries another from the crowd. The answers to multitudes of questions are at my fingertips, and I spout forth unstintingly except for classified info. One day I look up at the map in surprise and anger. Some wise guy has put a front line up around Berlin. Classified info such as name and strength of fighting units is under lock and key in my back room.

I am on guard duty. Instead of slinging my machine gun, I put my revolver in my pocket just to carry a lighter load. Gosh, I was sleepy. I slept till 10:00 a.m. the next morning. It's about a week since Gina died.

April 5, 1944

Went into work at 11:30 a.m. after early chow. Nothing to do and ended up reading a book that my sister-in-law Bea had sent me.

April 6, 1944

Another day off loafing around. That's the way it is around here now. Sometimes you work steady for a week and then don't do a thing for a week. I like it better busy. I wrote a few letters. No mail for two or three days now. This evening I didn't expect to do anything but luckily came into two opera tickets. I went to see *Amico Fritz* with another fellow. During the intermission, similar to my meeting with Maria, we met two girls and the aunt of one of them. The one I was particularly interested in was Angelina. She lived in Catania. I have her address and will visit her when possible. She says her aunt is a bit wary of soldiers and that I should wait.

April 7, 1944

Woke up with a bad headache and on my day off. Bought rations for myself and Klibee and three officers. The officers let me get cigarettes, which later went the way of most cigarettes. I sold about twenty-five dollars' worth of stuff and spent about twenty on a pair of binoculars with a few pairs of old socks and some soap thrown in. Walked downtown with Herman later in the evening and mingled with some friendly citizens in a large open piazza in front of the great *Duomo* Cathedral. A full moon grinned at us in a cloudless sky.

April 8, 1944

Today the first thing that struck me was the clean faces on many of the children around the school. They were scheduled for Easter holiday. I hardly recognized some of them. I worked on the masthead of the new newspaper called *Wingtips* putting it on a mimeograph stencil. I hope to preserve a copy for posterity. Tonight Sussman and I walked over the Transient officer's hotel downtown and chewed the rag with the interpreter there. He's an American who came here in 1926.

April 9, 1944

The first words that greeted me from the washwomen and children just outside were "Buona Pasqua. Buona Pasqua" ("Happy Easter"). It was Easter Sunday, and the sustained cleanliness yesterday must have been trying indeed on these children. For the people here, the holiday has the further connotation of making up with one's enemies. It was a day of rousing good spirit for all, infused with handshaking combined with an increased tempo of head and hand gestures, which even in ordinary times took second place to speech. The surprisingly gay finery was bedecking the citizenry from fine black to the cheery colors of a New York Fifth Avenue parade. The streets were crowded, and people congregated in small bunches everywhere, congesting traffic even more than usual. The streetcars had more people hanging on the outside than were on the inside. It was greater than any five o'clock rush hour jam I have ever witnessed. All this I absorbed after I was given the afternoon off at 3:00 p.m. to attend a dance. However, the dance never blossomed, so Sussman and I walked downtown to commiserate.

A couple of kids followed us to retrieve cigarette butts that we were about to fling away. After about six blocks, Sussman got sore. We told them to beat it. They were five of the smallest, dirtiest barefoot urchins in the lot who kept their eyes glued on the hand that held the cigarette, following it up and down as we puffed, like an audience at a tennis match. As they refused to leave and the butts were ready for disposal, Sussman stopped and menacingly turned, so their hungry eyes could see, tore up the butts, and threw the bits in their faces. They weren't angry. They merely took it as they took everything else. For them disappointment was to be expected—so in fear and desperation, they act without any tact. I was surprised at Sussman's cold rebuff. I'm a soft touch and would have cooperated.

This evening I managed to get to Angelina's friend's house in Ognini, a small waterfront spa outside of Catania, to speak to the girl I met at the opera the other night. She spoke softly, but with strength and sincerity, and no sign of timidity. Her straight, shoulder-length dark brown hair caressed a lovely elliptical, high cheekboned, clear-eyed face, altogether appearing tender and adventurous at the same time. It was a very modest-looking house, but I was cordially received by her aunt and friends, and I prattled convincingly in my improving Italian. They loved to hear about America. Her aunt is about sixty, healthy, and seemed quite active. Angelina was all smiles, and so was I. I waited for them to eat, which is quite late in these parts, drank some offered wine, and relaxed. It is poor manners to refuse the offer. We sat outside just off the Messina Road on the porch and, among other things, swatted the flies and fleas that were dive-bombing us. My cigarettes were welcome to the menfolk. The old-fashioned customs of the Grimaldis were noticeably gone. I had a chance to talk to Angelina a few times without some relative breathing down my neck. It was a relief, and I planned a future visit with her before I left. A sincere attachment was on the way.

April 10, 1944

Another draftsman arrived today. That is, two of them did, but one would be shipped to an interior group. He was to work in statistics; and Captain Morgan, the head of my section, asked me to interview them and choose one. Naturally I felt flattered that he had such confidence in me. The following is a text of the interview after we were left alone:

Me: "Say, where did you fellows come from?" I asked. "I'm from Indiana," said one. "I'm from California," said the other. Me: "I'm from New York myself, but would you like to be back home right now?" I asked as if I had the power to send them home. "You betcha," they both agreed, smiling. "You'll be home soon enough," I stated confidently. I learn from listening and observing. "Where did you study drafting?" I asked. They filled me in, and I soon discovered that both had more experience than I did. "What kind of work do you specialize in here?" they asked. "Oh, charts, classified map work, statistical charts, signs, and a lot of stuff like that," I replied. One raised his eyebrows; the other just stared, not much help. I had yet to make a choice, but I had no preference. They were both fit, so I offered a proposition. "You weren't buddies?" I asked. Them: "No, we just met in Tunis, and then were shipped over here." "Well, then you won't mind getting split up because you know we can use only one of you here. The other will go to one of the groups." I didn't tell them that one was in India. "Does either of you especially care to remain or leave here?" I asked, still looking for an opening. "How's the setup here?" they both counter questioned. "Oh, it's fine," I said, "but I imagine a draftsman will have it pretty easy anywhere." This seemed to lighten their spirits a little. I continued, approaching the climax of my proposition and looking about to see that Captain Morgan was not around. "Suppose we toss for it," I said. They agreed readily, and one pulled out an American quarter, which I had not seen for months. We tossed, and Walter Miller of Indiana won. The winner shook my hand vigorously, and I told the other that I was sorry that they both couldn't stay. We shook hands, and I left them to speak to the captain. "I think Miller will do," I said gravely, with the appearance of my emerging from a weighty board of director's meeting. "He'll have to pass a security check," I said. He thanked me, and I left.

April 11, 1944

Life goes on and on and on. Catania is becoming as familiar as Brooklyn now, and even the civilian faces have lost their novelty. Learning their language has improved our interface, our understanding each other. A common language makes it so much easier. Common calamity tends to unite its victims.

April 12, 1944

I prepared to get three packages off to home containing some souvenirs. On the way back to school, around 4:45 p.m., an Italian soldier approached me. He needed money for his sick mother. He backed up his story by showing me a telegram calling for his presence in Naples. He didn't want a loan. He had a .32 Berretta automatic and a holster to sell. I wanted to get rid of my revolver anyway, so we bargained up and back. I finally got it for forty dollars and two and a half bars of soap.

April 13, 1944

The USO show passed through Catania and played at our theater. Their MCs are pretty good. They had magicians, singers, accordionists, and jugglers.

April 14, 1944

Squadron dance at the Spring Bok. Same place we had it last time. We didn't have such a hot time then. This time the orchestra was Italian, and they played enjoyably. I didn't feel like going on guard duty at two this morning, so I found a fellow who needed five bucks, and he took my place. In the meantime, I have the next morning to catch up on sleep that I lost.

April 15, 1944

An inspection in the morning. Herman and I walked up the Via Septembre partway, and rented two bicycles. After riding around town for an hour, we decided that was enough exercise for the day. We stopped at the Red Cross and visited Strack out on the back porch outside the kitchen. Herman had brought a box of graham crackers along, and we had coffee on the house.

April 16, 1944

Today the first edition of *Wingtips* came out. I'm saving a first edition copy held for me. Only a limited number were printed for us and the attached units. Sergeant Klibee gave me the afternoon off.

April 17, 1944

I got thirteen letters today after a week's lull. No packages yet and no camera. Today Master Sergeant Brown asked me to be feature editor on the *Wingtips*, which I accepted readily. He didn't even ask me if I could do it. I wrote up all special events outside of sports, which was covered by a sports writer. Sussman, who was writing the gossip column, asked me to collaborate with him, which I did. I felt this extra activity would be a relief from the usual monotony.

April 19, 1944

I visited sweet and feisty Angelina this evening. I occasionally think of poor Gina, but Angelina is making strong inroads—an entirely different personality, strongly sincere and caring, and more like an open book.

April 20, 1944

This evening Sussman and I visited a girlfriend of his who, together with some of her college friends, is rehearsing a play to be performed on Sunday two weeks hence. Sussman has had some acting experience in radio, but he helped out in a limited way due to his inability to converse fluently with them. This is the second time I've been here, and I'm picking up more Italian that way. Sergeant Klibee saw me at lunchtime and asked me if I would go down to visit a castle in town in the capacity of a reporter for the *Wingtips*. The place was on exhibition, and since I was feature editor, I was to write an article on its history.

April 21, 1944

This morning I cut the stencil headline and wrote a short article in the news. On the way back to the school, a camera salesman stopped me, but he had little to offer.

April 29, 1944

Miller is the statistical draftsman and has little to do most of the month, so he hangs around my place. I made an ink drawing of a mess kit washing system used overseas for our medical department. It will be photostated and sent to different outfits in the field. I kept a copy for myself.

April 30, 1944

The boss let me go to the dance this afternoon. Not too many girls showed up, and most who did told their folks that they were going to the cinema.

May 1, 1944

At my last meeting with Angelina a few days ago, we arranged with her friend to bring along another fellow, and the four of us would walk around a bit near the seashore of Ognini. During the past visits, I spent some pleasant time, and we all enjoyed ourselves. I learned that Angelina was orphaned when her only remaining parent, her young mother, died in 1939. Fortunately, her aunt and uncle can provide her with her needs. I have taken more than a great liking to her, and I know she reciprocates. So I look forward to this period as a new turn in my unfolding destiny. Soft fading memories of past incidents and affairs haunt me at times, reminding me that as responsible doers and observers, we are at one and the same time actors and audience of a soul-searching play. Angelina may well be the star for a happy ending.

Chapter XIII

NEWS HEADLINE: ***May 9, 1944*****—Soviet Troops on Offensive Recapture Sevastopol**

At 4:30 p.m. I departed silently and unnoticeably from my office. I had a quick supper and proceeded to Via Septembre, hopped on a streetcar, and met Angelina and the other couple at the last stop, which was the beach. The late afternoon was sunny, and the walk was nice. The other fellow, Carlo, is studying medicine. He appeared more English than Italian. Our direction was toward the waterfront where I had my first good look at the Sicilian shore. It was really clear and blue. The shore is rocky, and lava hills come up to the water in cliff-like formations of about thirty feet in height. On the edge of one of these, a small patch of wild wheat grew. Everything else was barren and rock, but nevertheless picturesque in its oddity. No one lived here on the lava, but far behind, small settlements of fishermen lived with their families in squalid little streets. They looked at us quizzically, but not unfriendly in manner as we passed by their open doors or met them talking or mending their nets and boats. We sat by the wheat patch for a while. Later we descended through a tunnel in the lava to the shoreline where small waves broke into a fine spray over the rocks. Carlo and his friend took off their shoes and socks and began wading along the irregular coastline under the fringe of the overhanging lava caves. We chose not to follow, and after a few moments, we returned to the "topside" and waited for them. The sun was beginning to set now, but it was hardly chilly. Angelina knew little English, but we didn't have too much trouble conversing, our eyes sufficed. At about 7:30 p.m., we started back with another appointment on Wednesday.

This evening we had a VD lecture. I wouldn't mention it but for the fact that a new lieutenant was giving it and he surprised everybody. Instead of a dry statistical and threatening talk, he made us feel as though he was one of the boys, and his explicit demonstration was unique indeed. He got the idea across humorously and effectively.

At about 8:30 p.m., I again made my way back to an early chow and then returned to the corner of Via Liberta to meet Carlo who lived close by. We decided to go to Ognini together. We shook hands and then boarded a trolley. Handshaking is a very important courtesy here, and it is poor taste to miss shaking the hand even of a slight acquaintance. In fact, good fellowship goes so far as to produce grown men walking arm in arm down the street. We headed toward the waterfront to the same place and met Angelina and her friend Sofia. We just passed the time talking about this and that, and pulling wheat thistles out of our clothing. We then headed back toward the trolley and camp.

May 5, 1944

I met Carlo again. We went to a new spot in Ognini. Walking over a long rocky path, we finally emerged at a blissful cavelike setting. Angelina and I clambered over a path of dry rocks and for several feet over the water and sat on a tiny circle of flat black lava that kept us close together on our own private little island. The water was calm, clean, and blue; so we were in no danger of getting wet. The other couple scampered to change for a dip. At about 7:00 p.m., we left and sent the girls home apart from us to avoid disparaging civilian remarks. Carlo and I waited around twenty minutes for the next streetcar. I looked around at the surrounding cove that was formed where the water came up to the cliffs. Little fishing boats were arranging their night lanterns while it was still light. Small children were swimming nude and having a splashing, giggling good time jumping at little fish that came close. A few fishermen's houses near the base of some of the flatter sections of lava at the water's edge were like a little private village separate from the one above the cliffs. Here where the Messina coast road comes into Catania is a contraband inspection station. We throw a friendly wave as they eye us.

May 6, 1944

Spring is very warm here. I arranged another meeting with the gang for tomorrow, and I intend to take my first dip in the sea.

May 7, 1944

General Canon is making an inspection today; so we have started cleaning up, dusting, etc. He finally shows up at our office while I'm out to lunch. This afternoon, under pretense of going to the ARC dance, Lieutenant Jones let me off at two forty-five; and just as I got downstairs, I bumped into Carlo waiting for me. We boarded the next trolley and proceeded to Ognini, Toonerville, trolley style. It was rickety and crowded. My Italian is improving, and I try out my verb conjugations on our friends as we proceed to the beach. Angelina has her suit but doesn't like the water much. She shivers as she mentions it. My swim was chilly, and it was difficult getting out of the water on slippery rocks. We had a delightful sunbath after that. The trolley was filled to bursting capacity on the way back. An old gent in a jovial humor starts singing to the crowd as he forced his way in. In Italian he belted out "Plenty of room. All aboard. Bring the kids, have a good time." He got a good laugh, but no seat.

May 8, 1944

We met the girls again. I had brought two cakes of soap as a surprise for them. Can you imagine bringing your girlfriend a bar of soap as a gift and her liking it at that?

May 10, 1944

I got a letter from Private Thompson who has been in Naples Hospital for almost five weeks. He was there for observation as a result of mysterious fainting that overtook him at the most unexpected moments. Once he passed out just as he was getting off the back of a truck, and he severely injured himself as he fell. Another time, just as a movie show ended and the lights came on, Thompson, who had been sitting next to me, was frozen in his seat in a catatonic state. The doctor has confirmed it to be a psychoneurosis. Thompson will be sent home for further treatment. There isn't a kid in the neighborhood who won't miss his compassionate guard duty at our barracks. Candy is sometimes mightier than the sword for children whose fathers were mainly wartime prisoners or worse. He was a parent figure, and Thompson truly loved the children.

After supper, we went to a show with Sussman, and we always walk back the few blocks from Via Liberta. On Via Septembre, there is one of many open piazzas with benches, orange stands, and very kind people. These days it is difficult to find seats. Some are crowded with adolescent boys singing in happy unison while a quartet or so responds from the other side of the street in tempo. People play simple, gentle games. Some benches are occupied by families. They ignore the occasional light beam from our flashlights and usually respond to our "Buono Sera" politely. Many families, even with babies, are out until 10:30 p.m. Some benches have vagrants on them, the like of which you cannot imagine. Most are barefoot, filthy, and sick. Pieces of tattered clothing fall off. They are not drunks however. They would eat out of garbage cans if necessary. However, as long as I have been here, I have never seen a vegetable, leaf, or rotten apple discarded anywhere. There isn't even a stray piece of paper in the gutter. Storekeepers unapologetically wrap articles in old and torn paper. String is just as rare. If we chance to be tired and rude, we stand in front of a loaded bench, and pretty soon some of the people get the idea that we are looking for a place to sit and they get up. Their voices cease, and they slowly move over to make room. We sit and watch Catania go by, smoke, buy oranges at two cents a pound, and politely flirt a little even with the escorted signorinas whose boyfriends take no offense. Some instincts are very hard to resist. They all take it in good humor. We discuss a play that Special Services wants written for GI entertainment. We have an embryo idea, but not much else.

May 14, 1944

Over at the ARC saw Strack. He's a permanent hilarious attraction there. I expected Angelina and the friends might drop by to see the place. I had told them that I might be at the American Red Cross today. They showed up as I had expected, and I showed them around, and we danced. Angelina loves dancing—couldn't get her off the floor. I still haven't advanced much beyond the two-step.

May 15, 1944

Before going to the show in the evening, we (Sussman and I) stopped at the Arbiters, a singular and well-kept knickknack shop, the proprietor of which we knew quite well. I usually find the best souvenirs in town here. Bought two Spanish fans in a showcase—one of bone and the other plastic. The latter needed a new connecting ribbon, and he agreed to have it repaired by Wednesday.

May 18, 1944

Saw Angelina and friends again at the shore but didn't go into the water. It was too cold. We kept warm in the old-fashioned way.

May 19, 1944

Day off. Spent a while writing an article for the Sunday paper, the *Wingtips*, about a contest program. I actually saw the program come off, and I was proud to see that every word was mine.

May 22, 1944

Saw Angelina again. The poor thing wore an ankle bandage, having suffered a sprain the night before on a step. She figured that she could still make it out to the rocks anyway, so we went. I told her I was going to Taormina, our rest camp, tomorrow and would return in a week. She asked me to write but didn't like the idea of my being away.

May 23, 1944

First day of vacation began by receiving our orders for departure at about 8:30 a.m. in the morning. Sussman, Lopaton, and I were going together with two others. We hung around until eleven thirty when the bus arrived an hour late. Taormina was thirty miles away up the coast. The ride up was picturesque. As we climbed, I took a few photographs from the back of the truck and throughout the trip. We got many different views of Mount Etna. Going uphill all the way, we finally emerged at about a thousand foot altitude onto the rocky but beautiful cliffs off Taormina. We ate immediately upon arriving at the Hotel Miramar. The waiters were a pleasant surprise. The dining room had an adjoining terrace overlooking the Mediterranean Sea in true luxury style. There was every style and shape of dish with appropriate silver that one might associate with a fine hotel. After lunch we walked into town, about ten minutes away. It centers mostly around one long main street catering to the tourist trade. They excel in needlework of all kinds, and since the soldiers are now here, insignia work is their main output. Shooting off from the main street, the side streets lead one into the living quarters and the quainter parts of town—the few slums, the picturesque, the ancient, the novel, and the unexpected. Still, streets are hilly, and no two parts are alike. There are some beautiful villas that are situated in private places, commanding equally beautiful views of the sea. The town has a two-thousand-year history of Greeks, Romans, Saracens, Normans, etc. Each has left its mark in style.

On our first walk into town, we stopped at one of the typical shops and were attracted, naturally, to a signorina named Francesca hiding behind a pair of large sunglasses. Her aunt was also about, and we got along well with them. They spoke German very well because they had had three years of association with them. We bought a few knickknacks and then continued on down the street, talking to almost every shopkeeper along the way. Every barber played a mandolin. We thought that we would never reach the end of the main street at the rate we were going. There were several cafés with names like Red Lantern, Garden of Eden, the Red Arch, and others. They were colorfully decorated. After dinner, we again returned to town. Taormina is a rest camp town, but actually it is much more. Recreation camp would be more apt. Amid the splendid wonder of the scenery and free atmosphere, one has time to catch up, so to speak, on civilian life. Cafés are the natural result of this trend. In Catania, there are no cafés where one may dance and drink, but here the doors are flung wide open.

I mentioned hostesses before, and that is their nominal trade. Before or after hours, they are on their own. All women in town are required to take periodic physical inspections. There is one exception. Virgins are exempt, but how their exact number is known is a mystery. Girl hostesses wear convincing smiles and gab without end. At the hotel, in the evening, a scheduled dance came off with the elite gentry of the town; or so we were told. We danced in the dining room with most of the tables pushed back nightclub style. One Tom Collins left me sleepy, and I had to take off for bed.

May 24, 1944

Cloudy day. I awoke at seven o'clock in the morning, which always happens on vacations. Down to a breakfast of eggs, coffee, and orange juice after which three of us walked into town. We looked and photographed the old Greek theater ruins and further were about to take a few pictures when we heard a signorina calling down to us from high up on a steep hill. Our binoculars focused on a fair young face. We didn't know how to get up that hill, but we sure made it up darn fast and came onto a blissful scene of provincial antiquity where stuff and things were served out in the open. We had some orange juice and watched a Limey drink with a girl on his lap. The girls were a sort of come-on, so we left soon amid promises of the arrival of some more friendly signorinas. The foregoing report is rather a condensation of most of the weeks' activities. We did return to the Greek theater one day for photographic purposes and had our orange juice and cake in a little shop nearby.

May 27, 1944

We descended by truck to the Fiftiest troop carrier wing beach, 750 feet below. Instead of swimming, we decided to take a small sailboat out with an experienced fisherman. This was all gratis. It was rough, with whitecaps, but we started out nevertheless. The boat rocked badly, and although I didn't fear a swim back, I had two cameras and a pair of field glasses that I didn't want ruined. At five hundred feet out, in an attempt to turn to see some caves, a gust of wind caught the sail and threw the whole boat over on its side. The others fell into the water. The boat quickly righted itself but was full of water. I was in uniform while the other three were in bathing suits. By some strange piece of luck I held on and kept both cameras from getting soaked. Shorty, a friend of ours, had fallen in with binoculars around his neck. The fisherman remained inside and told us to keep calm. But Shorty couldn't swim! He began splashing around like a madman. If Shorty grabbed the boat, he'd surely turn it over. The other two kept their heads and stayed away from the boat. They were afraid to help Shorty because the fierceness of his fright might pull them all under! Shorty finally grabbed the side and began to scramble aboard. He was desperate to be safe, but I had to wait to let him on until he calmed down. When he got in the boat, it would sink a little lower. The choppy water made it difficult, but he finally came aboard while we kept the boat precariously balanced. I had awful thoughts of all of us going in, cameras and all. The water was up to my knees. We began to make our way toward the shoreline to a section of the beach that was closer, although rockier. Sussman got tired in the water, and we had to let him hold on to the rudder. About fifty feet offshore, we got out and walked over the rocky bed to the shoreline. Shorty, in a mad scramble for the beach, almost stepped on an undiscovered mine. It may have been dead, but we didn't care to find out.

Later I took the binoculars apart, prisms and all, and cleaned them. I had remarked to Sussman earlier that I wished I could find something to write about, and I certainly did. I think Shorty had aged a couple of years.

May 30, 1944

We left the hotel at 8:30 a.m. and returned to Catania. We never thought we'd be so sorry to leave a place as this. I will surely never forget that spot I know. It is only thirty miles from here, and with couriers running twice a day, you could spend a day up there. We didn't go back to work when we arrived in the morning. That would have been too much of a shock after those days of luxury. We walked about town and slowly got used to the old sights again.

May 31, 1944

Back to work, so to speak. I was happy to find another package that had come for me. I made guard duty for the second consecutive night from 6:00 to 10:00 p.m. at the motor pool. It seems they are expecting some political trouble. There had been some striking students causing unrest due to the coming elections.

Chapter XIV

NEWS HEADLINE: *June 6, 1944*—D-day Landings on North Coast of France
***June 5, 1944*—Allies Enter Rome**

June 1, 1944

Sussman, Lopaton, and I are making plans to return to Taormina this weekend. Today is anniversary day for our organization. In celebration, a dinner was given in the afternoon in the dayroom, and it was my job to write it up for the *Wingtips* newspaper. In the evening, there was a large dance. There were so many that one was held on the terrace and the other in the dayroom. It was a very successful affair. Refreshments came and went fast with the civilians running for touchdown.

June 3, 1944

We are all prepared to take off on the three thirty Taormina bus. Sergeant Klibbi says it's okay. We intend to return on Monday morning, took a few toilet articles along; and in an hour we were through the mountain pass on to Shangri-la, our very own Shangri-la. Before supper we walked through town; then we lounged on the outside veranda.

June 4, 1944

Swam before dinner and walked. Those beautiful mountains never cease to please me. The food is good, and the service is a pleasure.

June 5, 1944

Blue Monday all right, but after work, I went to Angelina's aunt's house to spend the evening in Ognini. She was neatly dressed and had just finished a day's work around the house. I had a little discussion with some of the men on politics. They did most of the talking among themselves because it was hard to catch their dialect. I merely gave them a few facts about the States with a good plug for Brooklyn.

June 6, 1944

D-day. Invasion day of France. Somber prayers here and all over the Allied world. A quiz contest this evening was cancelled out of respect. Deep thought pervaded for the men we knew would fall in this heroic attempt.

June 7, 1944

Made many changes on the invasion map. All eyes were glued to it.

June 8, 1944

Today is an important religious holiday here. Corpus Domani and many large processions go down Via Etna. Priests, crosses, soldiers, girls, flags, and music all pulled manually on large flatbed displays.

June 9, 1944

Went to visit Angelina again. From there we walked over to her friend Sofia's house right nearby and found Carlo there too and his Sofia. Angelina's aunt's house is not large enough for gatherings; that's why we came here. We played the phonograph, and Sofia's folks were very kind. I was telling them about Taormina, and they had been there many times and were not surprised that we loved the town and its ancient setting.

June 10, 1944

Today was a busy one. We had several things to do before I could take off to Taormina at 3:30 p.m., and the major came up with a map posting job at the last minute. That almost threw a monkey wrench in the machinery. Then I had to write the news for *Wingtips* because Sergeant Klibee was away at Taormina himself and wouldn't be back until tomorrow, but luck was with us, and we made the bus. Rest camp is closing on the fifteenth, so this will be the last trip up there. In fact,

Taormina will be out of bounds to all enlisted men from then on. We checked in at our favorite Miramar Hotel, dined like gentlemen, and relaxed.

June 11, 1944

Did little but rest and took in all the old Taormina sights for a lasting memory of this quaint, spectacular village.

June 12, 1944

Angelina is jealous of my visits to Taormina, but I kid her that I had two women one night. That joke was a mistake. She knew I was kidding but gleefully pinched my arm—a stinging, loving pinch—to remind me that it was just a warning prelude to a Sicilian Mafioso curse, the likes of which I was not ready to investigate. We didn't go to bed mad.

June 13, 1944

Moving rumors are in the air. This is something I have dreaded for quite some time now. Over at Angelina's house again this evening, I guess I was a little glum, and she asked me what was troubling me. I postponed the bad news for later. They were baking bread at the house this evening. The signora's daughter, a married woman with three children, was over to help from her house nearby. In the preparation, she sent the youngsters in search of dried branches for a fire in the oven. It was a very crude process. First the stone oven was heated, then the ashes withdrawn and the wet loaves inserted. A metal cover was then cemented over the opening with a kind of fibrous mud. After an hour and a half, they were taken out. During this time, there was a big discussion over something that was not at all clear to me. Once the daughter dropped her work and ran into the house to wham the daylights out of her brats who, it seems, are recalcitrant when led off to bed by their grandmother. When all was quiet again, it was dark, and we sat down to eat.

June 15, 1944

It's getting uncomfortably warm now, and I'm doing work on the new graphs for the A-3 section. After supper, I met Angelina at the streetcar stop. She had been in town for some shopping, and so we decided to meet and go back to her apartment together. The signora was sick in bed and was helped by her married daughter.

June 17, 1944

Moving rumors are in the air, but it is quite speculative as to where or when. It seems we are not going to Naples as we expected but probably to somewhere near Rome.

June 18, 1944

No work today, so I spent the day in Ognini. We went to the beach, and we rented lockers then met Sussman and Lopaton sitting at a table under the arbor. We joined them for a while. They had been swimming, and we didn't feel like going in just yet. After a half hour, we ate dinner there in the open. It was beautiful out in the sun, daydreaming, without any vestige of war around us. There was a little ballroom in the rear, and we danced later. Angelina was much depressed when I told her I was leaving. She wants to go too if it is at all possible. I was wrapped in thought wondering about the idea. I'm sure her aunt would object, but I think I could take much better care of her with me. It was a serious decision. We stayed awhile and lay in the sun. We were in the cove I mentioned when I first visited Ognini. It's filled with little boats, and a few in particular were dangerously overloaded with children from a church institution, enjoying a holiday. They did return safely. We returned about 4:30 p.m., dried off, dressed, and came back to town together—had two pizzas on a piazza bench. There was a small carnival on a street off Via Septembre, housing a daredevil motorcycle ride inside an upright cylindrical tank. We stayed, but Angelina could not watch the bikes defy gravity. We left and had some ice cream on Via Umberto.

June 19, 1944

A poison gas lecture in the evening was scheduled. Everybody was bored. I went to the wing movie alone. Catania is like an old hometown these days. People, mule carts, and the Italian language are almost as familiar as Fords and English. I find it quite easy to understand anyone who speaks clearly. Their customs are familiar too, and I have learned to eat an artichoke properly. I saw Angelina again tonight.

June 21, 1944

Western front is advancing better than we expected. There is a holiday spirit in America. Until the stuff is moved out of our office, there is little to do. I am packing up the drafting equipment to be sent off. I search for a parting gift for Angelina in my spare time.

June 22, 1944

I saw Angelina tonight. We have become very close. I don't want to leave her.

June 23, 1944

I woke at 9:00 a.m. and took a trolley to Ognini and spent the morning there. Angelina walked me to the trolley when I left, disregarding onlookers with her spiteful grimaces. The black market boys are now hounding us more than ever because they know we are moving. I'm starting to get my things together in case I'm told to leave suddenly.

June 24, 1944

Packing up at the office, I take a little time to see Strack at the Red Cross to say good-bye in case we are separated. I spend most of my free time with Angie. Our parting is imminent.

June 26, 1944

Little work this morning, so I went out to see Angelina. Later, back at headquarters, we were preparing the last boxes to move on Wednesday. I stayed in the office alone while the others took the afternoon off. After early dinner, I left again and met Angelina, Sofia, and Carlo. They were at the Grotto D'ulise, our usual spot where we swam once before. I saw them sitting at a far table. They had just bought some seafood that was prepared by the restaurant. Grotto D'ulise has scenic water views and is one of the most relaxing places I know. The soft sea breeze keep us comfortably cool under a moonlit sky and a sparkling cove lighted dimly by fishing boats, and the romantic songs of happy fishermen are heard. As of yet, I haven't told Angelina that I'm leaving Wednesday morning. I know she will cry, and I don't want her to do that. Tomorrow will be soon enough.

CHAPTER XV

NEWS HEADLINE: ***July 20, 1944*****—Assassination Attempt by German Officers Against Hitler Fails**

June 27, 1944

I hung around the dead A-2 section office, which was just like a morgue. Few men now remain in Catania. After supper, I rendezvoused with Angelina for the last time. I met her again in the grotto. She and her friends were sitting alone at a table, and she walked up to meet me. She was dressed in green with high-heeled wedges. Her expression cheered me. I sat down with them and munched on bread. Then I gave her the bad news. Tonight was the last night. She cried a little there, and I knew she was trying to maintain composure. We had some ice cream and then left for the signora's house. She didn't let her hair down until we got to the house. There she nearly soaked the place with her tears. She promised to come to Rome with my instructions on how to find me.

June 28, 1944

I woke at 6:00 a.m. and made a quick but sad departure. The truck picked up my bags and brought them down to headquarters. One of the young boys for whom I had retrieved some bread in the mess hall insisted on helping me load the stuff onto the truck. He wanted to go down to the airport to see me off, but there was no room for him. I gave him a couple of cigarettes, and he was happy. While I was waiting at headquarters for the furniture to be piled on the truck, I was surprised and pleased to see Angelina and her friend come walking up. She had said last night that she'd like to see me off in Catania. I had told her that it would be better if she didn't come in. Well, here she was, so I passed the few remaining minutes with her then left on the truck with the furniture. We sadly waved "Arrivederci." Her crying rattled me deeply, but I could not help loving her stick-to-it-ness of purpose.

At the airport, we backed up to our C-47 aircraft and piled everything in there. We flew off with Lieutenant Lingquester at the controls. After a while, he came walking back to the fuselage and laughed at our surprised expressions. He had the automatic pilot on; and Lieutenant Jones, who can't fly, was acting as copilot, just looking out the windows through a pair of field glasses, skirting the coast of Italy past Salerno and Naples. At Anzio, we turned over the military bridgehead inland at about five hundred feet and looked carefully at the inundated countryside. The Germans had flooded the area after Mussolini had gone to the immense trouble of draining it some years ago. The ground was pockmarked with shell holes and slit trenches as we progressed over broken buildings and rubble. The railroad station, Cisterna di Litteria, had a residue of smashed trains. Our troops took a bloody beating during the Anzio sea landing. An army truck crept by, cleaning up as we circled above. In a few minutes, we landed at Lido di Roma on the shore west of Rome, safe and sound precisely as the pilot had promised. We hauled the furniture out and resigned ourselves to wait in the hot dusty wind for transportation.

In a tent we found some Spam and bread and learned that a truck wouldn't be out for a couple of hours. It was coming by convoy. I lay down on a portable tabletop and slept in the sun. Others on the field who are also awaiting transportation were sleeping in the shade of the wings of their C-47 planes. First Sergeant Guzi came riding in on a truck at about 4:00 p.m., and it was grabbed by Major VanWinkle, our dentist, who had waited near his stuff with his dentist chair atop everything. All of his equipment required two truckloads. The road to Lido was pretty bumpy—concrete tank traps, barbed wire, etc.—which would require quick cleanups. Lido, Rome's rich playground, is several miles from Rome on the coast; and as we approached, turning left, I could feel the strangeness and solitude of an empty ghost town fall upon me. We rode down the main street past weed-filled gardens, smashed windows, and open doors. We stopped in front of a small people-less piazza situated next to our new headquarters. Desolation was everywhere. The Germans had been thorough in their destruction. Repairs to our quarters were under way.

We helped unload things for the officers, including an electric refrigerator for the colonel's villa. I found a room easily since many were empty as of yet. In our sleeping quarters, the floors were marble. This building was a better one than some of the other ones in town. The water supply was nil because plumbing fixtures were smashed. Faucets were ripped from the walls and toilets pushed over. No electricity either but water was trucked in. First things first, an outdoor latrine was quickly built. The glass in the buildings were shattered. Miller and I went out in the fading twilight after supper to inspect other homes along the strip. All beaches were mined and warnings posted. The sands were full of military debris. This city was once a famed resort for rich and political playboys—elegant restaurants and sumptuous bathing spas. A limited area has been cleared of mines for bathing.

As I said before, Miller and I began to look for some useful things in these abandoned houses. We had good reason to be fearful of booby traps. Nevertheless, entrance into the first house was an overwhelming shock. The floors were covered with papers, smashed furniture, food, trinkets, and photographs during a flighty exodus. Smashed beds, chests, drawers, mirrors, and plumbing were everywhere. People had been ordered to move out with only three hours' notice. From this observation, they took very little with them. We touched no light switches or window blinds and didn't look behind closed doors, but luckily most were open. In one house, the ceiling fixture was still intact. I assumed the bulb was still inside. Bulbs are rare right now. I was right and became the proud owner of two of them. We saved some picture postcards of Lido in prewar days; then we returned to camp when it started to darken and went to bed.

June 29, 1944

Much to be done. We worked hard moving crates all morning. The major let us go but to be back before 2:00 p.m. Miller and I decided to go for a swim. We got permission to use the mine-free beach. White tape lines showed the cleared areas. At the water's edge, the area broadened out to about a hundred feet wide. It was warm and shallow for quite a distance out. We had a brief swim and used an old locker room. We went back to work still tired but clean anyway.

Other work was soon completed. That evening I moved upstairs with Carter to a room facing the oceanfront. We both stepped out to do a little scavenger hunting after supper. We tried new places, but the same spiteful damage was everywhere. We did find brackets and lights and, among all the breakables, a few good full-length mirrors found, which we would not touch. In the empty houses, you could tell who had lived there from the photos found. We expected to bump into them and their asking, "What are you doing in our home?" This former amusement area of bars, gambling spots, and hotels came to phantom life as we sat on one of the islands in the center of the beach road and fantasized while the surf roared behind us. We imagined prewar people swarming about us on a June night such as this, carefree, pleasant, and coming out of those broken hotel doors. Only they weren't broken then. The brass was polished until it gleamed with a doorman swinging it open and giving a cheery "Buona Sera!" Couples would be wandering in and out and perhaps dancing on the very veranda over which was now a fallen tree trunk and shattered masonry. They might have sat on that sofa there in the corner that was now torn apart, with its contents littered about. Friends might have parted on those steps saying "Arrivederci!", "Until next year!" but next year was never to come.

June 30, 1944

Work is beginning to come in thick and fast—new direction signs have to be made. Working together with Miller is convenient because we can fill in for each other. Carter says he saw an electric stove in one abandoned house two nights ago. After supper, Klibbi, Carter, and I go out for it; but someone beat us to it. Generators are supplying electricity now.

July 1, 1944

We've got our electrical connections set up and a little furniture for our rooms. It is quite comfortable now. All day and for the past days, there is constant shooting and explosions. Parts of the beaches are being cleared of mines, and sometimes the explosion shakes the building. Tonight there is a USO show in Rome. My first glimpse of Rome, even though it won't be much. As we approached outlying districts, it feels strange entering so famous, ancient, and historic a city. There are no Roman togas swishing about of course, but I am slightly disappointed nevertheless. Before I know it, we are upon the Coliseum. Well do I remember its picture in public school hallways and history textbooks. It is within the city and is visible from many directions. The large "wedding cake" monument at the Piazza Venezia is the most colorful spot in the busiest part of town. Instead of police, MPs are directing traffic. It would drive anybody but a former New York City policeman batty in five minutes. Such is the volume. The city is crowded with soldiers of every kind. Civilians are better dressed than in Sicily, but I learn that there is little food. Eggs and meat are almost extinct. One-half pound per family of bread is the Italian rationing from the Americans per day.

July 2, 1944

I got two five-gallon cans that we can use as water reservoirs in our room. Otherwise we have to run downstairs and fill our helmets from the water truck around the corner. Cold showers have been set up in a small courtyard behind the headquarters building. They consist of a framework over which rests three fifty-gallon oil drums with shower heads attached. They serve the purpose pretty well, and the temperature of the water is of little importance in the warm sun. In the evening, we go to a movie in a bombed college building. The auditorium is in good shape and makes a good showplace. There are paratroopers camped here, and they make up a good part of the audience, a rugged lot, always running and singing daily.

July 4, 1944

Sussman and I took today off. At 6:00 a.m., we awoke, dressed, made some Spam and cheese sandwiches in the kitchen, and got the six forty-five truck that goes into town to pick up the civilian help. We arrived in Rome at about 7:30 a.m. and got off at the Coliseum. Nobody was there except a few caretakers and guides. We refused the latter and poked around by ourselves. It was quite impressive but in very forlorn condition. Broken pillars lay around in a disorderly fashion. There was no center floor. It was probably made of boards and had rotted away, leaving many subterranean hallways leading to dressing rooms. Cages made of iron bars along the lowest level were probably where the lions were once kept. Imagined trumpets heralded the imagined entering gladiators. We left and found a tailor to alter a pair of pants that Sergeant Carter gave me that were too short for him but three inches too long for me. Offers for our packs of cigarettes brought little compared to the Sicilian market. We decided to hold on to them.

A July 4 celebration just as we arrived at the big wedding cake monument (Piazza Venezia) consisted of raising the American flag that flew over Washington when war was declared. In the piazza, Secretary of War Stimson and Major General Hugh Johnson (the Rome area commander) were making newsreel speeches. We window-shopped on Corso Vittorio Emanuele, a busy boulevard. It was wide, treed, and spotted with many expensive Fifth Avenue New York type boutiques. Still roaming, we returned to the tailor shop run by a Jewish family. They told us much about the German inquisition, lucky to escape with their lives. All of their goods were taken. The mother fixed my pants and refused any payment. We offered them some of our sandwiches, and they brewed some black coffee for us.

We finally dumped our cigarettes at a depressed price. At the same time, we were looking to rent an apartment so that we'd have a place to rest up when in Rome, or if we got a three-day pass. However, there was none found in central Rome. Our friendly tailor said she'd look. We walked through Parco Di Traiano and sat down for a while to eat the remainder of our sandwiches and bought some flavored seltzer at a kiosk as an aid. A little girl came over from a nearby bench and stood before us silently and pathetically watching. We were aware this might happen, but we gave her a bite nevertheless. Prior to this we had passed a store selling, to my surprise, drafting equipment. I picked up a drawing pen and some lettering stencils. A little while after 10:00 p.m., we boarded a truck going back to camp. Along the route, we picked up several paratroopers and infantrymen who had had a little too much partying.

July 6, 1944

Big heavy formations of bombers flew over us this morning. They were headed for northern Italy and the south of France I later learned. In the evening, Sussman and I returned to Rome and went up to the Red Cross, which was mobbed. Long lines extended out from the main snack bar, so we threw in the towel on that one. Some units are beginning to clear more mines from the beach. There was a terrible accident today when one man was killed while removing a detonator. Miller, who had gone down to see the results, said there were chunks of flesh scattered about. We pondered the terrible price paid for clearing mines.

July 8, 1944

Inspection today and there were no problems. Strack, my old roommate, was punished because he didn't police up his room; and he moaned "What do they expect? The Germans wrecked the joint, then they bawl me out 'cause there's some dust on the window sill maybe." He's so philosophical. During lunch, Miller and I looked up and down the beach for some chairs for our office. We can't find anything. Still plenty of work at the office. A few civilians are starting to move back to town, and the place is starting to look slightly normal again. Clothes are on makeshift clotheslines, and cleaning up is in progress. You have to be careful now before entering a house on a scavenger hunt. Booby traps!

July 9, 1944

We are awakened almost every morning to the tune of exploding mines and gunfire, and we hope, safely. Still plenty of work at the office. Lieutenant Jones, pert as ever, came up to see how I was doing. He told me about a special job in a day or two on a map overlay. These jobs are a relief from the printing. Sergeant Fountain, an orderly room worker, asked Sussman if we would donate blood tomorrow morning. There was a monetary compensation of ten dollars thrown in. We agreed with several others because a notice on the bulletin board announced a critical shortage.

July 10, 1944

Off to the blood bank. There are five "wing boys" and fifteen Signal Corps men going to the Twelfth General Hospital just on the other side of Rome. At 9:00 a.m., the doctor confirms our presence, and we proceed into Rome. I can get a good idea of the size of this city because we had to drive completely through it. On the side of a grassy courtyard is the hospital, and quite a large one too. We put our names on slips of paper at the blood bank and in a small adjoining room are cots where the blood is taken. The doctor there gave us each a slip, which allowed us a drink of whiskey at the laboratory. Sussman and I decided to stay in Rome after we were through. Before going back, we ate at the hospital and then waited for a lift back to town. Some kids annoyed us for the usual items along the way. However, we had nothing to give. The jeep picked us up and let us off at our direction. At this siesta hour, 1:00 p.m., most stores are closed; and we couldn't do much. We did have some ice cream, and after some walking, we waited near the Coliseum for a lift back to camp.

July 11, 1944

Feeling fine this morning, we get up at 7:00 a.m. these days, which is wonderful, and we are quite busy. It has been windy lately, and the coastal waters are churned up to a muddy brown. Several ships, or convoys, passed our shores. Quite often I try to make out better details with my binoculars, but things are too distant. We all expect that troops are in preparation for a landing in Southern France. I inquired about a Catania-bound plane in operations section for tomorrow, but nothing is available. That town holds many pleasant memories for me and Angelina.

In the evening, Miller and I walk the shore road along the ocean to the end of town. There are many concrete fortifications facing the sea. It seems that the Germans were trying to make the entire coast of Italy "tank proof." We rummaged around in more houses, finding much trash. The sea is rough and sends a salt spray over the entire area, making our hair sticky.

July 13, 1944

All flea and scabies bites have disappeared; I am extremely happy to announce. We all had little respite from them. The clean sea breeze here helped, I think. Today I met a fellow who is a professional goof-off, cum laude. Private Schulman is a member of the Signal Corps but actually does nothing. He is short and somewhat bald, and his attitude in brief is a shrug accompanied with words "So they'll break me?" He repeats it twice. "I go here, I go there," said Schulman, "I'm all around. If somebody gives me something to do, I do it." "But nobody seems to know exactly what you are doing," we respond in chorus. "Well, when I used to go on the truck with the boys, they wouldn't let me do anything," he responded, referring to the line maintenance crews. “Finally, they wouldn’t take me along altogether!” Schulman was slightly indignant. He had already presented his defense, and it seemed useless to argue. This ended the interview, but not Schulman’s well-planned idleness.

Schulman, Strack, and I then repaired to the bar, but for some lemonade only. Most of the other boys there already were half stewed to a mellow degree of conviviality and wouldn’t even have noticed if a German walked in. Strack and I went up to my room, and for about an hour, he told me what he did all day, especially in instances where some Italians were helping him to fix up the Red Cross equipment. One incident had me rolling on the floor. A high-pressure hose being held by an Italian tore loose from his hands. He grabbed the writhing hose but didn’t know what to do with it, so he tried to put it through a window thinking that it was open. It wasn’t. It backfired all over the poor guy. Then he tried to run into the toilet with it next. He was completely soaked from head to foot when Strack came in to see what the racket was. All he did was fold the pipe over, and that stopped most of the water. There were several other stories along that line, which finally blended into stories of his prewar job in the shipyards. I guess I’m his best listener, but he is good entertainment because he knows how to tell a story with a good tinge of New York sarcasm applied to bungling helpers.

July 14, 1944

Big important conference here today with General Williams. It was held upstairs in our secret room above the A-2 section on the roof. I remained at the foot of the stairs with orders to allow no one to go up. I was nervous until it was over. After, my mind rotates to Angelina. I try to find out more about a Catania-bound airplane. Everybody gives me a different story, but I’ll get one soon. I want to see Angelina again.

July 15, 1944

Very unusual day. Sussman and Lou found an apartment within town, together with an officer. If the officer leaves, I’ll take his place. Bigshots are all over the place, the Twelfth Troop Carrier command has arrived from England. Big things should be doing soon. Russians should be into Poland on their way into Germany now. I’m listening to a phony German broadcast about how they are annihilating us and how insignificant Allied invasion gains really are. Unfortunately, their boasting of the terrible effect of V-1 rocket bombs on England is mostly true. Those broadcasts never had the intended demoralizing results but rather belied their own frustrations. Like a game of chess, the successful invasion into France should call for their military resignation and a "checkmate, this bloody game is over!"

July 16, 1944

Working on my last piece of assigned work today, perhaps. With my Italian grammar, Miller tested my verb conjugations. I did well.

July 17, 1944

Found out from Operations that there was a plane going to Catania Wednesday that might fit us in. Meanwhile, whole groups of paratroopers go double time running; and as far as I can see from the window, they never slow down. They also may be seen taking many hikes with full equipment. Today we learned that a vegetable plane was going to Catania tomorrow morning. Miller and I, though pleased to go, also learned that it was coming back the same day. We had two days, and we were hoping that we could use them in Catania. Takeoff was at 5:00 a.m. from Lido di Roma field, which is a ten-minute ride from here. We felt that we would chance coming back on the second day with another plane. Sergeant Guzi was going also (basically for wine purchasing), and we decided to take a chance and ride down to the field with him tomorrow morning.

June 18, 1944

The CQ woke me at 4:00 a.m. That must have been the first time a CQ has ever been thanked for waking anybody. All I had to do was dress. All my stuff was packed, cigarettes, matches, and candy. Major Tower drove us in a jeep with a trailer attached. "All you fellows want to go?" he asked, "I didn't say you could all come." We are overloaded and carrying a jeep. Someone asked if we could go along and come back on some other plane. "Can't promise," he said. We all hopped in, not giving a damn how we would come back. One disturbing item was my remembering Captain Jones telling me the other day to be sure of two-way transportation before I went. All I happen to care about right now was that at least I could get to Catania, and Captain Jones could go blow it out of his barracks bag if I came back a little late. "He owes me one," I rationalized.

So with the soldier's conception of a clear conscience, we started out in the blackness for the plane. The field is very dusty, and the flight section is living in tents. Every time a plane takes off, they are hit with a sandstorm. We took off at 5:10 a.m., and I slept part of the way. It was odd to see two men in a jeep onboard, flying to Catania without using a drop of gas. Landing at 7:40 a.m., I watched as they rolled the jeep out, started the motor, and drove it some distance away. Everything was unloaded; then Major Tower and a few us got in and rode into town. There wasn't a GI to be seen anywhere, and half the English were gone too. The major told us where we could eat and sleep if we wished. We were near Piazza Bellini, famed black market hangout, and we figured it was a good time to make a deal. However, we first shaved in a barber shop and refused an offer of eight dollars a carton from the barber.

At Bellini, the usual throng was gathered. We and our haversacks were the object of careful scrutiny. Pretty soon whispers of "Cigarette?" wafted to us on the gentle breezes; and amiable, if not very profitable, contacts were soon made. In short, we found ourselves surrounded by brats, young boys, men, and old toothless octogenarians all waving money at us and cursing at each other for the fierceness of the competition. The inertia of the mob soon carried us into an out-of-bounds area and into a barn for carriages. Some of the followers fell by the wayside, but the entire group remained more or less intact as they steamrollered along, picking up new recruits along the way. Once inside the teenagers managed to kick the brats out, and the men began shoving the young boys out. Soon we were left with a cartel of about fifteen seasoned black marketeers. They would come to blows sooner or later, I had good reason to suspect. I only hoped that they wouldn't turn on us, and I was a little sorry that I hadn't brought my gun.

After much bickering, we cleared about a hundred dollars. We didn't have enough for everybody, and they began haggling about how much each deserved. One of the men got the bulk of my cigarettes. Suddenly a strong hand grabbed one of his packs, demanding it, and said he would pay the other for it. I had already been paid, so I didn't give a damn who got it. The other, to whom I originally sold it, loudly demanded its return. Then they started pushing each other around. There was a horse in the barn, and I thought that with the terrific clamor going up, he'd be frightened into a stampede over us, so I began yelling in Italian "Basta! Basta!" ("Enough! Enough!") and we finally got them apart, both mad enough to chew razor blades for dessert. I didn't bother to find out who got what for fear that they would start in again and perhaps ask me to mediate. During all this, the kids outside were kicking on the door—some crying, others cursing in the foulest language. One of the men inside would occasionally open the door and let loose with an oath and a kick that sent them flying, only to return later and carry on again. The padrone, the boss of the barn, came up at the finish asking for a cigarette and some respect. I figured that he should have been honored to have us gratis. Where else in Catania would Americans single out a barn in which to foster better Italian-American relations? We felt like Admiral Dewey opening up Japan during the 1800s. Nevertheless we soon left with apologies to the disappointed children and started out toward Ognini.

I intended to surprise Angelina, but I had no idea whether or not she was at home. We took the streetcar from Via Etna. Before walking down the road to the house, I checked for her at the Grotta Ulisse—not there. Just around a bend in the road, I noticed a horse carriage carrying an old man and a young girl coming toward us about two hundred yards distant. They were proceeding at a walking gate when they suddenly stopped. The girl jumped off and began running toward us. I knew it was Angelina as soon as she got off, but I was so surprised. I just stood dead still. She ran all the way down, and I must admit that our meeting couldn't have been sweeter. She ran right into my arms, and Miller applauded, a bit embarrassed. I'd never had anyone so happy to see me. We kissed while her throaty, sexy voice murmured loving words. I was bewitched. She excused herself for not running any faster because she had her wedges on. I couldn't help but hug her all the more for her saying that. I introduced Miller to her. "Walter" was difficult to translate. We walked arm in arm back to the signora's with Angelina laughing and telling me her intuition foretold my coming. Her dark-lashed eyes fluttered as she spoke. There was the signora puttering as always around the garden, who I hugged when we came up to the cottage. She was pleased with a chocolate bar. Even then, I was thinking of a distasteful parting tomorrow, but only tonight mattered. Miller gratefully accepted a glass of wine and some cheese. He was glad to see us happy.

At noon we walked down to the grotto for a meal. We sat outside in the open air arbor as we had also done so many times before. The place was still the same except for the noticeable lack of soldiers. We were undecided on whether to take a boat ride or go to Catania for a movie. The movie was Italian, and I only went because she liked it. A streetcar brought us to the theater. At 7:00 p.m. we remembered the RAF hotel nearby, and we had a bite. "I missed you terribly, Angelina," I said as I reached for her hand, "You don't know how lonely I've been."

"I miss you all the time, Milton. I must come up to Rome soon. You're the only one for me, Milton. That will never change."

I understood her Italian perfectly. "I wish you could fly back with me tomorrow, sweetheart. It would be so easy."

She stared defiantly. "Don't you worry, Milton. I'll be there." Back at Ognini, after some wine—all to bed for a pleasant night. Next morning, a tearful good-bye. We hitched a ride with a Limey chauffeur who drove us to the airport in grand style in a classy sedan. At a snack bar, I had tea and salmon sandwiches. A plane finally did arrive that was going to Lido and had room for us and arrived two hours later. The runway is rather short, and the plane drops like a rock. We bounced badly and gasped when I saw our right wing tip over momentarily. Nevertheless, we ran off the runway into the stiff weeds but still arrived safe and sound, except for our composure. We reached camp at about 5:00 p.m. but then a call came in from the orderly room that Captain Jones came in from Naples with a load of maps and needed me and Krotec to help him unload.

July 21, 1944

No time off for late guard duty anymore since it only comes once in a while. This evening we had a *Wingtips* tabloid staff meeting and worked until twelve midnight.

July 22, 1944

More civilians moving back to the other end of town. They were full of stories about what had happened while the *Tedeschi*[9] were there.

---

[9] Italian word for Germans.

They were given three hours to leave, and just as I had said before, they took very little. The train running to Rome was packed, and they had no room for baggage.

July 25, 1944

Much increased activity in the area. Every kind of outfit passes through. I can tell by my work that big things will soon pop. A Catania plane is going out. Captain Jones says he can take us in but not bring us back due to a heavy load. We will take our chances as usual.

July 26, 1944

Got up early and went to the airport with the line boys right after they had eaten breakfast. A paratrooper captain and his friend were sitting on a broken-down sofa on the field waiting for a ride to "somewhere." The plane to "somewhere" had already left, he learned. I was bringing some sugar as a present for the signora and Angelina. We didn't get into the air until 9:15 a.m. I asked the pilot if he'd have room for me going back. He thought so. We all agreed to meet at 6:00 p.m. for the return. They were trying to figure a way to stay two nights, but no one had a brainstorm, so we let it go. I hopped onto the streetcar for Ognini and arrived there at about 2:00 p.m. this time. I walked all the way up to the house without seeing anybody. I walked in and found Signora, Mario, her son, and daughter; but Angelina was not there. She was in a nearby village, Acireale, with some friends, where a fiesta was in progress. I got a hitch on a truck going there. This town, Acireale, had a well-earned reputation for its ingenuity in serving ice cream platters in artistic designs and colors simulating such culinary items as fried eggs or lasagna, or sausages.

There were a couple of ice cream parlors on one side of the street, and my first hunch was right. In one of them I found her sitting at a table, gave her a big kiss and a hug; then we all had some ice cream and left for Ognini. We ate dinner at 8:00 p.m. as darkness was beginning to fall. A couple of kids ran up and asked, "Do you want a little boat?" No, we didn't want a boat, so we just walked on. We strolled past a small carnival from whence came Neapolitan strains of music, and up the winding road we stopped, and I had a shave while she watched. She had a good laugh when I forgot to close my mouth as he started spraying my face with aftershave lotion. Angelina always gave my spirits a boost. We got home at about 9:00 p.m., horsed around, and went to bed.

July 27, 1944

The clock swished around to 9:30 a.m. before I got out of bed. At twelve we slowly returned to the grotto. Angelina was quite pensive as we walked along. She wanted to know as much as possible about Lido so that she'd know what to bring. Pointedly she asked me to be sure I wanted her before she came and that I wouldn't change my mind later, not so much that she'd be left alone in a strange place, but that it would be a crushing shock. "You're my one and only." I reassured her as best I could. We had a long discussion also as to the propriety of her coming along, and I told her that I'd arrange for her to board with somebody or some family, and she needn't worry and that I could take much better care of her than her aunt could in Sicily. We finally agreed on certain details, traveling, etc. I'd arrange to get her a letter saying she was promised work in Rome by the Red Cross. That wasn't a difficult matter. We had walked all the way into town and down to the hotel where our men were assembling and the jeep would leave shortly. We waited just around the corner until leaving time when she boarded a streetcar for home.

We finally left, trailer and all plus a tipsy crew chief, for the airport. The plane was very heavily loaded with seven thousand pounds when we should be carrying only 4,500 pounds. The back was pretty heavy, so all of us got up to the front over the wing for the takeoff. In an effort to take off, the plane ran down almost the whole length of the runway before she rose up. Nevertheless, we were okay. We sweated out our time over the Mediterranean, but it was smooth as a baby carriage ride, slept part of the time on vegetable baskets. We landed just before dark, and I found that I had packages waiting for me.

July 28, 1944

Hope to prepare something for the *Wingtips* meeting tonight. I'm working on a Rome gossip column as an experiment called "Roamin' About."

July 29, 1944

Wrote up the news for *Wingtips* edition tomorrow since Sergeant Klibbe quit suddenly.

July 30, 1944

Archbishop Spellman from New York was here today at our college theater leading the mass at 10:00 a.m. Sorry I missed him. We went for a swim on the beach. It was warm and a beautiful moonlit night. We took it all in seriously and thankfully.

Chapter XVI

NEWS HEADLINE: ***August 4, 1944*****—Anne Frank and Family Arrested by Gestapo in Amsterdam, Holland**

August 2, 1944

Lucky day. Strack and I go down to the airport, after getting three-day passes, looking for a ride to Catania. We got to the airport about 7:45 a.m., and there is supposedly an eight takeoff. The Red Cross girls are there too. When the pilot arrives, we show him our passes.

The trip was two hours and twenty minutes. At the field we inquired at Movements Control for planes leaving for Rome the next day, and there was nothing right now, but I could call later to check about tomorrow. It was hot in the city and that old Catania gourmet food aroma was stronger than ever. We rode in on the airport bus in the morning. Strack and I got off near Bellini Square. I had fifteen cartons of cigarettes, but unfortunately we began to deal with some kids who tried swindling us by handing over the roll of money and pulling out the middle once we handed the cigarettes over. I caught one at it and was tempted to belt him. A mob the width of the street was now following. Some kid got gypped out of a carton by one of his pals, and he yelled bloody murder. He was ready to call the police. So we gave him a carton to get rid of him. We parted ways and left for our respective destinations. I took a streetcar to Ognini for the third successive week. I was beginning to feel like a commuter. A lift by an English ambulance got me right to the front door. Angelina was sleeping in a back room, and I surprised her. She jumped out of bed saying she dreamed I was coming. We smooched a little and went out for a walk. Slow carts drifted by. Many drivers relaxed while their mules clip-clopped ahead. One had three men sitting upright, all fast asleep. They carried marketable junk of all sorts to sell along the Messina coast road. Occasionally, autos would zoom by raising a little dust and sometimes disturbing them.

Only a few seconds would elapse before the driver was once more fast asleep and unaware of the undesirable elements surrounding his daily existence. From my experience in Sicily, I can really believe that a person does not always miss what he doesn't have. Walking along this country road made me think of all of that and how we sometimes place importance in the wrong areas.

August 3, 1944

It was quite damp at the signora's, and we made ourselves as comfortable as possible. She put a melon on ice, and I looked forward to the evening when we'd cut it open. Supper at the grotto. That is another place that will prove hard to forget. Eating outdoors along the water's edge in the cool evening is something that not many soldiers will be able to boast about. We were thinking of seeing Strack tonight at a nearby café, but since it was too late, we walked back to the house. The carnival was operating, but the shooting gallery ran out of candy prizes, so we kept on going. The watermelon was deeelicious!

August 4, 1944

I went to the airport last night, but they still had no information on departing flights. So we decided to check about it in the morning. We got up early, and I made a call from a nearby ice cream parlor. There was a B-17 leaving for Galera near Rome just at the moment, so we were out of luck. Angelina had met us and walked us down to Via Etna, and we continued on while she took the streetcar back. A hitch got us to the airport, and an hour later we were on a plane back to Lido. The crew generously offered a feast of beer, beans, and salami.

August 6, 1944

Slow day. Went swimming this evening before supper with Miller. I made a few signs for a new chaplain assigned to our wing.

August 7, 1944

Brought my laundry in this morning. No work at all right now. I got a job later from Major Johnson. He needed some map overlays made.

August 8, 1944

Plenty of work today. Food is a disappointment. C rations most of the time and most of the condiments are spoiled. Hamburgers break the monotony occasionally. We had another little feast tonight in the doughnut shop with peanut butter, jam, tomatoes, and bread borrowed from the mess hall, and of course doughnuts and coffee. Went to bed very tired.

August 9, 1944

More overlays for Major Johnson. A large number of paratroopers were on an inspection parade this afternoon. Paratroopers and airborne artillery are beginning to leave in trucks. I drew up a professional diagram for the major from a rough copy of the coming invasion plan as far as the troop carrier work was concerned. That is where paratroopers and light artillery and gliders will be dropped in Southern France, showing all routes to be used. The landing will be near Cannes. This document is classified as top secret "Bigot Dragoons." *Bigot* signifies that its contents are for officers only. *Dragoon* is the code name for the coming operation. This evening Sussman and I went into Rome. He had an apartment with Lopatin who wanted to give up his half, but I was not interested any longer. All around were houses of lesser height with many good views.

August 11, 1944

The paratroopers have all left, and the seats from their theater are being moved over here. World-champ boxer Joe Lewis is coming here to Lido next Wednesday, and the signs from Special Services are asking for sparring partners for him and also asking for next of kin to be notified.

August 12, 1944

Another inspection day. This time with special emphasis on mess kits. Most are pretty dirty, mine being no exception. But with some soap I saved from the States, it is cleaned up quickly. Actually, our mess gear washing equipment is not good enough to remove all the grease.

August 14, 1944

Invasion day is coming at last. Tonight paratroopers will be dropped over Southern France, and from then on we can read about it in the newspapers.

August 15, 1944

Invasion came off. This morning Carter was working all night getting reports from participating squadrons. One C-47 crash-landed but with few injuries. Glider operations were good. However, one glider got caught in the slipstream of a C-47, and the tail broke off. That was over the sea, and although rescue boats went after them, there was little chance of finding them at night. More paratroopers will be dropped tonight together with more gliders carrying airborne artillery and troops.

August 16, 1944

The operation came off as expected. No opposition at all. Just a little flack near Toulon. No planes lost. Swimming this evening. Took pictures. Sussman and I came back from Rome to see Joe Lewis. He boxed a captain two rounds, and we took pictures. The captain survived and got a good round of applause. We had good front row seats.

August 17, 1944

Sussman needed a stove. There was none left in town. We remembered that the paratroopers had pulled out and had maybe left something behind though much is thrown away. We knew that there must be a couple of stoves about. They are efficient but heavy. We walked down to their area and saw the supply sergeant. He showed us some battered stoves that might be repaired easily. He slyly suggested that he could use some beer, and we readily complied.

August 18, 1944

We went back and found a perfectly good stove. It's heavy, so we got a lift on a truck after we got out of the gate. I repaired the second stove after cleaning it up. I am resigning from *Wingtips*. I don't feel like spending so much time on it. I'll continue to write the news however.

August 20, 1944

Major Solomon made lieutenant colonel. Pretty soon there won't be any officers below the rank of captain. When will a few stripes be handed out to us lowlifes? War news looks pretty good. Paris ought to be falling any day now. I used to get up early on rare occasions and walk over and smell the orange groves along the roadways. A few sleepy pedestrians dotted the road walking, bicycling, or hitching rides on carts; and they watched us whizz past with envious, tired faces. This evening Sussman and I went into town and had a little refreshment at the American Red Cross. Rome is not very dark at night in some localities, and plenty of people are strolling along the Tiber River that snakes silently through the city.

Sussman and I were off today, so we decided on a little sightseeing. This afternoon we visited the Vatican. It was the first time for both of us. Although we could have taken a crowded streetcar, we walked so as to have a look at the residential sections of Rome. It is much like any other large city. The people love their city just as much as people do elsewhere, and the blonde traits of northern Europe are much more in evidence. They are polite to soldiers and eagerly give directions, sometimes accompanying us part of the way. That is how we reached the Vatican. We approached it from a side street that fenced in a section of Piazza Saint Peter. A man prayed before a statue of the Madonna in a wall niche. The sun was very hot there, and there were several GI trucks parked around the entrance bringing in tourists from out of town. Sightseeing is greatly encouraged by the army, and they provide many Red Cross tours throughout the city—not only GIs, but Poles, French, and Indians. Saint Peter's is certainly impressive with its central obelisk and two sculptured fountains. The cathedral to the rear is small in comparison to the area that lay before it surrounded by a rotunda of columns in front of it. Many people sat in their shade as did two Napoleonic dressed guards on horseback. We walked up the long steps and into the great hall running to the spiraled columned altar at the rear of the building. Several large double doors lead off to different areas. A priest was gathering together a number of visitors in preparation for a tour, and we joined them. He pointed to different statues relating to

Catholic history. We saw rooms decorated by Raphael. The ceiling of the Sistine Chapel decorated by Michelangelo was our next stop. A relatively small place, it housed treasures of inestimable value. The ceiling depicted the creation of the world, requiring two years lying on his back. Wall murals took five years each. There is a collection of books in the center of the room that contain all the signatures of the bishops of the world, agreeing to the creation of the world by God. We learned that Churchill was there and about to have an audience with the pope. Sussman and I left the group and returned downstairs. I took two interior pictures of the Sistine Chapel and several more out in the Square of ourselves. We left to eat at the GI restaurant on Corso Umberto. We both had headaches from lack of food and the sun, so a meal of C rations and potatoes was satisfying. At least we were served at a table by a waiter for ten cents. Music was supplied by the restaurant's musicians who passed the plate around for contributions. Parents watched from a nearby bench as we chatted with their children, in a setting like New York's Central Park, buildings all around the perimeter. Then we began our weary way home.

August 24, 1944

Someone gave me startling news that Angelina was waiting near the beach. I couldn't believe it. She was waving her arms as she saw me just behind the headquarters building. But there she was in a weakened condition but so happy to be with me again. An elderly man had accompanied her part of the way. She had hitchhiked some before she got to Rome. She said she hadn't eaten for two days. Her leg was infected by a minor accident she had before she left. Her skin was pale. I blamed myself for encouraging the trip but rejoiced with her. I checked to see if a room I had reserved was ready—it was not—but a barber and his wife, relatives of the owner, took her in for the night and gave her supper that I brought with some blankets and food for all.

August 25, 1944

Angelina was ironing out some wrinkled clothing, but she didn't look much better than the previous day. I had bought some medicine from the dispensary for her leg the night before, and she changed the dressing while I was there. The barber's wife was helping Angelina clean out her new apartment and getting things in shape. Luckily, none of the walls was damaged, and the sink and stove were in good condition. The apartment was shaping up and wasn't half bad but would not be ready for another day. For light they used gasoline wick makeshift burners, which gave off an orange light and a little smoke. I brought as much food as I could get from the mess hall. Our cook, Sergeant Pesce, was very understanding. This evening a couple of GI paratroopers were over by the house; and I saw that they were selling food to the barber besides cigarettes, matches, and everything else. These two conveniently worked in supply. They were "friends of the couple" and had brought a radio with them for a little entertainment.

August 26, 1944

Angelina's new apartment was clean now, and she could sleep there tonight. The barber carried some beds over, all the way on his head. I'm trying to get a truck to pick up some more furniture. They are good people.

August 27, 1944

Today the open air theater was going to open in the rear of our headquarters, Special Services asked me to make and paint a large triangular Twelfth Air Force insignia for a decoration at the foot of the stage. It was a little out of my line, but I was willing to try anything once. I finished it about 4:00 p.m. in the afternoon, and it was just about dry. When we put it up an hour later, I got a picture of the whole stage. I took Angelina down to the show at about 8:00 p.m. as part of a special program there. There was music by the Fifth Army band plus some of our own entertainment by the 908th ABS battalion. She liked that, and I had a lot of translating to do for the movie that followed, which was quite difficult. We walked out in the middle. I should say that I could see that she was a little homesick for Catania. I told her that I might go back there one of these days, and I could pick up some of her clothes and bring her regards to the signora, her aunt.

August 28, 1944

Life goes on, and I am still carrying mess kits full of food to Angelina when I go to see her. She looks much better now. She and Leda go bathing practically every afternoon to keep herself busy.

August 30, 1944

No PX rations this week, and the boys are starting to roll their own and mooching cigarettes like nobody's business. This evening I told Angelina that I was going to Catania tomorrow, and she started to cry about wanting to go back. Everything was still so new to her. I told her to look at how far away from home I was, and I couldn't go back, but she could. I cheered her up as much as I could with my improving Italian, and it was times like these that I really noticed how much I had learned. It's not like ordering food or asking for directions. At the movies she snapped out of it, and at the house she wrote a letter asking for certain things at a friend's house that I would pick up in Ognini. I was to take along with me the valise she had brought with her. Sussman was bringing along about twenty cartons of cigarettes with him and was going to bring back about fifteen quarts of olive oil, which could bring in a good profit. I dug up six cartons of stuff, not my own, and agreed to take it in for a commission. No use carrying an empty valise.

August 31, 1944

For this trip we had to get orders and a pass that stated that we were on official business and so would facilitate a return transportation in the event that it should need facilitating. We couldn't return on the same plane because it was to be loaded with vegetables and a jeep with trailer. Captain Rimmer was our pilot, and he loosely swore that he'd take nobody back. He capitulated later. Our first stop on the trip was Bari on the Adriatic Sea. Two medics had to be dropped off. We arrived there shortly and then had lunch at the transient's mess, which was a real nice setup with plates and waiter service. We had steak. Two hours later, we landed in Catania.

As before, we rode the jeep into the Moderno hotel and walked up Via Etna from there. Then we walked over to a jewelry store. The female owner who was a good friend of Sussman agreed to buy the oil for him. She suggested some salt too on which could bring a good profit. Then we strategically refused to eat supper there and left. Our next stop was Angelina's friend's house in town. It was on an unusually narrow street and not very sweet smelling either. I found the house with the aid of a kid who then hung around and waited for some kind of a tip. The landlady believed me but couldn't read Angelina's letter. A shoemaker working on a bench just across the hall who must have been the neighborhood scholar undertook the task of translation. They all smiled as they heard about Angelina, and after she gave me the clothes, they all sent "Tante salute" (best regards) to all. We were planning to leave that section, which was out of bounds to us anyway. That same kid was still waiting, and we still had nothing to give him for a tip.

Miller and I stopped in at the RAF hotel where we once lodged and took a room there for the night. Seventy cents with three meals. Then we started for Ognini by streetcar after inquiring as to the rates a carriage driver would want for an all-day hiring. Five bucks was asked, so we refused. In Ognini we got a lift in a truck and were at the old homestead in a few minutes. The signora was combing out her long gray-black hair and tying it into large bundles over her ears. "Caro mio, Milton!" she joyfully exclaimed on seeing me. She was outside, and we walked into the shuttered house, which was quite cool. I broke through her Sicilian dialect enough to tell her how happy Angelina was and not to worry about her in Lido. I got the clothing and shoes Angelina asked for, refused her offer of food, left rather quickly, and got a hitch back on a truck to eat at the hotel. A good steak was there with vegetables, potatoes, pie, and tea. Later we picked up the oil at the jewelers then came back and locked up both valises in the hotel before going out for a walk. We sat in the park for a while where a café had been set up, and we had some ice cream.

September 1, 1944

Because of the heat I woke up many times. Even though we had mosquito nets, something kept biting me. It was at one of these times that I remembered what I forgot in Ognini. It was a yellow jacket that Angelina wanted. I decided to get it first thing in the morning. We had breakfast at 7:00 a.m. I then left and got a lift to Ognini. I picked up the jacket and a letter and was on my way back by 8:00 a.m. We left for the airport at 9:00 a.m. but found nothing available as of yet for a return flight to Rome. We waited, ready to put our bags aboard any plane that even came close. I had brought some cheese with me that sister-in-law Hannah had sent in case we ran short of food. From our own plane yesterday, we took some tomatoes and peppers and had a meal. About 1:30 p.m., we found a booze plane. It was one that came for liquor from the Sixty-second group. It was leaving in an hour, so we booked ourselves on it and waited. While waiting, we watched a P-38 load up with booze. The pilot carefully put bottle by bottle into the auxiliary wing tip lockers. We took off at 3:00 p.m. There was good transportation to Lido from Rome. When I walked over to see Angelina, she was upstairs in the apartment I originally intended to rent. There was an electric light on the porch. Angelina stuck her head out of the window upstairs and called for me, so I went up. Everybody was upstairs, including new friends Marcello, Augusto, and Leda's kid brother, all of whom slept in one room (but not with us).

Outskirts of Tunis, North Africa
Happy Arab Boy + Sweets, plus Author Donor 1944

Sicily 1944
A Young Restoration Worker Rests on the Bombed Streets
of Catania—Bombed House Below

Catania Sicily—A Busy Old Back Alley Commercial Street 1944

Taormina, Sicily—(Military Rest Area)
A Friendly Shop Owner, Francesca, On the Main Street.
Luo Lopatin (Left) and Author (Right)

Ostia Antica (Near Rome)
CPL Walter Miller (Left) and Author at Archeological Diggings
Between Rome and Lioo Di Roma on the West Coast, 1944

Rome-Vatican 1944
Author seated at one of the fountains in front of the immense fountain & rotunda area leading to the great steps fronting the Cathedral Entrance

Rome
Wedding of Good Friends Leda & Marcello 1944
Notice Angelina, left side, top row with hat.

Siena Italy 1945
My Friend Abbe Sussman and I enjoy a joke at the Siena Barracks (Converted School) Notice: Only "Well Connected" Persons were permitted the sought after Low Cut Officer's Shoe Issue, rather than the Heavy High Cut Boot like Battle Issue—Not really made for dancing.

Siena Italy 1945
Continuous natural running springs fill in nicely during water shortages. Kids love to play there even with icy water.

Siena February 1945
At work on my drafting table at headquarters

Rome
Early growth of Communist Party after Liberation.

Venice—Italy 1945
Happy Times in Venice—A Street Photographer catches us in a brisk walk. I am hatless

Siena—Italy 1944
Our "War Room" in Headquarters, author at right.
Foto was permitted due to lack of any specific details shown.

Mains—Germany 1945
War Booty—The Devil's Coat of Arms.

Chapter XVII

September 2, 1944

This afternoon I got Harry and his Red Cross truck to go down to the empty orphan asylum. With me came Marcello and Augusto. We picked up some bed springs and a few bits of furniture. The reason for this was that the fascist landlord had escaped from here when the going got bad. Now that things had cooled down, he came back like a smiling Cheshire cat, looking for his apartment. He had lived in the apartment and wanted his furniture, and he had the permission of the Carabinieri[10] police to take it. Lido is now a communist community, and maybe that is the reason that they don't pay any rent. It seems that if you are a party member, like Marcello and Augusto, you have that privilege. So they let the old boy have his furniture, which you couldn't give away back home, because they felt that it might be a little compensation for his losing the whole building. Two paratroopers were in the house at the time consummating a little deal with Marcello on a roll of wing fabric. They gave me twenty yards of

---

[10] The national military police of Italy police both the military and civilian populace. Although the Carabinieri are known to have assisted in the suppression of opposition during the rule of Mussolini, they were also partially responsible for his downfall. Many units were disbanded by the Nazis, which resulted in large numbers of Carabinieri joining the Italian resistance. The Carabinieri have been one of the four Italian Armed Forces since 2001.

it before he sold it. Getting back to the landlord, they didn't like the old guy very much and thought he had a helluva nerve asking for his furniture. If he were a young fellow, I think they would have punched him out. Anyway, he got a hundred and seventy-five dollars for the stuff but only a part payment. It's getting chilly now. It looks like bathing days are over for the most part.

September 4, 1944

I have been bringing doughnuts around occasionally and some condensed milk, both of which are very popular especially since people have been eating hard brown bread and never see any milk whatsoever. Water supposedly undrinkable, but nevertheless drunk, is procured from a common long pipe in the street where all sorts of tubs, pots, and barrels are assembled when the water is turned on. Special drinking water comes in a tank truck from Rome, I don't know how often, and is dispensed in a more or less orderly fashion. Angelina is going to make some bedsheets and a dress from the material the paratroopers gave me. It's half silk and half rayon and is extremely tough.

September 6, 1944

Took a day off and, in the afternoon right after chow, Angelina and I started walking toward Ostia Antica, the famous archeological ruins that are about two and a half miles inland on the south side of the Tiber River. About two thousand years ago, it was a thriving business center of the world belonging to Rome. The ruins were unearthed at the beginning of the twentieth century in an orderly dig. It had been looted in many places for its valuable marble some years before. A lieutenant gave us a lift and were directed by some people to the site of the old city. Very few buildings have roofs, mostly stubby short rough brick walls. Everything is marked. I had a guidebook and had no trouble finding things. The place has not been taken care of for a few years now, and grass is growing wildly over many parts. Parts of that ancient city have not been excavated yet. Behind the old amphitheater there was a great deal of prized snails attached to weeds, a favorite Sicilian dish when properly prepared. Angelina collected a handkerchief full of them. She tired quickly, and we returned at about 4:00 p.m. after seeing less than a quarter of the place. I expect we'll be back.

September 7, 1944

Erminea, who is our cotenant in the apartment downstairs, is going into Rome today. We gave her a piece of the material that the paratroopers had given us. In the afternoon, I learned that I had made corporal, together with Sussman. Miller who had been sweating out PFC didn't make it and was properly indignant.

September 8, 1944

During the night, there was much lightning and thunder. The town got a well-deserved cleaning, and I was glad to see that Angelina's roof did not leak. The quartermaster is getting my stripes in, and Angelina will sew them on. Naturally that called for a celebration, and we all agreed on a wine drinking spree. Marcello said that there was electricity in the house, so I brought him some wire and a bulb to connect up. That evening the current was on, and we had a light for the first time since those smelly gasoline lamps.

September 9, 1944

Walls are beginning to be built around the outdoor showers, in preparation for the upcoming winter, I guess. However, that's no indication that we are going to stay here. This morning I worked down in the darkroom making photographic copies of a map overlay. I had early chow, so I didn't bring Angelina anything for dinner, but she eats with the others once in a while. In the evening, I came up to the cheerful sounds of singers keeping up with the radio. Angelina and I danced awhile before supper, which began about 8:00 p.m. We didn't go to the show but napped almost directly after we were finished.

September 10, 1944

Got up a half hour later than usual and at the office made up a new heading design for *Wingtips Gazette*. Miller got permission to take the afternoon off. I didn't, but I took it off anyway to make up later. He and I decided to go to see the ruins. After chow, we got a lift to Angelina's and gave her lunch. As I feared, she wanted to come along. I finally talked her out of it with a handful of candy, but she was still mad. The only reason I didn't want her to come along was that sooner or later she would get tired or thirsty, and we planned to stay until about 4:30 p.m., which I don't think she would have liked. I promised to go with her soon, and she could pick all the snails she wanted. We finally left, and she watched us from the side window, slightly miffed.

We got a lift on the Rome truck and then walked up to the "new" Ostia neighborhood and stopped near the old castle where some people lived just outside its tremendous walls. Some overanxious kids offered all kinds of information for a price. There was a very ancient church near us inside of which we were told lay the body of a sixteen-year-old boy who was unfortunate enough to come upon a mine while investigating the interior of the castle. There is supposed to be an old man inside who conducts something like a tour for anyone who is interested. He was the grandfather of one of our child guides. The kids decided to follow us into the ruins, and they kept jabbering all the way. We entered by one of the rear streets and searched around the "window box" coffins hung on walls, for souvenirs. All we found were a few chalky old bones. Some other boys had previously told us that they had found some interesting things but wouldn't tell us where. We decided to let it go for a while. After a while, the kids left, and we searched around ourselves. We reached what used to be a museum. Although it was marked off-limits, a man outside showed us around. Most of the stuff had been buried somewhere so that the Germans wouldn't find it and was now being returned piecemeal. On the way out, we decided to cut across the open space between the town and the Rome road instead of walking back the way we had come. It was a distance of about a thousand feet. We later found it was not cleared of mines!

After supper, I showered. It's getting pretty chilly; and while I was dressing, Smitty, of the orderly room, told me that since Strack had not returned and should have been on guard duty tonight, I was to take his place. I didn't mind much. When I told Angelina, she offered to come down after supper and keep me company. While on my post at the motor pool only one block from the house, I talked with Vincent who is our interpreter. He was born on Sullivan Street in Manhattan, and his father brought him here when he was seven years old. He is going to Naples tomorrow night in order to clarify his American citizenship status. Later we spent some time in our friend Erminea's apartment below. She needs cooking gasoline. That's their only source of fuel other than wood branches. I procured two tin cans from friends at the motor pool.

September 11, 1944

Slept very well, in fact, too well. I got up at 8:30 a.m. and beat it down to the office as quickly as possible. I saw Quartermaster PFC Cooper and asked him for some blankets. Angelina was pestering me for some photos, which I made at the darkroom for her. Later, Cooper gave me two blankets. I had hoped for more, but a good general knows when to retreat.

September 12, 1944

Two new soldiers were up to the house in the evening at Marcello's invitation. He had met them on the beach and probably thought that he might buy something from them. He's a shrewd article and does this once in a while. Before the night was over, he got a carton of cigarettes and a pair of civilian shoes from them. I usually act as an interpreter when the GI can't speak any Italian, and I always tell the guy to jack up the price because I know that Marcello and company can afford it. We are very easy with them, and in turn they think us overly naïve. Their concern for immediate matters is expected and plausible. I never discuss anything but the advantages of democracy.

September 13, 1944

Took the day off and slept late. Met Augusto, the friendlier of the two between him and Marcello, and we went to the casual camp of the 322nd to see about a military barbering position at the regal rate of ten cents a haircut and five cents for a shave. The first sergeant agreed and told him to come back tomorrow when they'd have a place fixed up for him.

For some shopping, Angelina and I went into Rome. She bought some elastic for garters and a hair ribbon, but thread was so poor that she didn't buy any. We got tired and stopped in at a café for some ice cream. In the *Stars and Stripes* was an ad for a variety show that Angelina said she would like to see. It was at the Teatro Galeria on Corso Umberto, a short distance back. We got there early and as a result got good seats up front. Strangely they charge more for balcony seats than for orchestra. It was a good two-hour show, all vaudeville, in which both Italian and English were spoken, although all were Italian actors. I took her to a restaurant later where we each had a plate of spaghetti, fish, and some wine. Then about 7:00 p.m., we walked over to the Tiber River and sat down on a bench with the stony Castle Sant'Angelo in the background. The bus going back was scheduled for 11:00 p.m. We thought we'd try to get something else because we were tired and a little chilly. We reached the Coliseum at about 9:00 p.m. and waited an hour for one of our trucks that went to Lido. The driver told me to hide her in the back.

September 14, 1944

Marcello, Leda, and Marcello's sister are still in Rome in preparation for their wedding. Augusto couldn't start work today because a barber room was being cleaned out for him. He is a trainee barber. I had early chow and then got a ticket for tomorrow night's dance to which Angelina was anxious to go. At about 1:30 p.m., I brought food over to the house. Some civilian friend of Augusto was there, and he asked if he could get work in the camp. I don't really have any pull, but I'll ask. I took his name and address.

September 15, 1944

Today is the regular biweekly dance day in Rome. Angelina was getting all ready for it even to a pair of silk stockings. Marcello came back somewhat bemoaning the fact that his remaining free days as a single man were fast running out. They ate some of the food I brought over at lunchtime and left the rest of it in a plate on the shelf together with a few other such plates that were in the cupboard. There is no refrigeration whatsoever. Marcello mentioned that he was trying to get work at the same place that Augusto was as a barber. They don't care much about the money that they make. It's the food they are after. Civilian workers eat army meals. Augusto once mentioned that he'd even cut hair for practically nothing just to get in. After supper we waited out on the street for the Lido truck to pass so we could get a lift. Marcello waited also, and we had a drink of wine at a nearby café. In spite of all their *vino* drinking, I have never seen an out-of-control Italian.

The first truck passed and was quite full, so we waited. Then came a weapons carrier with room for two, and we took it. The open seats were quite windy, so I gave her my army cap to keep her hair from blowing around. She looked just like a WAC. We arrived about 6:30

p.m., checked our things, and went on to the dance floor. The house provides a bar; we provide eats. The guard at the door was having a little difficulty keeping out unauthorized persons, but he was firm. An Italian orchestra played for about two and a half hours. A few WACS were there on pass and were quite popular. Harry the Red Cross boy drove us back home. There are no chaperones at these dances as in Sicily.

September 16, 1944

This morning I contacted Harry, and he promised he'd drive the truck for me this afternoon to pick up some more furniture down where the 509th paratroopers had moved out. After chow, we drove back to the house. I gave Angelina her food, but Marcello and Augusto were both out. They were all set up for barbering nicely with mirrors in a small outside building. We traveled slowly on account of the bumpy streets. There were plenty of things to be picked up, but the driver only had time for two loads. We picked up lots of furniture and mirrors. The paratroopers seem to be great artists. Every available bit of wall space had been covered with Varga's[11] type girls, but usually with less clothing.

Two *carabinieri* watched us but didn't say anything. The whole job was finished at about 2:30 p.m., and then we carried the stuff upstairs while envious neighbors looked on. We assembled everything in its place, and then I left to eat supper. We've been getting some pretty good meats lately, and that makes it hard to get extras because they don't get much of it. Therefore, I can't always get something for Angelina. In such cases, I bring vegetables and spinach, which she oddly enough is crazy about. Italians don't miss meat very much. After chow, I returned, and all the furniture was cleaned up, and it certainly looked different; it was so shiny. A couple of boys were up with some beer. Marcello always sees to it that they bring something.

Tonight the clocks were moved back one hour.

---

[11] Girlie cartoons painted in the style of Alberto Varga. These types of pinup girls were wildly popular between 1942 and 1946 and were featured in *Esquire* magazine.

September 17, 1944

Strack finally got back last night after being in Catania fifteen days with a friend. They couldn't get back here on a five-day pass because their orders read "Motor Transportation" by mistake instead of "Air Transportation." As a result, nobody would give them a lift at the airport. An Englishman finally flew them to Bari, and there they met a Lieutenant Gibson who fortunately flew him back the same day.

September 18, 1944

A lot of replacements are around Lido these days. My roommate, Sergeant Carter, has gone home. His wife was very sick, so they sent him home. He was gray around the temples when he left.

Sussman went to Rome on a five-day pass and probably lived the life of Riley or better. He came back this afternoon, with his girlfriend Sarah, to spend some time on the beach. Another soldier was at the house this afternoon, and he was intent on studying Italian, and to that end Augusto had agreed to help. We had a lot of fun, especially when it came to dirty words through mispronunciation.

September 19, 1944

Had a lot of darkroom work to be done again with the Balkan operation. That took all day; and since they were in a hurry, we had to work until 9:00 p.m., Captain McKee told us to take an extra half day off tomorrow. Hot water has been started in the shower room, and almost all the pleasures of home are once more enjoyed.

September 20, 1944

Decided to work this morning and take the afternoon off. The day was quite rainy, and it seems like summer is over. Angelina, Marcello, and a few strangers were sitting around the dining room table talking about Italy's future. They were optimistic. The wet weather and the constant drone of their talking just about put me to sleep as I lay on a daybed. Marcello suggested that we all take a ride into Rome. I agreed and told him I'd have to go back and get a pass. On the way back, it started to pour. I learned that Erminea and Leda had just returned from Rome, so that cancelled our trip because we preferred their company, and it was late. I left for supper shortly after, and I met Strack on the way upstairs. He was thinking of moving into my room, which I had suggested previously. Upon returning to the house, I found it completely surrounded by water, due to the heavy rains and broken sewage system, so I whistled up to the window; and soon Marcello, Leda, and Angelina came down with flashlights. We tried all sorts of plank crossings. Luckily, there was a small wagon in the courtyard, and I ferried across in that. We began our English night school, played the radio, ate supper, and passed the evening pleasantly.

September 21, 1944

The weather was bleak with an occasional spot of sun through the low, scurrying black clouds. We walked, singing to cheer ourselves up.

More tragic news. In northern Italy, because of the lynching of an important German officer by Italian partisans, 320 innocent Italian hostages were executed by the Germans in gangland style. All were shot in the head. Civilians are shot summarily in gross numbers, in reaction to partisan attacks. It is to their enduring bravery they knowingly accept these risks. "God help them."

September 23, 1944

Stayed in Rome all day and returned at about 7:00 p.m. What a fantastic city—like to stay there for weeks, seeing the artifacts and famous temples.

September 24, 1944

Woke up a little late and had no breakfast, which I later found out was nothing worth eating, namely chipped beef on a large cracker, which is far better known as "shit on a shingle" and with a taste to match.

September 25, 1944

War news has slowed down some. Got a letter from my friend Al Mozell who is a daring Signal Corp photographer in battle-torn France. I've known him since elementary school days. He lives and breathes photography. Ugly rumors are starting about bed check, roll call, drill, and calisthenics due to an increased venereal disease rate. In the face of these things, our outlook is naturally gloomy considering early morning winter wake-ups. The doctor examines all genitalia, called a "short arm" inspection. One man tried to explain his runny penis as a cold. "Let me hear it sneeze," chortled the doctor. He was lucky to have penicillin available.

September 26, 1944

Notice on the board this morning stating coldly, flatly, and in equally cold typewritten letters that we are to rise at 5:30 a.m., breakfast at 6:00, and drill and calisthenics from 7:00 to 8:00 a.m. I could think of better ways to begin a new day. On a lighter note, *Wingtips* staff members, including myself, got certificates of merit for second place in the Twelfth Air Force newspaper writing contest. Bravo!

September 27, 1944

Today begins a new era in our camp life. The early rising is reminiscent of those back in the States and the early days of Catania. Things look gloomy and disheartening, but we've been through similar periods like this before. The weather has been damp, dull, and murky, which is no help either. Captain Weatherbee, a human relations military officer, came into our little room and together with Sussman, Lopatin, myself, and Miller had a friendly discussion as we warm up to postwar life and the future. He's from the south and one of those head-wagging common sense boys who could make you believe he's been through it and seen it all. There was no electricity tonight, and Marcello fooled around for half an hour trying to get three batteries and a flashlight bulb together without using a flashlight case. It only seemed to work when he kept his hand on it; and after uttering several smooth-flowing, futile oaths, he resorted to the old reliable oil lamp.

September 28, 1944

Calisthenics for five minutes and drilling for the rest of the hour. Our first sergeant marches us past the officers' quarters as we count cadence, shrieking ballad ditties at the top of our lungs. This is supposed to build morale. Then we brought the curtain down with a few off-color songs, which always seemed to arise spontaneously from the guys, as if rehearsed. Our muscles feel slightly sore from yesterday's five minute workout, and many are the grunts and groans and cracking of knee joints and knuckles as we go through these simple paces. It's been a long time, but we've been through this before.

Chapter XVIII

September 29, 1944

When I came over to the house after dinner, Angelina and Marcello were eating spaghetti that he had just bought with his ration ticket. Each one had a big plateful, but he complained that it was hardly reaching his stomach. They added the stuff I brought, and soon he belched and left. Angelina was becoming homesick again. This evening, Leda, Marcello's future wife, came back; and Angelina seemed to snap out of it. Her comfort and happiness are my only concern.

September 30, 1944

In spite of a late guard shift, I still must be at roll call and calisthenics. After that I hit the sack and awoke late. Angelina, Leda, and Marcello went to Rome today—the latter to make out a preliminary marriage contract and Angelina to buy something. She told me all about a wonderful spaghetti and pasta sciuta (dinner) she and the others had in Rome.

October 1, 1944

By order, neckties go on today and some good news at roll call. Lieutenant Crowley lifts restrictions as no new VD cases have come up. Later, I walked over to the Red Cross, spread the news, and saw Strack making his coffee for the boys. As today was my day off, I hung around the house, helped them get some water, chop a little firewood, and be a pest. In the evening, I had the misfortune to fall asleep until twelve thirty. As I came back late into the barracks, I had the further misfortune of bumping into the first sergeant when I tried to see the CQ so he'd take my name off the missing list. The irony of the situation was that the CQ hadn't even taken a bed check at eleven thirty and my bumping into the first sergeant might not have happened.

October 2, 1944

I thought everything had been forgotten about my missing bed check. On my way downstairs, Lieutenant Crowley saw me and asked me to step inside the orderly room. I knew he wasn't going to pin a medal on me, so I prepared for the worst and got it. He said he'd recommend my reduction in rank. I had no real complaint I guess except that Sergeant Guzi discriminated against me in favor of his bosom chums, to whom this never would have happened. I don't know what he's bucking for as he already has six stripes. However, I already have some enlightening notes on drill and first sergeants, so enough said. I told the news to my civilian friends who remarked unanimously that the CO and the first sergeant were both unfair. I guess I'm really to blame, though, because I failed to develop influential friends, outside of my work.

This afternoon, Leda, Marcello, and Angelina are to go to Rome to do some additional work on their upcoming marriage and are to be back this evening. At about 6:30 p.m. while I was looking for Miller in the street, a soldier told me that a girl was looking for me just around the corner. It was Angelina, and she explained that they couldn't get a truck into Rome that afternoon, so they'd have to wait until tomorrow. It was cold and windy, so I gave her my raincoat and went back to the house with her. She shivered all the way. Not expecting them to be here this evening, I had not brought any food, but they were preparing some pasta. Leda is rolling and cutting the stuff into small pieces, and Augusto is squeezing them with a fork to thin them out. Erminea helped also in making tomato sauce. When I left, I made sure that I didn't oversleep this time

October 3, 1944

Last day of calisthenics much to everybody's relief. I learned that one of the Red Cross women from Catania (we knew her as Blondie) came up to Rome unexpectedly in search of some work, and Strack has agreed to ask the boss about it.

October 4, 1944

I have a slightly sore throat and may take tomorrow off. When I brought the regular afternoon chow over to Angelina, I met her near the spot where Augusto does his barbering at the 322nd Squad. He and Marcello change off occasionally, a great convenience. I walked her up to the apartment and stayed about half an hour, listened to the radio. She was going over to a hair dresser for a shampoo and haircut or whatever else they do. The weather tonight was poor and put an end to our desire to see a movie. We listened to the radio and gabbed.

I had something that I had to say. I pulled her close to me, and we sat down. She trembled. “You’re so serious, Milton” looking at me soulfully. She kissed me as if to cheer me up. “I’m not unhappy, sweetheart, just the opposite. We’ve been together a long time.” Looking deeply into her eyes—“I love you very much. Would you leave Italy and family and go to America? I want you to marry me.” That was putting it bluntly, and not quite as romantically as I had hoped.

She hugged me. “I would go anywhere you go, Milton. I love you. You don’t have to ask. You take good care of me and give me everything I need. But that is not the reason I love you. I am happy just to be with you. You are unselfish. You worry about me. You cheer me up and make me forget my worries. I think I am lucky.” Then laughing, “Besides, you like to shop, like pasta, like kids, don’t argue much, and oh yes, not a bad lover.” She pursed her full lips, winked and tossed her curls, to emphasize her meaning. I was overjoyed, loved her all the more for her little speech, and caressed her warmly.

October 6, 1944

Spent the morning at the house helping out Angelina with little odds and ends. I went back to chow and then returned after getting a pass to Rome. We thought we might go this afternoon. It was after 1:00 p.m. when we finished eating, so we missed the Lido truck in. The city water truck pulled out just before us and already had a full complement of bicycles and running board hangers-on, so we cancelled out.

October 7, 1944

Hardly any mail for anybody from anybody. I had early lunch today, and there was nothing I could bring Angelina but a little can of Vienna sausages, which she fried in olive oil. That was her entire dinner. This evening Marcello went to Rome, and I brought over a lot of pork chops that I had happened to see lying around in the kitchen. Angelina asked one of the kids downstairs to get a bottle of wine across the street, and when she returned with her little sister, we gave them some meat and bread, which they beheld with popped eyes. When they took it, I thought they would hide it for a rainy day. Their mother came up later to light a candle and thank us.

October 10, 1944

A few hundred English troops have moved into the old paratroop building and are cluttering up fair Lido di Roma, our hometown so to speak, with their clippity-clop hobnailed shoes. They add considerably to the drinkers already here, and they are beginning to drape the once-fair streets and gutters of Lido.

A picturesque common sight around the back of the mess halls are little children waiting with pails hoping to get the leftovers of a GI's mess kit before he dumps it, in rain or shine, barefoot or shod. Surprisingly healthy looking, they collect their scraps regardless of condition, their little faces seriously intent on their missions. It's seldom that we see an Italian child playing. He or she is usually engaged in a house chore, minding one or several babies, building a fire, fetching unbelievably heavy buckets of water or scrubbing clothes near the street water fountain, living what we might call a drudge's existence but with a mature nature and pride of accomplishment.

The porter in our office building told me that his child had never tasted a piece of chocolate and could I please get him a piece. I was happy to find a few pieces in my pocket. However, the children around here do not bother us for sweets as much as the Sicilian kids did.

October 11, 1944

Marcello told me this afternoon that he was inviting the first sergeant of the outfit he works for up in the evening. Marcello, who was always is a man with a purpose, had this up his sleeve. He'd like me to ask him why Marcello can't get a meal at the outfit's mess hall. When I arrived, I shook hands with him. "Sergeant Chapman," he said, and I answered slightly unabashed, "Private Pashcow." I was about to add "at your service" but thought better of it. He ran true to form as far as first sergeants went, lanky and slightly impenetrable. However, I didn't ask, but I believe that he came from a city rather than a farm. He was looking through an English-Italian dictionary I had left at the house. Marcello told me that he was trying to learn Italian, and that was about all they had in common. That is, Marcello said he would teach him some while intending nothing of the sort. Finally, Marcello gave me a go-ahead look, and I popped the question about the food for Marcello. He said he spoke to the first sergeant at the 322nd where they eat but without any luck. He suspected that Marcello and the mess sergeant must have had some argument. Marcello denied this and added that the barber at the 322nd ate two or three meals a day and why not him! I could see that First Sergeant Chapman didn't wish to pursue the subject any further, which lack of desire probably sprang from an agreement among all first sergeants never to barge into another's "sphere of influence." However, he apologized and was nice enough to accompany us to the movies. Only two civilians are allowed in with a GI, and we had three. Angelina's smile did the trick.

October 12, 1944

Columbus Day but it is surprising how little Italians know about it. Tonight a squadron dance is coming off at the Sala Pichetti where outside vengeful hair cutters try to trim the heads of signorinas who come to dance with Americans. MPs stopped that quickly. We got a lift on a truck going in, and as we climbed over the tailgate, an old lady started to mount up behind us assisted by two men. They were evidently under the impression that this was a civilian truck, so with her one leg over the tailgate, the driver ordered her to get out. With some difficulty, we all helped lower her down. She was offended and loudly indignant. I congratulated her on her spryness.

October 13, 1944

Angelina feels like going into town. She, Leda, and I went to Rome this afternoon and got there about 3:30 p.m. Leda went home. Angelina and I went to the Galleria Theater. We saw a two-hour vaudeville show and got a lift back in Harry's ambulance at the Coliseum. I had a bad headache.

October 14, 1944

Olive drabs clothing is given out brand-new. The fellow who cleans our office asked me to give him my old ones. He thanked me. The place is as dead as a doornail. I forgot to mention that last night two German planes came over, took some photographs by light flares, and also dropped artificial Italian money nearby on which was printed "The Allies promises are as worthless as this money." Marcello is heading for Rome tonight as he feared a bombing. PS No bombs.

October 15, 1944

Marcello keeps reminding me about next Sunday being his wedding day and that he wants me to come. I would take some pictures. Mail is very slow these days. No packages for a long time now. I got a little job to do today printing on some folders to be used as covers for a "Campaign Summary" of the wing's activities for the last few months. One goes to the adjutant general in Washington. Sergeant Klibee urges me, "Do a good job, Milt!"

October 16, 1944

Finished the covers for Klibbi. Weather is getting colder. This evening we had a squadron meeting where the bar, dances, crap game room, and other innovations were discussed. We're to have dances every Wednesday from now on. No outsiders are allowed into our crap games.

October 17, 1944

Ahh me! No work again. Read the *Stars and Stripes* every morning and adjust our big wall map. I got a new blanket for Angelina from Supply this morning, and I also picked up our repaired shoes. What lousy work! Each shoe had a nail sticking up in the heel. Angelina will have a coat made of the blanket by Marcello's sister in Rome. Of course, it will be dyed a different color.

October 18, 1944

There is much preparation of material evidence for a request for a presidential citation for the wing. While I had no training in art, I made colorful covers for this material.

I managed to buy a couple of extra boxes of vanilla wafers for Angelina, my little Lina.

October 19, 1944

Marcello is in Rome today seeing to his last-minute wedding arrangements. He would also probably have a last-minute fling if the poor guy had a cent in his pocket. I returned to the house at eight thirty after picking up a new chess set at Special Services. I'll try to teach someone; I don't think that it is Angelina's cup of tea.

October 20, 1944

Rainy and wet. Not going to the movies anymore while it remains outdoors. In the evening, Angelina and I went "downtown" to the business section of Lido and bought some blue type dye for the blanket. On the way back, we saw Erminea, the woman downstairs from our apartment, who offered to dye the blanket for Angelina. I forgot to mention that we also inquired as to the cost of making the coat in a tailor shop; but Signora Agosto, who was to dye the blanket, said she had a friend, etc., etc., etc. In the meantime, Angelina was getting ready to go to Rome for the wedding.

October 21, 1944

Received a package from home with a fountain pen and pencil and a few other things. At 1:00 p.m., we got on the Lido army truck headed for Rome.

October 22, 1944

Today is Marcello and Leda's wedding day. It will be one of the few happy days they will be able to look back on in times like these. Love conquers all. Today there will be no skimping, saving, and conniving. It is a day, unlike most other days, of goodwill and cheer and merriment. A day of unstinting, mutual promises of infinite love and devotion, secured only by unbounded faith, really a celebration in the true sense of the word regardless of our troubled times. For me, it will be my first attendance at an Italian wedding, so I look forward to the experience about to unfold as we ride into town on the mail truck at 9:00 a.m. this morning. Of course my camera is ready too. The Roman countryside at this early morning hour never fails to impress me with its freshness and unaccountability. At every turn, an unexpected sight holds my attention, and the irrepressibility of the people never ceases to impress me. A man futilely pleads emotionally with his beloved burro to move on. Farm hands wave as we drive by.

At the gates of Rome, this panorama ceases almost abruptly, passing a few suburbs, a general market, and into Rome proper. We alight near the Rome to Lido station built for Mussolini's friends. A few seconds later, we are with Marcello's sister who is also named Angelina. It is 9:30 a.m., and the ceremony will take place at 10:00 a.m. The trolley stopped running a half hour ago, so we have to walk presto to a small outlying section called Garbadella. That is Leda's true home. We follow the car tracks and skip the puddles, dodge the pedestrians and traffic, which all seems to be coming against us. We pass a large apartment house that is sheared in half by a stray American bomb meant for a nearby bridge. In the same vicinity, the walls of the stores and the buildings on both sides of this busy street are pockmarked from gunfire. Retreating Germans entered the city when our troops landed at Anzio a few miles to the south. A few overturned and charred autos lay on a central embankment. Erminea once told me she was there and how she dived into the gutter when the Germans opened fire from the roofs with machine guns on the civilians below. We reached Garbedella a few minutes later, made our way through some courtyards to Leda's mother's apartment three flights up in one of the buildings.

There was a large crowd of relatives and guests milling about, but few gifts. Prices are high, and reasonable gifts are too scarce for poor or middle-class people to buy. There was an electric iron, handkerchiefs, something that looked like a tapestry, some china, and a few pieces of silverware. An extended bouquet of chrysanthemums decorated a long table in the middle of the dining room on which was neatly set cake and wine on a white tasseled tablecloth. The young children, like all young children, ran around in spite of our constraining attempts. Nothing was eaten before the ceremony however. Leda was dressed in white and looked very rosy and happy. Marcello dressed quite well in a blue serge suit with a surprisingly accurate fit. There was a three-petal white flower on his right lapel. He was very proud today and rather handsome. A few minutes after I arrived, we began to leave for the church. There was quite a traffic jam in the narrow halls of this railroad flat. People were trying to pick up clothing in all parts of the house at the same time. Leda and Marcello are finally ushered into a waiting carriage and sped off to church a few blocks away. People everywhere watched. Angelina was wearing a broad-trimmed blue hat that Lada had loaned to her, and I walked down the middle of the street with everybody else. It was sunny, and everything sparkled after an early morning rain brightened the dark lava paving stones.

The church was moderately large and well kept. Many people there were neatly and properly attired as was to be expected. As special guests of the family, Angelina and I stood up before the railing before the first row of pews. Marcello and Leda were on bended knees before the altar. I took some pictures from this position. There was a great ceremony, and when it was all over, we and the family and relatives repaired to a different room where the marriage was officially entered into the church books. Several times during the ceremony, Marcello looked back and smiled a little, but quickly turned back so as not to appear undignified. The kids also had to be kept in line by a priest who periodically pushed them away from the front railing before the altar. If they were strangers, he reprimanded them and strongly resisted the temptation to cuff a few of them. I took a few pictures outside, and then the four of us got into the horse carriage and drove back to the house.

There was no shortage of wine at the feast that followed, and the cake wasn't bad either. Leda's mother had made it, and Leda's father was in good spirits, seeing to it that nobody ran low on wine or cake. He was smiling as good naturedly and as happy as if it were his own wedding day. Marcello had most of his nine brothers and sisters there. Occasionally a relative would breast-feed a baby out in the open without covering herself with a handkerchief. Anyway, the sight became so common after a while that I didn't even look twice. Leda's mother invited everyone to a nearby restaurant where she was well known, and they prepared the table in banquet style. The first course of dumplings came out with potatoes and strong Italian grated cheese on the side. I took mine but deferred on the cheese. Beefsteak, fried potatoes, and tomatoes were next. Wine flowed profusely. Two accordionists and two guitarists played for us. There was happy dancing and singing, and then we all left to go back to the house,

Leda and Marcello to pick up a valise, for an overnight honeymoon. Thumbing for a ride home, a few military cars stopped, but none would take civilians. Luckily, a major and a nurse drove by in a jeep and picked us up just as it started to drizzle. When we arrived in Lido, there was a bright moon to put an end to a wonderful affair.

Chapter XIX

NEWS HEADLINE: ***August 25, 1944*****—Liberation of Paris**

October 24, 1944

Angelina's blanket has yet to be dyed. She is not feeling well. I have a cold also. We nuzzle together happily, recuperating together.

October 25, 1944

Not much doing. My cold is worse; Angelina too, her back giving her the most trouble. We may have to call a doctor soon. She is under a heavy pile of blankets. This evening when I arrived, the doctor was already there, a young fellow of about twenty-eight years old and coincidentally a friend of Marcello. He happened to be in Lido today. He said that she possibly had nephritis, a kidney ailment, and would have to go to the hospital for a week or ten days. I told them I'd try to get permission to take her in the morning to Rome on our truck.

October 26, 1944

I got the okay for Angelina and the doctor to go along on the truck about 9:00 a.m. Marcello is going along too. Luckily, it is a sunny day, and we won't be bothered by past rains. The truck stopped in front of the house, and I ran up to call them down. Angelina was dressed, and a minute later we all got aboard and left. As we drove along, the bouncing truck's jolting worsened Angelina's condition. I suggested that she sit on the blanket that was covering her legs, but she preferred to just lie against my shoulder as we drove along. We got off on Viala Tritone.

Our accompanying doctor Bruno got her registered and into a ward in about fifteen minutes. Angelina cried a little when we left, but I promised to be back tonight; and then Marcello, the doctor, and I walked downtown, got on a streetcar, and headed back to the Saint Paolo section. It was very crowded with everybody yelling "Permesso! Permesso!" ("Please! Please!") as they forced their way up the middle of the car. The streetcars here are quite modern in contrast to the Catania antiques. I kept a steady watch on my wallet. Then from Saint Paolo, we walked a block to the doctor's house. I offered the doctor money, but he surprisingly refused to accept any. When I returned this evening, I stopped at the doctor's place first. It was anything but what a doctor's office should look like. I later learned that he worked in the hospital four hours a day and did very little practice in the house. We only remained a few minutes and took right off for the hospital along a street that I had never seen before. They had some interesting ancient sites on them, and Bruno explained them as we went along in the moonlight. He's a good tour guide.

Saint Giacomo Hospital is right off Corso Umberto, and it took us about twenty-five minutes to walk at a fair gait. At the door, I passed out several cigarettes to the boys and all the red tape that might normally bar a visitor after visiting hours, especially at night, vanished. Regular hours are in the afternoon only. We walked through a courtyard and into another wing. A nurse quietly directed us to the proper bed. Angelina had an ice bag on her head and was still suffering from bad headaches and fever. She didn't say much, and Dr. Bruno and I stayed only a few minutes. In our short stay, I noticed an altar at the end of the wing where any patient might pray and where the priest said prayers for them. There were also a few black-garbed sisters who helped as nurses. When we were halfway down the street, Dr. Bruno realized his error in misreading the clock and regretted leaving so early.

Instead of going directly home, I went with him to a little *osteria* and came upon a singular group of people within. First thing that impressed me was their similarity in type. They were all middle-aged and older. They all seemed to know each other well. Bruno's father and younger brother were there also. His father was a small, thin man who wore a felt hat and a cheery, spirited smile of welcome. He looked me over from head to foot and was later engrossed in my air force shoulder patch insignia. I heard him ask Bruno if I were Brazilian. Why I don't know, but when he heard I was an American in the air corps, he seemed pleased and pulled up a chair and leaned closer to me. The whole atmosphere was that of a backroom hangout. During the wine and conversation that followed, I learned that Bruno and a sister, whom I had not yet met, were partisans and had been hunted constantly by the Germans. As a result, they took to the mountains and returned only a few days before the Germans left Rome. He has a large scar across his forehead and was wounded once in the arm. They are, and have always been, anti-Fascists and had been beaten up several times by hooligans. His father had been jailed here in Rome for a year as a hostage for his son's return. The pair had always been a staunch anti-monarchists and republicans ever since Buffalo Bill made a circus tour in Rome in 1904. Buffalo Bill made many speeches praising the American form of self-government. They referred to him admiringly many times throughout the evening. Bruno, with medical knowledge and training, had helped many of our paratroopers and infiltrators. The father had studied French and English about thirty years ago, and though his French was good, his English was very limited although his accent was quite good. I left about 10:00 p.m. quite full of wine and democracy.

October 27, 1944

Steadily increasing rains and wind. The ocean is rough too. I visited the hospital again, and she wasn't feeling much better. We walked back to the osteria again, and Bruno's old man started complaining about the wonderful democracy they could have if it weren't for the king. It was going back through history to hear men plotting the overthrow of the monarchy for a republic. It makes one really sense a parallel with our colonial history. I don't know if they were expecting something out of me in pursuance of this movement other than a few cigarettes and favorable testimony upholding democracy, but they confided in me to such a degree as if I were a charter member of their organization. Some were loudly demonstrative. I believe it was only the shortage of glassware that prevented a violent glass smashing jamboree when they reached an emotional climax. Others played cards, and a good deal of the time, it was by the light of a bright, canned gas flame. They resembled a collection of the town's more intelligent ne'er-do-wells whose political ethics were sincere but ineffective. They drank incessantly but with no serious effects. What they needed was a little action behind them, which I think they were expecting from the town's youth. Perhaps after all is won, they will lean back in their wine-stained chairs and proudly hail themselves as the fathers of the Italian democracy in the same class of great Italians like Garibaldi and Mazzini. More power to them! They may very well prevail.

October 28, 1944

I took this afternoon off and found Angelina much better. Her case was now analyzed as malaria. Quinine was given, and she was coming along just fine. Some of the nuns are becoming quietly indignant at my untimely entrance into the women's ward. This permission was given to me by a doctor after four packs of cigarettes were seen to change hands. Bruno and I went to a movie. We saw about ten minutes of it when the power shut off and refused to come back on. After twenty minutes, we left. On the way out, passes were given to us for a return engagement. We went back to the hospital, but first I ate at the GI only restaurant, without Bruno, made a sandwich, and carried it out for Angelina. I met Bruno at the door of the hospital, passed out a few cigarettes, and then we both went in. Bruno returned to the door a little later to wait for a doctor friend's advice on this case. Angelina was feeling very bad tonight. Headaches, backache, and a temperature of 104 degrees and naturally no appetite. When I left, the other doctor who spoke to Bruno told me that Quinine didn't seem to agree with Angelina's stomach and if possible I should bring Atabrine from the camp. Her condition added fright to my helplessness. It was raining outside, but we walked back to the little barroom again on Via Grotto where we had been the last two nights. The same gang was there, still playing cards. Angelina didn't eat the food I brought her, so I gave it to Bruno. I left at about 10:30 p.m., and Bruno waited with me until I got a hitch to camp.

October 29, 1944

Without seeing Dr. Bruno, I brought the Atabrine directly to the hospital where it was quickly administered. We kissed, hoped for the best, and I left.

October 30, 1944

This evening as Bruno and I went into Rome, two English soldiers asked for directions. I had my raincoat on and wore no hat and was mistaken for a civilian. They insisted on speaking broken English to me in spite of the fact that I spoke perfect English to them! I wasn't very much flattered when one of them said to me, "You speak pretty well. Speak good English." I decided to keep my nationality secret. When they left, they offered us a cigarette apiece. Bruno was practically doubled up in laughter listening to them talk to me. We needed a good laugh. Angelina is coming along fine now. In the meantime, I disposed of some merchandise, walked around town, ate lunch, and brought Angelina some chicken. During our walks, I had a good chance to see one of Rome's poorer quarters, famous for the poet Dante's birthplace. Late in the afternoon, Angelina seemed completely recovered and was discharged.

October 31, 1944

For privacy, I had moved Angelina to a new apartment in the same building. However, it was in a different wing, so all the stuff had to be moved down three flights and then up four flights on a separate staircase. Marcello and I did most of it, with Leda, Erminea, and some kids carrying the lighter items. We have an extra room here, but there is no heating system in the building. Even if there were, no fuel of any kind was available.

November 3, 1944

These mornings Angelina's cheerful looks cheered me immensely as we got her room straightened out finally. Angelina and I had some material saved up for bedsheets and a lining for her coat, and I suspected that Marcello must have stolen some of it during the last week when Angelina didn't sleep there. My suspicions are correct. I found about ten feet of it missing, and I felt that something had to be done about this very soon. I don't like her living with such people in spite of our friendship.

November 4, 1944

Today is Italian Unknown Soldiers Day here and a sad holiday, as Antonio our office cleaner explained. This afternoon we decided to dye the blanket. First, we had to find wood to build a fire. It seemed simple at first, but these days it's hard to find any wood with everybody searching. We lucked out. The result looked quite good. It was a time-consuming job. This afternoon when I arrived, they were eating a little horse meat, which came into town as an unexpected windfall, if you could call it that. Some poor horse had the misfortune to step on a mine in the neighborhood. However, better an animal than a person. The stuff quickly sold out in the local butcher shop and without any rationing points. Blondie, Strack's friend, came over this evening and wondered why Strack hadn't been over to see her. That's quite a story. He got slightly burned up when she spurned his affections in spite of the fact they were blessed with good food and PX supplies. There were some others over also, friends of Marcello and Leda who promptly partook of a good pile of meat I had brought over.

November 5, 1944

This morning, Smitty, in the orderly room, told me that the new commanding officer, Captain Ware, wanted to see me. Uh-oh. I immediately went to see him and couldn't imagine what I had done. I was greatly relieved to learn that he only wanted to see me about some signs he needed. This evening I had a most unexpected surprise. While walking out of the mess hall, it was twilight, I thought I imagined a figure that looked like a Brooklyn friend named Eli Brody. He apparently recognized me first and said firmly, "Hello, Mr. Pashcow, I presume!" as if he had ended his long search for the missing Dr. Livingston. He was a medic on a ship. We went back to my room, and he liked the nice setup that we have here. I told him to be sure to tell my folks just how everything is here if he ever got to New York. Then we went down to see Angelina, and I asked that he not mention Angelina's presence for now. We talked most of the evening about his experiences as an army medic on ships. We inquired as to a plane going to Naples where his ship was docked. He had to be back on time as it might pull out at any time. The courier leaves at ten fifteen every morning. I decided to go back with him as I had not yet taken any of my accrued leave time. Angelina understood. We put our names on the flying manifest.

November 6, 1944

Lieutenant Colonel Solomon said that because Sergeant Klibi was ill in the hospital, I could take only two days. He was sorry, but he said it wouldn't count against the five days I'd get later. That didn't do much good, but I took it. This afternoon Eli and I took off for Rome at one. First, we took in the Coliseum, then Piazza Venezia, the home of Mussolini's famous balcony pulpit. From there we hit the Pantheon and then to Vatican City. We trailed along on a tour for a while inside the great cathedral. Later, an English-speaking priest showed us around with some interesting explanations. Michelangelo's most-perfect signed work is here. All paintings are really mosaics of exceptional workmanship. It is the largest cathedral in the world being six hundred feet long and holding six thousand souls. Then we hopped into a carriage and rode to the San Carlo restaurant. The driver first wanted a dollar and a half but after trailing along after us finally accepted sixty cents. From there we got back to camp in two lifts. The second one brought us to an accident in the road. It seems that an unlighted English truck smashed into a furniture-loaded wagon, and a pregnant woman was injured. We got her to her home a few miles ahead where a male nurse was found that took over. My friend Eli slept in Sussman's bed tonight.

November 7, 1944

Election day at home. We reached the airport at about 9:30 a.m. and looked around the airfield for a while. At 10:00 a.m. the courier arrived, and there was some unloading before we took off. We arrived at Naples airport less than an hour later and then got a lift into Naples eight miles away. The city reminded me of Sicily. Naples is very busy. Along the dock areas, there is almost complete devastation of houses, rubble filling up more than a floor in each building. The same poverty, filth, and indifference is rampant in public. However, Naples had more food and clothing than elsewhere. Military traffic is almost of a convoy concentration. We finally get to Eli's ship and, after hiding my camera, get it in the dock area. The boat is a Liberty ship. After lunchtime, we picked up a snack of bread and butter to last until supper. Then we walked to the Red Cross, and a girl is playing the piano for the boys who crowd around. I ask info on how I can get a lift to the airport tomorrow. I pick up a Naples “tourist” folder; then I pick up a pair of shoes for Angelina. Shoes here are about half the price of Rome. She needed a pair, and I figured I might as well get them here. There are shoes for ten bucks or less, but they are not leather and are poorly styled. I didn’t take those, but a really nice pair. In the evening, we went to a movie at a theater on the docks.

November 8, 1944

On the ship, I slept on a nice mattress and sheets; and in the morning, we had a breakfast of eggs, potatoes, baloney, etc. We ate with a crew of sailors and maritime men. We got permission to buy PX supplies and bring some back to camp. I brought eight cartons of cigarettes, four dozen Baby Ruths, two bedsheets from the ship, and other incidentals. The ship was being loaded with a great deal of K rations. I picked up eight cans of cheese. All and all, I had a nice bundle. Before chow, we took a walk around the docks, which were loaded with all kinds of military supplies. Cranes were busy unloading ships. They worked twenty-four hours a day. Scuttled vessels, none American, were here and there in the port waters. On the top of some of them, loading platforms were constructed so as not to waste space. Then we returned to the ship, ate lunch, and prepared to leave at a few minutes before 1:00 p.m. I said good-bye to Eli as he and a friend prepared to go to an opera and I got a lift on a truck. Just previously an MP asked me what I was carrying out, and I showed him the permissive note the lieutenant gave me. A lift got me to the airport just five minutes before the plane left. The weather was becoming foggy, but visibility was still good. At 3:00 p.m., we landed at Lido di Roma, and Harry drove me back in his Red Cross truck. In the evening, Angelina was much pleased with the shoes and gave a cheerful hug. I think it was more than she expected.

November 9, 1944

I see that President Roosevelt is reelected for sure. Happy days are here again. He deserved it. Nothing to do in the office. Mine is becoming a very enviable position. Got three packages yesterday from Mom and Pop.

November 10, 1944

Wrote a few letters. Got a package from my good pal cousin Mary, whose bosom friend is lusting for me. Tonight I'm on guard from 7:00 to 11:00 p.m. Angelina comes down at about nine and stays with me the remaining two hours. At 11:00 p.m., after I was relieved, I drove back in a weapons carrier and dropped Angelina off at the house on the way. Angelina tells me that Marcello was saying things behind my back. When I bring doughnuts, he gets slightly irked if I eat one, and he expects me to bring the contents of all packages I receive from home. He is too nosey in general, but I still like him.

November 11, 1944

Besides being my twenty-sixth birthday, it's also Armistice Day. I don't know what kind of celebration they had in Rome, but I'm sure they had one. I saw Strack this noon hour, and we decided to go apartment hunting. That's a continuous occupation. After I brought Angelina's chow, Strack and I searched up on the next floor and found a penthouse locked up and empty, but as we looked around, a woman came up and told us that somebody was moving in soon. There was some furniture there that we took because we didn't believe her. This evening Marcello had an English paratrooper up for some entertainment. Marcello has something up his sleeve, I'm sure.

November 12, 1944

Getting pretty cold now. There's an award being given to the 807th Medical Group outside right now. A two-star general is pinning the medals. Strack and I looked around again. We found another usable apartment, but smaller. There would also be rent to pay, probably ten or twelve bucks a month. One room had unbroken windows. This evening at Marcello's apartment, he had some English soldiers over for entertainment and dancing. There were about a dozen, and I didn't like the whole thing. Also Marcello is thinking about selling two big mirrors and writing up some phony contract about his having purchased some of the furniture so that I could not take it out of the house. I expect to beat him to it by moving out tomorrow, with my furnishings, while he and Leda are out.

November 13, 1944

Today I arranged with Strack to get a Red Cross truck for moving. Marcello and Leda are supposed to go to Rome at two o'clock. I intended a very unpleasant surprise for them when they returned to find only the bed and radio. We stopped at an apartment we had looked at before and spoke to a woman who lived there. There was nothing in the apartment in which she lived. No lights, nothing. She was glad to have somebody come in with her, and it seemed that here too nobody paid any rent because the "boss" never came around. The place would require a great deal of fixing. This lady worked in a relative's store of some kind and was around the house on and off during the day. We told her that we'd move in later today. She'd be away, but the landlady of the entire building would see that we got in all right. Back at the other place, Angelina was all alone. Leda had just left but didn't take her valise. I didn't want her to return and interrupt us. Because it was late and we didn't know when she'd return, we let the job go until tomorrow. Seems Leda didn't go after all because no transport was running.

November 14, 1944

It is raining a little but not enough to stop our moving operations if all goes well today. It took three ambulance loads and four Italians to help for almost two hours. I gave them each a pack of cigarettes. We quickly arranged everything, but candles had to be used. The place looked pretty nice in spite of everything. The tenant returned and helped Angelina. I asked the woman if it was safe here at night with everything broken open. She told me not to worry and that the two of them would be all right.

November 15, 1944

On my way to the new place this afternoon, Augusto met me, and the questions flew. "Why did you take my china closet? My table?" I reminded him that I owned those items, and Marcello was going to sell them behind my back. He denied it. I firmly told him that I found some other furniture to replace it and I'd give it to him. After all, he wasn't a bad guy, and he did help me out when Angelina first came to Lido. I told him to meet me Saturday afternoon and I'd tell him how we'd move it. I told Angelina about my meeting with Augusto, and she told me about her meeting with Leda early this afternoon. Leda was yelling out of the window all sorts of threats about the missing furniture calling the cops, etc., etc. She was even mad because I took my own electric lightbulbs with me. They are expensive, if you can find any. Angelina was against returning the furniture, but as I figured that Augusto was to get it, we didn't mind much.

Tonight Strack and Blondie came over. He brought a quart of vermouth with him, and we poured it into cut coke bottle "glasses."

November 17, 1944

Strack and I got all the lights fixed up in the apartment. We gabbed while we worked about the spite damage done by the Germans. Angelina impishly loved tickling my leg whenever I'd be balanced on a chair, which was on top of a table. Bernardo, the landlady's husband, is a very amiable old cuss who likes his wine almost as much as his wife. We brought him some pipe tobacco and some coffee and sugar. One night I found them eating dry wheat shells in an effort to convert it, by what alchemy I don't know, into coffee. The stove downstairs throws a very cheery heat, and most of the neighbors are welcome to come down and sit around. They all bring something to do, usually sewing or eating chestnuts.

November 18, 1944

I got this afternoon off, and Strack and I finally got the truck. We returned to pick up the furniture promised to Agosto, half expecting to find most of it gone. We found only a few pieces gone and the glass of a china closet smashed. While we were busy carrying things out, a boy came into the house and watched us. He came up with the not-so-good news that this was his house. "Not anymore," I said. I tried to soften the blow by offering some goodies as a foolish swap. He wasn't convinced, and he rather convinced me instead of I him. In every apartment we entered he gave out with a thumbnail sketch of who previously lived there, detailing family job and marital status. As long as he kept quiet, we didn't care. I just hoped that he wouldn't run down the street yelling or trying to warn people about what we were doing. We loaded up three times and then dropped Augusto's furniture off at his house, all by late p.m. We sure had plenty. The Italians who help out at the Red Cross, under Strack's guiding hand, helped us graciously with all the loading. These guys sure can work when they want to. Angelina is not feeling well again. It seems like malaria relapse with back pains again. I hate to see Angelina sick. She has gone through so much, and it is so unbecoming to her cheerful normal self. "Don't worry, darling. I'll be better soon. I don't want you to worry." I still worry.

November 19, 1944

Angelina was in bed the whole day, improving all the time after taking Atabrine. The landlady helped her a great deal, always checking up on her.

The wing is putting on a play tonight called "Hurry Up and Wait." I will try to see it tomorrow.

November 20, 1944

To my relief, I found Angelina out of bed at lunchtime and ready to romp.

November 21, 1944

Strack had an extra stove, and we could use it in the house "if it was repaired." He and Angelina took it to Rome. We hoped to see a movie if we got done early, but we lost the road twice, and it was three o'clock before we found the place. We must have driven halfway to Naples by the time we got back to Rome. Anyway, we saw some of the surrounding country from the ground for a change, including an old Roman elevated aqueduct on the Apian Highway No. 7.

November 22, 1944

Strack had to go back this afternoon to get the stove. Angelina is still a little sore from yesterday's ride, but tomorrow is Thanksgiving, and I won't have to work. I'd try to get away to go to Rome with her. We got the stove, but he forgot a pump, so we let it go till the next day before trying it out. I brought my little paratroop stove over to warm her up.

November 23, 1944

Today on Thanksgiving Day, we all awaited anxiously our special Thanksgiving dinner. Colonel Manning was there and had just made brigadier general. After a little speech we fell to, and it was certainly a fine dinner—plenty of white turkey meat, good stuffing, cranberry sauce, peas, mashed potatoes with cheese, and hot buns. It was one of the few times that we all found it difficult to get up from the table. We were never so satisfied. I got plenty of meat for Angelina, and naturally I gave an explanation what our holiday was all about. She certainly enjoyed it and purred like a pussycat. We had enough left over for the next day. The stove worked, and it gave off a dandy heat.

November 24, 1944

I still feel quite full. The landlady's husband, Bernardo, went to Rome this morning. Last night he asked about a ride there. Our truck now picks up civilians in the morning to Rome, and they would give him a lift. I wrote a little note and gave it to him just in case they couldn't understand him at the motor pool.

November 25, 1944

Got a fruitcake the other day that my mother sent and also a rare letter from my father. The people who usually hang around the landlady's stove are making shoes out of material cloth and eating chestnuts. They were certainly experts at sewing. These shoes are only worn around the house to save their outdoor wear for more important occasions. This evening when I returned I found that running water was in the house, but pressure was very low because the town engineers can't repair much. We have no faucets in the kitchen and so may not stop the flow. We didn't know how long it would last, so we filled up a five-gallon can immediately, and then Angelina took the opportunity to clean up the house.

She cooked up some spaghetti for supper on the little stove. She just loves to cook. She's thin as a model and walks like one.

November 28, 1944

Day off. Slept until 11:00 a.m. then I went back and told Angelina to get ready as we would go to Rome this afternoon. We began to eat out of trays today (progress). I still bring my canteen cup and fill it up for Angelina. We got a hitch on an English truck at about 2:30 p.m. and got off at Piazza Venezia. As we passed shops, I noticed a great deal of new goods displayed. Suits, overcoats, kitchen utensils, underwear, etc. Angelina ate in a civilian restaurant. Many restaurants are off-limits to soldiers, so I had the owner make up some beefsteak sandwiches and ate them outside. When I finished, I walked around and saw a "pro station" in which there might be a stove there where I could warm up a little. I was lucky, but also found an interesting storytelling refugee who was running the station. By the way, a pro station is one of several special dispensaries where any soldier could treat himself with a prophylactic solution after intercourse. It was greatly encouraged by "Take a pro" signs hanging everywhere, sometimes around the necks of statues of Italy's most revered heroes.

The fellow running the station, who is a Jewish Czechoslovakian doctor, spoke English very well besides German, Italian, and French. When he told me he was Jewish, I said "Shalom aleikhem" (welcome), and he smiled like an old paisano. I then returned to the restaurant, and after paying the bill, we walked back toward the Coliseum. It was a clear night now and starry, but still chilly. A short wait for a lift home. When I returned, the orderly room was a drunken mess. The only sober character was W. W. Cooper, "Charge of Quarters." I was told I might see him in the morning, meaning I might miss bed check, and he said sure. He's going to give me two more woolen top shirts. He's really the kind of guy a fella needs once in a while.

November 29, 1944

First news this morning is that I am now under the jurisdiction of Captain Morgan of statistics and with whose office I have been working with Miller. That means that I am now a part of statistics but still assigned to A-2 intelligence section. I couldn't seem to find Strack all day today, and something told me that he was up to no good. The ambulance was gone too. Angelina told me this afternoon that she heard that Strack was drunk and on a little spree. Seems he brandished a pistol and was about to shoot it out with a policeman but backed off.

November 30, 1944

The MPs finally caught up with Strack and took away his gun. The commanding officer gave him seven days of hard labor, but because his back hurt, his sentence was commuted to reporting to the CQ every hour from 5:00 p.m. to 10:00 p.m. for seven nights. Tonight we attended a squadron dance in Rome. There was a large crowd, and we enjoyed ourselves. We came back in Harry's ambulance (not as patients).

December 1, 1944

Borrowed Strack's stove this evening, and it felt great.

December 2, 1944

The landlady asked me if I could recommend a few customers to her for laundry, and since Captain Morgan was looking for a recommendation, I gave her a plug. The weather is getting a little colder now. Strack took the stove back. Too bad, because we sure could use it now.

December 3, 1944

Angelina finally got her coat made, but it seems a little snug. The dying job was good.

December 4, 1944

Brought over a mosquito net to the house. Angelina wants to make an evening gown, but for what reason, I don't know. From what I've seen of her sewing and alterations, I believe she can do it.

December 6, 1944

I would have taken the day off, but Captain Morgan was off somewhere in Siena, I think. I'd have to wait until he got back. Angelina washed out a piece of my tracing cloth in hot water and found some excellent grade of linen in it. I had thought of this as a source of material for her for the last few days now, and she liked it very much. I'll bring her a roll of it soon. We attended a dance, and I was somewhat angered at the civilians' food grabbing. Not only did they line up again after immediately getting a sandwich, but they pushed the GIs out of the way before putting the sandwiches in their bag and then leaving. I don't feel like coming back.

December 7, 1944

Third anniversary of Pearl Harbor and a minute of silence in memory.

December 8, 1944

Everything quiet. Seems there are some ridiculous rumors that Blondie, Strack's friend, is a spy. The FBI is checking up in some manner.

December 9, 1944

Getting colder now. That is, you almost have to wear gloves. We don't go to shows because of it, and it is so nice and warm in the landlady's apartment that it is hard to pick ourselves up and leave. It seems that the property owner was around and asked that she begin paying the phenomenal sum of four dollars a month for rent. I didn't see him myself, the landlady told me. I said okay naturally as I didn't feel like carrying all of that furniture out on my back. It seems that the civilians are having some of their rights restored.

December 10, 1944

This afternoon I brought over a twenty-five-yard roll of tracing cloth, and we dunked it in hot water to clean off the gelatinous covering. Later it was washed and pressed, and it looked very good. It's supposed to be linen, and Angelina says it's worth four to five dollars a yard.

December 11, 1944

Captain Morgan said it was all right to take eight days off now anytime I wished. I'll probably start Friday. Tonight we all played "twenty-one" for one to three cents. Easy way to pass the time. Sicilian card decks have only have forty cards, one to seven, and three pictures on each clubs, hearts, spades, and diamonds. I won a few cents then quit. One of the other women who live in the house is there every night and constantly sews, making clothes and shoes for her kids out of old, thick materials.

English paratroops are drilling these days, and all kinds of detonations echo around us. On almost every street, you will see a small group of them drilling and firing into sand holes.

After chow, the tailor sent a dress made from some new material that Angelina had had for some time. It was light with a flowery design. This was in preparation for the dance tonight. The dance was as usual but perhaps with a few more civilians. Krotec dressed up like a girl and, being stewed, promptly began insulting the commanding officer as a "chicken shit." The commanding officer has his own headaches in the form of a chaperone who sits at his table together with his date. They smile grimly at each other and have a terrible time. On the way back, we had three tipsies in the ambulance who serenaded us all the way home.

December 14, 1944

Went to work today, but my thoughts were on the next eight days off. I helped Miller a little, and as Major Morgan wasn't around at all, a pleasant time was had by all. At about 3:00 p.m., I asked Mr. Ellis at the orderly room for my eight-day pass, which he promptly issued. Angelina was ecstatic over our coming time together.

We decided to go to Rome and got on the truck after a little haggling about some matter of permission that nobody seemed to know anything about. Like all other women, Angelina was quite happy to window-shop. She was interested in buying a watch, which at the moment didn't make me very happy. I sidetracked the issue temporarily. I "accidently" walked up Via Tritona and past the PX store. I thought I'd try getting some rations, which I knew I was entitled to buy. I got cigarettes, tobacco, soap, two boxes of figs, and some candy and matches. I figured it would be good for the purchase of a watch if it seemed inevitable. It was. Angelina had great fun trying them on. What fun! A final selection was made, which she wore proudly on her wrist, and of course after giving me a great big kiss. "Fungiuto mia," (my sweet lips) she exclaimed. I got a year's guarantee for the ten-jeweled watch. After a sumptuous dinner in a posh restaurant, we took in a vaudeville show. Comic and straight man teams are boisterous and experts at facial distortion. Very enjoyable. At about eight thirty, we left and walked in the direction of the coliseum hoping to get a lift home. We lucked out with a lift in a command sedan. It was like old civilian days riding on a soft bouncy backseat with your girlfriend. Captain Weatherbee was up front with the driver.

December 16, 1944

Sussman was having Sarah come out again, and we asked him to have her stay at Angelina's apartment while she waited for him. They looked over the apartment, but I could see that Sarah didn't exactly like the layout and that she would rather stay in Rome instead of coming out as she planned. She and Sussman argued about it, and Sarah decided to stay in Rome for a while. At about 3:30 p.m., who should arrive but our new "landlord." He came in with two women who were taking measurements of windows and figuring repairs. We thought he intended to move in, and that soured us. We tried to think of a few angles. There is a temporary housing rule that a tenant cannot be evicted if the owner has somewhere else to live.

December 18, 1944

Sergeant Pesci, the chef, got sore when I tried to take out some food before feeding everybody else, so I waited until 5:45 p.m. While the folks played cards this evening, I heated up some water to wash out some tracing cloth, which yields some very nice linen. I'm doing it myself now because the last time that the landlady did it, four yards were found to be missing when I remeasured it. One of the tenants had swiped it while it hung out to dry. I made a makeshift clothesline in the apartment, and we hung up more than thirty yards.

December 20, 1944

We visited the diggings at Ostia, hiked, and scoured the back streets of Rome where we bumped into Marcello and Leda, the "honeymooners." I told them I'd have their wedding pictures soon. We're still good friends. We spent some happy time together. Angelina and I became closer, and I was convinced that we could ride out the rough seas ahead of us.

December 23, 1944

Back on the job again. Very busy. That "movements" section of the A-3 department gives me a pain. They always ask for a sign with the officers' personal names on it. Highest rank on top. By the time it is finished, somebody's rank has changed, somebody has left, or somebody has come in. The commanding officer isn't around, but we can't relax. He'll probably be in tomorrow, and I'm wondering what kind of days off he'll give us for Christmas.

December 24, 1944

No bed checks tonight or tomorrow night. Shorty Carsetti has been drunk for three days now and is telling everybody to go to hell and worse, regardless of rank. He has one or two amiable, mellow companions supporting each other in a buttress-type formation. Nature does protect its helpless. Krotec for some mysterious reason has been going around as sober as a judge. This afternoon Morgan was in and gave Sussman and me a carton of cigarettes each for a present. He also told me to go and take off now and come back Tuesday morning. I went over to the house and found Angelina in the street with the two kids of the "lady who sews." We went down to the landlady's apartment. She told me that a new owner of the apartment had arrived together with his entourage, which contained an American captain. He is connected with the postal system in Italy. He inspected the place and to our relief wanted to see others before deciding. The fellow who lived next door was also there. They looked and selected his apartment. He was badly shocked over being evicted and asked for time. They left after giving the landlady a buck to keep an eye on things.

December 25, 1944

I volunteered for Christmas guard duty from 3:00 to 7:00 a.m. Two other Jewish boys did the same. For dinner had turkey and dressing similar to Thanksgiving. I brought back a lot of it to the house not knowing they had their own dinner, and so we saved it for later. Then a young boy with an accordion came over, and we went inside the apartment downstairs and danced awhile. We certainly do a lot of dancing. Angelina had drunk different types of wine and felt giddy.

December 28, 1944

Miller is trying to learn Italian the hard way by studying vocabulary and pronunciation but is making less progress than a snail going uphill. He has never studied a foreign language before. I like teaching and was glad to help. No work at all today, not even a Please Flush sign. Several other fellows, including another pal Brooklynite named Epter, congregate in our room because it's out of the way at the end of the hall. The room is like a madhouse at times with some soliloquizing, singing, drawing, mimicking radio programs like "The Lone Ranger." This evening I found friend Dodge, the stove maker, to place an order.

December 31, 1944

I was busy, and Angelina was at an informal gathering of new neighbors. I later joined them. It was only a few blocks away. The gathering was in a room about twelve feet square with three of the walls lined with chairs and had a radio and phonograph, over which hung a bare, bright electrical bulb. Present were several police, one civilian, and one other GI. Wine, nuts, etc., were immediately put before me after I entered and greeted them. This hostess was a woman who seemed happy to have company and made herself very convivial. The other GI was a hillbilly and didn't feel like dancing. He said, "I only know those mountain steps like the square dance." The men danced with each other, not for lack of women, but by custom. When twelve o'clock struck, there was no shouting or carousing, but we shook hands and wished all a "Happy New Year." I was pleasantly shocked at having every man in the room kiss me on both cheeks, including Angelina.

"Angelina, what do you wish for or want for the new year?" Her deep brown eyes flashed and without hesitating, "I already have everything I want or need. Just you, always to be there for me, and to make you happy, next year and forever."

"You don't know it," I said, "but you have changed my life, given me purpose and direction in ways you cannot imagine. Stay with me always." I knew she understood me. We embraced just as the new year ticked off.

The Rome radio station was rebroadcasting the American programs, all of which sent New Year's greetings to the servicemen in Italy. I knew it was actually 5:00 p.m. in New York. We left soon after another hand shaking and kissing event.

January 1, 1945

Work today for a rush job and with today comes the sad news that most every rear echelon man must hear at one time or another: "You are moving up." These words really shook me, to say nothing of the surprise. We were moving to Siena, an ancient city and the birthplace of the Italian language. As I was later to learn, it was a living museum. It was like Florence, a center of Italian art and culture. Many problems are popping into my head. What to do with Angelina? The apartment furniture? To say nothing of finding a new place up in Siena for her if she comes. I'd like to go up there and see what's up there first. Miller went up there yesterday, and I asked him to look around for a room for Angelina. Bernardo and Erminea, our downstairs neighbors, are also downcast about our moving. We got along so well that Bernardo feels as if his own son is leaving him. I sort of like the old loveable reprobate myself, even if he did drink a little and have small, halfhearted arguments with Erminea about it. That's the worst part about moving, leaving new "old" friends. A few months of friendship here seems like a year. Such is the hospitality. That is the one bright light in this miserable war. Here they say, "Ti voglio bene." Literally it means "I wish you well." Actually it means that you are part of the family and welcome to anything they have. It is an affection for strangers unequalled to anything I have ever seen anywhere. Romantically it means "I love you" but is so deep-rooted as not to be anything of a temporary nature or anything casually applied. Therefore, when you are the object of these three little words, you may rest assured that your best interests are with them, and you have reached something far more valuable than an ordinary friendship.

January 3, 1945

Horsed around working feverishly on those insignia for section A-1. They want five-wing insignias in color, not now, but yesterday. I don't know when I am leaving yet, but within a few days, I should guess.

Chapter XX

NEWS HEADLINE: ***January 26, 1945*****—Soviet Troops Liberate Auschwitz Death Camp**

January 4, 1945

I'm to go off to Siena by plane tomorrow to see what space we get and direct the goods as they come from the airport to our office. I should be back Sunday after the other fellows come up on Saturday or Sunday morning. Strack may go too to see about Red Cross matters. Angelina seems determined about moving up here also. Miller came back at about 5:00 p.m. and had anything but good things to say about the new place. The city had a medieval look about it and was more like a fortress than a city. However, I hope to see for myself when I go up.

I brought over a sack of pine cones to burn in the stove. They give out tremendous heat and a wonderful aroma. The stove also seems to thrive on a diet of broken tables and smashed furniture.

January 5, 1945

Got up and got ready for the plane trip and was greeted by a wind and rainstorm that kept all planes grounded. Angelina was happily surprised to see me at lunchtime. At the office we began packing our equipment.

January 6, 1945

We're to leave today. The weather is rainy, but we finally did get off. The trip was uneventful, and we landed at Maliginiana airfield about five miles from Siena. It was in the midst of some beautiful mountain scenery, about five thousand feet up, in the rolling soft green hills. A jeep from headquarters drove up and told us where to have chow. At the field, the mud was thick as we trudged our way up a hill behind broken-down hangars to eat. We were starved and ate fried Spam like it was beefsteak while we waited around for the truck to unload. It was sunny, but cold, and we hoped to get going quickly. Our truck finally arrived, and we left the airport quickly. The roads were narrow and hilly, and it was an indication of what to expect in Siena. We drove through the ancient entrance gate preserved in a modern brick supportive wall, and we were inside the city. Narrow winding streets were the first impression, and they are paved with square flagstones; then the hills begin, and it looks like the truck won't make it, but it does, after much grinding and backfiring. Pedestrians put fingers in their ears.

We ride up a short but very steep angled street to a former technical institute, now our headquarters. It has a very wide central stairway, and the building is in good condition. We help unload the A-2 section and then go to the barracks, a former school, which is practically empty. We select a large room that will hold eight or nine men and put our things in them. The day is cold, so we decide to carry our beds into another room where a woodstove has been set up. A few of the boys who have been up here since January 2 give us the lowdown on the city. The difference between this and other Italian cities to the south is the manner of the people. They are much more formal, almost cool to us, better dressed than other towns, and many faces are of Nordic feature. They speak the purest Italian with no dialects, and their speech is breathy and very pleasant. The town is steeped in culture and is so old that many sites could easily serve as ready-made movie sets. The cleanliness is also outstanding. I have not seen any garbage dumped randomly. We are on the side of a mountain, and the houses are bunched together as if holding on to each other for support. Streets run in every direction. One can lose his way quickly. Houses are built on archways over the streets at certain places. A couple of kids ask us for the same old chewing gum as always, but they are clean and fairly well dressed.

January 7, 1945

Today is Angelina's eighteenth birthday, but she's in Rome, and I'm looking for a gift. "I can't give you anything but love, baby" would fit if I could sing. There was nothing I could find on short notice. Flowers would always be appropriate. I found a bunch of daisies while we searched for rooms. I landed one, furnished, for twelve dollars a month. After chow, we went over to the Red Cross. It's large, busy, and volunteers are friendly.

January 9, 1945

The big trailer arrived at headquarters early, and we carried stuff up to the third floor. Then Strack and I took off for the airport and got a plane for Lido. Captain Ware, our commanding officer, was at the stick; and he is a sort of hotshot pilot. We hit turbulence and a snowstorm over the mountains, and he rolled the plane to a ninety-degree bank toward the ocean to avoid the snow. Our heads grazed the ceiling. Later I had to work fast to get the bulk of our furniture out of the apartment so that it could be loaded onto the truck going to Siena. I had seen Angelina in the meantime, and she was ready to come up. "Angelina," I said, "I missed your birthday while in Siena. Let's pretend it's today. Happy birthday, honey." She planted a kiss on my nose as I gave her the daisies. Unlike most of her gender, she took it calmly with understanding. "I'll make up for it when I get to America," she slyly threatened. We toasted each other in deep affection.

Really, nobody wanted to buy the things in our apartment because they were afraid that the real owners would eventually see it someday. In the evening, I met a guy who bought seven pounds of cheese, an old pair of Angelina's shoes, and the last few pieces of our old furniture all for forty dollars. Angelina would sleep over at Blondie's for the week.

January 11, 1945

We got up early to catch a plane, and Angelina left for Blondie's apartment. It was snowing lightly. That was the first time Angelina was in the midst of it, and she loved the flaky beauty of it. Strack and I ate breakfast; then we got on a plane with a little baggage, and just as we started up, a snowstorm closed the field. We hung around the operations tent for a while, and at 3:30 p.m., Captain Ware loaded up a PX ship and had no room for us, so we went back to town. The girls were surprised to see us, but it was nice to be back again, even for an overnight in Lido.

January 12, 1945

When we arose this morning, there was an inch of snow on the ground, and it was crystal clear at the airport. We took off and landed uneventfully forty-five minutes later at Maliginiana, in Siena about 11:30 a.m. and later met Miller and Sussman at the mess hall. They said Captain Morgan was a little sore about my being late this afternoon. I explained the snow to them, and everything is okay now. I got to work immediately.

January 13, 1945

Office furniture is beginning to arrive. The room is filled with furniture and looks like a bargain basement. The new office isn't bad even with the A-1 section with us. This afternoon at chow time, I told the new landlady when Angelina might arrive.

January 14, 1945

Very busy on the stat report and, while I was working, Strack came up to the office and told me that Angelina had arrived (by some unknown means) and was waiting outside. This was certainly a surprise to me. I took off, and sure enough there she was with another girl about a block away. They had hitched on one of our trucks on the way up. They had started out about 4:00 a.m. this morning, had eaten little, and were waiting for a place to go. The other girl was Bill Cooper's wife, Yolanda. I brought them both to Angelina's apartment until Bill came over. Later I brought over her valise and a barrack's bag full of her stuff. Angelina and Yolanda looked tired, and they needed rest.

January 15, 1945

The war news is looking better, and the Russians seem to be launching a new offense in Poland. I hope it ends in Berlin. The landlady has an oil stove she isn't using and has agreed to lend it to us. I can get kerosene from supply. We are getting ready for our first Siena dance this Wednesday. This town is a little chilly and damp. It's the rainy season, I guess.

January 16, 1945

Angelina went on a little shopping spree today. She bought a dress, shoes, and a few other things to the tune of ninety bucks. I almost hit the ceiling, but she needed the stuff, and since we had sold the furniture, it wasn't too bad on the pocketbook. She went to town with the landlady's little niece because she was afraid of losing her way. This evening I saw what Angelina had bought. It was a fine, white with pink polka dots, chiffon knee-length dress. We're beginning to have movies in our mess hall this evening. The electricity is unstable in these parts, but we have plenty of candles ready.

January 17, 1945

I feel a little headachy, but I went to the dance anyway. The dance tonight was a rather simple affair. Siena has no large dance halls, so what we had was a small hall whose walls were lined with benches. An orchestra came out with some American music. The women were a disappointment; that is, they were friendly but didn't know the art of makeup or dressing. Strack was there, and he was neat as a pin. There was no bar, much to everybody's regret. We walked back after the sandwiches and cake. Hope things will improve.

January 18, 1945

The landlady is skulking around for more rent. She has undertaken a bit of thievery in the way of a cake of soap and some kerosene, which she spilled all over the place. We didn't care much, but we agreed that we'd have to move since we've already had experience with stealing.

January 19, 1945

The Russians sure are plowing through the Germans in central Poland. Plenty of statistical work and I don't see the end of it yet. I expect to get seven days off beginning February 1. No trouble getting food. Jones gave me some extra chicken and bread today. The landlady gets the willies every time Angelina lets the sun in on her "beautiful" bedspread, fearing fading. "Don't sit on the bed either and be careful of the linen." It's all patched up. She blabs away about all these things. The poor lady's husband is dead, a casualty of the war, and so is her sister. Whenever she speaks of them, tears roll down her cheeks.

January 20, 1945

I looked at the surrounding country through my binoculars, and one can really appreciate the vast expanse of fertile land that lies beyond and somewhat below Siena. In the distance, rising up over the rolling valleys and small grassy plateaus are the Apennines, covered with soft blue-white snow. Summertime should really bring out the real beauty of a different season. Raining tonight. I had a little argument with Angelina about going to the movies. I wanted to, and she didn't. I went alone, but about twenty minutes later, she came in quietly. We held hands; neither the rain nor the movie mattered much.

January 21, 1945

Strack is settling down to a quiet life taking things easy. "Just wait till I meet the right girl," he says. A statistical report we had to do is boring as all hell, and I would rather dig ditches. Major Morgan tried to talk Sussman out of marrying Sarah as was his military duty for all such soldier requests. Sussman seems to be ready to go through with it.

Section A-2 is putting out a morning news bulletin as they did in Catania. I'm helping.

January 22, 1945

Pretty rainy these days. The landlady is beefing about washing the linens. That's because linens around these parts cost around a hundred and ninety dollars, she says. She feels like changing the sheets only twice a month.

January 23, 1945

Sussman left for Rome today for five days to see Sarah. Captain Morgan is leaving for Naples for a few days, and we should have a good rest. The report was finished tonight. First Sergeant Guzzi also took off for Rome, and that's a load off everybody's mind because he's tough.

January 24, 1945

Dance night again and new WACS to boot. These darlings are the homeliest I've seen yet. The orchestra was quite enjoyable. Jones, one of the cooks, and his girl were there. Angelina seems to get along well with her. We walked back through the wet streets, arm in arm.

January 25, 1945

I've got my eye on those "rushing Russians," and it's pretty hard to follow them too. I forgot to mention that since Captain Morgan wasn't around, Miller and I took off at three when the stores opened and did a little shopping. I bought Angelina a pair of rare silk stockings and some postcards for myself together with a history booklet on Siena. This afternoon I looked around for a new place but found nothing, not even a hot lead. After supper, Cooper's wife, Angelina, and myself sat around the kitchen stove discussing all sorts of topics from politics to the black market to cooking and passed a pleasant evening.

January 26, 1945

This was my first real day off here. At about 10:00 a.m., Sylvia, cook Jones's girl, came up and stayed for a while, and then she left and said she'd help us find a different room later for Angelina. I had a piece of that so-called linen in my pocket for pricing. We found no room but got a couple of hints. Then I went about my business and got offers of about four dollars a yard for the material, which is all right. After supper I went over to Sylvia's house and saw Angelina. After they finished eating, we talked awhile and then left. Jones speaks no Italian, and Sylvia's broken English gives Jones and me plenty of laughs.

January 27, 1945

We had an inspection today, and nothing happened as usual. The landlady got wind that I could sell the stuff in town, and she is already calling me names because I won't sell the stuff cheaply to her. "C'est la vie, mon ami."

January 28, 1945

I got a letter from home; and I see that my friend, Eli Brody, is back in New York. I'm glad he finally made it. Now the folks will have a much better report about me after seeing him in person.

January 29, 1945

When I came over to the house at lunchtime, Angelina was selling a can of butter to some friends of the landlady. I could have sold them the clothes off my back if the price were right. Sussman finally got back two days late, and he had settled things up pretty well with Sarah. She is quite well-off financially. I hope that doesn't stir his ardor.

January 30, 1945

Lately, selecting what incidents to record represents a dilemma. What may seem trivial or routine today may one day recall some dramatic moments with new intensity from a long-lost past. I continue as always, still in a dilemma state.

Miller was going downtown with us for a while. He wanted me to look at an offering of some postage stamps because I was an old-time collector; however, he changed his mind and didn't go. Angelina and I then took lots of highly desirable linen and got a very nice price.

January 31, 1945

Another dance tonight and tonight is really not worthy of special comment. The new hall, or rather nook, was just outside of town. The interior was about thirty feet square including the orchestra in that space. There were no windows. When we entered, I saw a dearth of women and several drunks tottering around. Adjoining the dance hall was a small room used as a bar. Cognac was popular and second to wine. Captain Ware, Mr. Ellis, and a few other honored guests were present. (We were never invited to their dances.) We drank a little of Strack's private stock of vermouth he had brought along in case the party got dull. It got dull amazingly fast, and the rumbling began.

The trouble all started with Jones's girl who refused to dance with a couple of drunks. One pulled her up from out of the chair. Jones handed him a right to the jaw, and then everybody jumped between them to avoid a bloody brawl. The fellow Dodge, the drunk, was whisked away while Jones was furious at his disappearance and continually eyeballed the room looking for him. I calmed him in a few minutes. During the fracas, his girl screamed and collapsed on the floor. Three men picked her up and carried her somewhere. It seems Dodge is just as mad as Jones and broke out of his "pen" where several guys had been holding him down. Jones met him in a corner where everybody charged into the scene to prevent the fight. However, one smash to Dodge's face by Jones set his whole face bleeding. By now the captain and Mr. Ellis were in the fray trying to establish some civil, if not military, order. In a most unceremonious surge, all officers and unlisted men alike went down in a heap. While Captain Ware struggled to his feet, Dodge, bleeding badly, was pushed up against the wall. Captain Ware then got a hold of him and bellowed some orders, which quieted him down until the cordon of men steamrollered him back out of the room. Jones was quite unflustered at the whole goings-on. The orchestra played on for a while, but even they soon lost heart and stopped to watch. That ended the fight. Sandwiches and cocoa were issued to the combatants and guests alike. We went back with Strack soon after and swore that we wouldn't go to another affair for our wing again.

February 1, 1945

We all expected and found a notice saying our presence at a squadron meeting would be appreciated this evening. Today was also the first of a seven-day pass I had fallen into luckily. The two additional days beyond the regular five were due to me from past months. The meeting this evening was a mild bawling out by the commanding officer for last night's brawl, and the news that we'd have no dance for a month suits me fine. He forced us to sit through a depressing sex hygiene film as additional punishment.

February 2, 1945

Today was the final day in the lives of twenty airplane passengers who had the misfortune to be on the wing courier this afternoon. Three escaped; two were badly injured when the plane, which was suddenly surrounded by fog, crashed into a mountainside before it had time to gain altitude. Some of the fog here in Siena is thick in the mornings. Major Apple of our A-1 section was among the dead, a great loss. I had seen him many times each day. Nurses were among the sad fatalities. "Rest in peace," I murmur.

Found a new room for Angelina today and made arrangements to move in a few days—a great improvement.

February 3, 1945

The landlady's son and I held some preliminary talks prior to the formal opening of trade relations concerning certain contraband items: prices, terms of delivery, etc. We understood each other quite well now. Namely that he is trying to skin me and that I am trying to skin him. He is a worthy opponent. This brisk trade keeps things lively, and he will buy anything that is not nailed down—and maybe even that. I haven't much stuff myself, but Strack has accumulated a pile of no mean proportions ranging from condoms to razor blades and toothpaste. I am his designated agent for the present.

February 4, 1945

I am taking the scabies treatment, which has been bothering me for some time. I have become quite used to the fact that it is part of wartime life although they modestly claim few cases here in Siena. Angelina will move into the new place tomorrow night. Italian lessons are to be given in the headquarters on the company time, both elementary and advanced. I expect to start on advanced soon when I return to work. I bought a treat at the Red Cross for Angelina. She has a sweet tooth. We packed up all the stuff to get ready for the big move.

February 5, 1945

I attended funeral services for the plane wreck casualties today. Then after a respectable pause, I closed a few deals, mostly with the landlady's relations, prior to taking off for the new place this evening. Her son is very sneaky or shrewd. Every time he closes a deal, he says, "How about throwing in a cake of soap or a package of razor blades?" I always tell him to get lost or else to top it off by returning an extra buck or two. Then we grin at each other and withdraw with a limp handshake. At about nine, we carried furnishings over to the new diggings and plunked an American flag in the new ground to claim sovereignty. The new landlady wanted to announce Angelina's presence to the police according to the law, but so far we have talked her out of it. She lost her identification papers, which prevents a lot of foolish questions. Angelina may also eat with them at times if she'd like to buy food occasionally. Mess hall dinners have been poor lately, so that's fine with me.

February 7, 1945

Last day of my vacation and I'm plum ready to go back to work. In the afternoon, Angelina and I walked over to the Red Cross and bought some cake and oranges, a can of tomatoes also. Right now we were all well ensconced in the new landlady's kitchen with a coke fire. They are playing cards, and the young daughter of the landlady is studying Latin.

February 8, 1945

Sergeant Guzzi is going home at last, and a farewell dance is being arranged for next Thursday. I don't usually eat breakfast most of the time when there are no eggs, so I didn't miss much. The bed is comfortable, and I hate to get out of it.

The Russians are at the Oder River now, and the Germans and Russians are having a fierce time, with terrible losses on both sides.

February 9, 1945

The former landlady of ours is still buying a few items from me, and we are getting along like nobody's business, which is just the way I want to keep it. Strack is helping me out by supplying some necessary items that he has accumulated and that I pass off for him. Suffice it to say that a good time is being had by all. Some of the food I bring over is not eaten by Angelina, and she gives it to the others, and this helps keep good relations.

February 10, 1945

The sun is coming out a bit, and it isn't quite so cold now. I went to an Italian lesson class this afternoon, and it was most interesting. We have a Professor Fiore, of about fifty years of age and gray-haired. He speaks good English, having spent time in England. There are only about eight in this advanced class, and so instruction is one on one. He speaks only Italian to us and uses English only for a grammatical comparison. I understand 99 percent of what he says.

February 11, 1945

The city water is off today for some unknown reason; and the good burgers are carrying their pots, pans, bottles, and drums and line up to fill at the few running fountains. There is a constant line always.

February 12, 1945

Today is honest Abe Lincoln's birthday, an inspiration from a common man for future generations. Today Miller's camera was ready. On the way back, we met Angelina and her young girlfriend going to a movie. I am glad she keeps busy. When we returned, the bulletin board had a notice of quarantine due to a diphtheria case. That meant no leaving the area.

February 13, 1945

I brought Angelina some tender juicy steak tonight, well seasoned. I am happy to see her enjoying her food. She ate with the others who shared her meat. The wine was plentiful, and the old-boy Bernardo was in his cups. He whipped the cork off, throwing the bottle in the air, and catching the neck with a dexterity that approached sleight of hand. You could see his eyes savoring the contents even before the red liquid filled the glass.

February 14, 1945

There was no inspection this morning. In fact I got up just in time to catch lunch, and then I went over to the PX and made a reservation to buy a watch and cigarette lighter. That done I returned to the house, and at about 2:45 p.m., Angelina and I walked downtown. I forgot to mention that Angelina had sold the last remaining linen cloth for a nice price and was casting her eye about for a dress. Of course she found one, and I was happy for her. I also have another roll of tracing cloth ready for Angelina's personal use. We had no drafting use for tracing cloth, so my guilty feelings were greatly assuaged.

February 15, 1945

I look back over the long period that my notes have covered and wonder how many more there will be when my final words, as planned, will be "I am now walking down the gangplank thrilled to be home with family and with visions of a frank at Nathan's hot Doggeria in Coney Island." This morning, as any other morning, began with necessity of my getting up. Waking up is not a very simple operation but one that is very often tied to reflections that are difficult to cull during other periods of the day. It is a time when I know deep down whether things are going right or whether my conscience is clear. It is a time when thoughts too soon to be disrupted by the daily chores are pinpoint clear, and when I know what bothered me yesterday and what may bother me today. It is my period of confession when I am at once the confessor and the confessee. However, very soon the cold floor is against my bare feet, my fingers are forcing buttons into tight buttonholes and shoelaces into shoe eyes, and the icy water on my face and scalp tortures the last sleep out of my stubborn body. We are ready for the usual day's work but never for the unexpected.

Tonight a dance was to be held; but instead of hiring a hall, we used the mess hall, which was elaborately decorated for the purpose. Ferns, crepe paper, and even some newly painted walls perked up the joint beyond our expectations. Strack and his Iginia, the landlady's comely widowed daughter, and her two teenage children accompanied us in search of a little entertainment; and we were glad they came. That was near 11:00 p.m., and we thought it was time to go. Frank had been dancing with Iginia. Private Straub, another friend, was amusingly tight but trying to cut in on Strack's girlfriend. He was quickly rebuffed and retreated in the face of Strack's strident manner and a clenched fist. I got our coats, and we left.

February 16, 1945

Back in the morning, I brought Angelina a tiny stuffed puppy. She loves stuffed animals, practically squeals over them.

February 17, 1945

I received a package from Hannah and Bernie, my brother and sister-in-law, with a salami in it among other things, all of which were enjoyable. Sergeant Guzzi and some of the boys, after a cheerful and envious send-off, left for the States today. We were just as happy to see him go as he was to leave.

February 22, 1945

I'm writing on my drafting table. Outside it is unusually foggy toward the mountains and the valleys. The clattering of the typewriters in the A-1 section is giving me a headache. I think the wing is due for some kind of a change soon, either in location or who knows what. Captain Morgan asked me to make a sign Ladies Only for a bathroom door. The A-3 section gives me a job, and then the medics want a few charts. Everything happens at once. Because of the dance, we quit at about 4:15 p.m. and early chow. Iginia, Strack's lady friend, doesn't go along tonight; and Frank oddly says it's all the same to him. We had a very fine orchestra of fourteen pieces. Aside from the usual drunks insulting all of the officers present, especially the commanding officer, it was a nice affair. We had sandwiches, coffee, and candy. Lopatin was clutching his girlfriend while she pretended to get away. Many of the boys had their right pants legs rolled up a few inches as a sign of a college fraternity password. At one time Sussman had both his hairy legs rolled up almost to his knees in humorous competition. The dance ended without any incidents similar to the fracas that brought last week's dance to a tumultuous close.

February 24, 1945

Today, we displayed our gas protective equipment. A group had rifle range practice. In Italian class, the professor told us what happened to his villa just outside of Siena when the Germans pulled out. He had some good English books in his library that, among all other things, were destroyed. He had two sons, one dead and the other a Russian prisoner, and three daughters who are all studiously inclined. He speaks English and gives the appearance of a well-lettered man. He brings out language differences quite well, and although our progress is slow, I know that every bit of it is worthwhile. Even just hearing him discuss things in Italian is worth the trouble to come and listen to him; so well does he speak.

When I bring lunch over to the house for Angelina, the young fellow, Nino, Iginia's son, always grabs the newspaper comics, which I explain to him as best I can. He is a cartoonist himself. He saves them all and pulls them out when a friend comes over. Then they both chuckle and laugh together in typical Italian hysterics.

February 25, 1945

The landlady is becoming a little anxious about Angelina's presence in the house without an announcement to the police as required by law. She heard about a couple of people who got in trouble that way. I tell her I'd find out about the possibilities of getting a pass.

February 27, 1945

Miller is working on the cover for next month's report. I heard that PFC Gianette of our dispensary was to be commissioned as a second lieutenant in the medical corps. The jump from PFC to second lieutenant is very unusual. We congratulate him on his newly acquired status.

Angelina went down to see the police station. They agreed to make out an occupation permit after closing an eye and opening a beckoning pocket.

February 28, 1945

Today is payday or more aptly "petty cash" day. I rise promptly and go down to get my rations at the new PX store in town. I go out a little later on a few business deals while Angelina goes out on a buying spree. Iginia has been filching a few little pieces of candy as the latest look at the candy box shows. Her figure is beginning to show it too. I lock the dresser upon going out.

March 1, 1945

Tonight at the dance, I ask Corporal Allen, who runs the dry cleaning section, if he could use Angelina. The situation didn't look good, but he'd try to give a note to the boss saying that she was needed. If there was any space later for her, he would take her on. That worked out pretty fine eventually.

March 2, 1945

At the house I woke Angelina, and she got dressed quickly. We went over to the city hall where after a few minutes she emerged and said that the residence permit would be ready tonight. I arranged to have her come down to work tomorrow.

March 5, 1945

After breakfast I came back to take Angelina to the dry cleaning quarters. Corporal Allen was inside, and we arranged for her to stay at the desk and accept and give out clothing instead of doing any real work. Then I left with him in a truck at nine in the morning. There was a light rain as I alighted and went into the office. At lunchtime, I saw a note on my bed asking me to call Allen. He told me that an officer objected to Angelina being there and drawing of an extra meal ration. That sounded like plain chicken shit. Allen said he could give her ironing tomorrow, and that helped. He told me that Chef Flanders said it was okay for her to eat if Allen hired her, and Allen approved.

March 6, 1945

It seemed odd not seeing Angelina at lunchtime, and I hardly knew what to do with my time. Angelina asked if I could still bring food up to the landlady. I didn't like the idea but said that if someone came down to the barracks at lunchtime, they could take it back with them.

I didn't even want to do that, but for the present, it's a small bother. When Angelina returned, she was slightly tuckered out, and her left arm was sore from ironing many pairs of trousers. It will probably be tiring for her for the first couple of days. She did want to keep busy. Strack came over, and we had a big discussion about our future and how lucky we were, in spite of a war.

March 7, 1945

I got up early so that we could be near the beginning of the PX ration line. I hope to get a watch and a cigarette lighter. There were no watches, but a cigarette lighter, yes, and some witch hazel. I went to Italian class in spite of it being my day off, and then Sussman and I took off to some new neighborhoods in town. Angelina returned very tired this evening and didn't want to go to a movie. I hope the job hasn't gotten her down already.

March 8, 1945

This evening another dance and nothing much happened. There was even a dearth of drunks. Mr. Padavich, head of the motor pool, was explaining the difficulties of keeping men of unequal rank on friendly terms. All of which was over a glass of cognac.

March 9, 1945

Italian lessons are challenging with translations on the blackboard from English to Italian as a part of our exercise. It is excellent training and simpler than any language I have ever studied in school. The natural outside street talk with shopkeepers makes it all the more effective. Our new first sergeant seems to know his business, and life is much easier without Sergeant Guzzi. Angelina's job seems to be all right now, but the tempo of business has slowed a lot. She gets a lift out to work every morning on a GI truck at about eight in the morning in front of headquarters.

March 10, 1945

Today I amassed many pictures and sent them home. Here's hoping they get through quickly. The weather is springlike, nice and warm. The war news looks good. The Allies are in Berlin.

March 11, 1945

Captain Morgan gave me the afternoon off, and I spent it at Angelina's. From out of the blue, "Do you miss me, honey, when I'm working?" she titillates, trying to provoke me. My eyes lock on hers. "I miss you all of the time," I respond, smiling, "even when you're in the next room." I feel her purring as I stroke her cheek. "I'll never leave you, I promise."

March 12, 1945

I wrote a letter to Eli sending Mozell's letter to him. Mozell is a Signal Corp cameraman and my good hometown friend. I also got an Easter V-mail prepared for mailing home. Nothing to do in the office. I went on sick call this morning with an eye ailment. The doctor says it's a cyst on my upper lid. He will operate in two or three days.

March 13, 1945

Still no work of any sort. The doctor saw me outside the barracks and, after examining my eye, said he'd operate tomorrow.

It's nice and sunny outside these afternoons, and that's about the only chance we get for some sun. Strack was up this evening, and while he spoke with Iginia, the others played cards. Strack may not be serious about Iginia, and I warned him to be honest and open. They sat around the kitchen table with one shaded electric light just above their heads. Jagged flashes and shadows result when bumped.

March 14, 1945

I arose early, ate breakfast, and then at 8:30 a.m. I went over to the doctor's office. He started on me almost immediately with some local anesthetic that made me feel quite sick. I later learned that there existed two cysts on the lid. He removed only one of them because I began to feel nauseous, and I soon threw up. Now I'll have to go through the whole thing all over again. He made me rest half an hour before I went back to the office.

March 15, 1945

There's a USO show at the air force service command theater at eight in the evening featuring an all-girl orchestra. We decided to go.

Allen, the corporal in charge of the dry cleaning section, told me there is so little work these days that Angelina would have to quit for at least a week to see what develops.

March 16, 1945

It was nice having Angelina back again. I'd rather not have her work there anyway, especially not that kind of work, but it was the only thing to do at the time.

March 18, 1945

We played around with the baby chicks this evening. Not much to do at the Gianni household, Angelina's place.

March 19, 1945

A notice on the board announced a meeting tonight. The dodo who wrote it didn't say it was compulsory, and so hardly anybody showed up. In spite of the reason, Captain Ware was very upset. He called the roll three times while ranting and raving, not behaving as an officer or gentlemen, and in desperation swearing to punish the absentees. (Captain Bligh could have learned from him.)

March 20, 1945

The weather is warming all the time, and something like spring fever is creeping over us. We watched the kids in the Teresa Children's Orphan Asylum in the courtyard below playing games. There was nothing to do this afternoon, so I walked down to the house with Walt, where he picked up his new blouse, having had it pressed.

March 21, 1945

I returned to see the doctor this morning. He will send me up to Florence where they have a good eye man at the hospital. I'm to go tomorrow. Later I got to thinking that maybe it would be for the best if Angelina returned to Rome to get a pass and then came back. Then down to the police department to inquire for a pass to Rome. He said he could give her one to Rome, but it was up to the Rome police to allow her to come back. After thinking it over, we cancelled the idea.

March 22, 1945

It's dance night in Siena for the wing. Many come, and few don't. For those who come it fights overseas boredom. Some have used alcohol so often that it becomes an addictive palliative, in spite of all the attempts by the Universal Services Division to provide other forms of diversion. It is no joke. Americans can expect to open their arms to a greater number of returning drunks than it would dare to believe.

March 23, 1945

Miller and Sussman are away on five-day passes. Only one other and I are here. A little work helps me keep occupied most of the day. This evening Angelina told me that Santa, Metz's girlfriend who is also from Rome, was arrested by the English military police because she had no travel pass. Someone tipped them off, and she spent the week in jail awaiting trial. Not only that, she was found with military articles in her apartment. The result is two months in jail or a three hundred dollar fine. Metz doesn't have that kind of money now that he's not in the quartermaster section, so she is in jail much to his sorrow. He now walks around drunker than usual while her brother, a young fellow, got kicked out of his job with the army and keeps hounding Metz to do something to try to get him some work. It is a tragic situation, and I worry about the possibility of it happening to me and Angelina.

March 25, 1945

Allen came, and we walked to his apartment, which was on the way down to the junior officers' quarters. There was hardly anybody out on the streets at this noon hour on Palm Sunday. Linda's job is still up in the air. I came back to the house at two, and Angelina had just finished cleaning up the room. Before I left for chow, I heated some water for her bath.

March 26, 1945

I went on sick call at 8:30 a.m. and was sent to the 154th medical dispensary. I was soon on my way to Florence. One WAC patient accompanied me, and a few friends of the driver came along for the ride. The weather was drizzly and the road bumpy. It shook up our organs so that we all could have used a checkup on arriving. We passed a French soldier's graveyard, and amongst a sea of little white crosses were a few Americans buried. In Florence we entered the Twenty-eighth General Hospital grounds at around noontime. The fellow at the desk told us to eat first and gave us directions to the mess hall. It was filled, naturally, with patients in bathrobes, jackets, and combat shoes. Instead of us picking up our own food, the trays came off an assembly line, all fully loaded. Just pick up a tray and move on. Separate tables are reserved for VD patients, skin disease patients, etc. There was no place to sit, but at the VD table, keeping my distance and a little bag of toilet articles in case I stayed overnight. Back in the waiting room, I noticed a few signs. Check Your Guns and Ammo. Not Allowed in the Wards. Makes sense.

I asked them to take care of me as quickly as possible as the ambulance was leaving at 2:00 p.m. The clerk said he would try. If I didn't make the ambulance today, I might have to wait until Thursday when he returned. I sat around in a treatment chair up in the eye, ear, and nose section for three hours. The doctor was examining a colonel and took their sweet time. In the meantime, the ambulance was waiting for me, hoping I'd get done any minute. He started at three thirty with anesthetic and was finished at 5:00 p.m. We all rode back, I with a patch on my eye, and the trip almost made me sick, but we arrived all right at 7:00 p.m. I picked up a can of salmon and a box of salted biscuits from the barracks and went to the house. Angelina was over at Yolanda's place and arrived about a half hour later while I was eating. "Just like a pirate!" They laughed on seeing my eye patch. "It's not funny, smarty," I said.

March 27, 1945

I went on sick call this morning as the doctor in Florence suggested that Captain Black wash my eye. He gave me some solution so that I could do it myself every couple of hours. Miller is back, and he started on that beastly summary again. Another job came in, but I'll let it go as long as possible. It's one of those semipersonal time wasters. I took a hot shower after supper. Somebody told me that Angelina was over at supply with Yolanda and Bill. I met them there, and we walked back in a drizzle. She was very quiet this evening. Maybe because she is thinking about her coming trip back to Sicily and my impending move out.

March 28, 1945

PX day. At nine fifteen Miller and I left with one of the fellows in the office and went for our rations. We waited on line about a half hour before the doors opened and after that only let in a few at a time. We take great delight in observing the busy passersby—the teenage girls, especially, who pretended restraint on seeing us and were somewhat giggly. The old tramps bend down and reach between our feet to pick up cigarette butts. The young boys lean toward the Russian style of dress with large side-buttoned high-necked shirts, balloon knickers, and leather boots and a swaggering air. Some well-to-do businessmen avoid the crowds as much as possible while sporting alpine feathered hats, a short fur-collared coat, neat military-type knickers, and slick shiny boots. When I say "well-to-do businessmen," I mean nothing more than a man who has his own little business and is not suffering. What the rest of the people do is more than I can fathom. Yes, some work as sales help, porters, street cleaners, and peddlers; but for the major part, they seem just to be keeping their heads above water—and oh yes, crafty horse trading, and just sweating out the war for a quick end.

March 29, 1945

Another quiet office today, which seems to be very often. Sussman is back after seven days in Rome. It's nice down there, and Sarah is well and happy. In Italian class this afternoon, instead of the usual grammar lesson, we have some simulated involved conversation practice. The professor started off with the Easter holiday and asked us our religions. To me he asked about the Jewish Easter, which he knew fell at the same period, and then he asked me what was that white, stiff, flat bread that they were giving out on the chow line. I explained about the Passover matzo substitute for bread, and he was very impressed. He had some Jewish friends here in town. He told me about some who were rounded up by the Germans and others who escaped to hide somewhere in the woods. He also said that Mussolini was never prejudicial against the Jews; in fact, he made Saturday the legal Sabbath for them.

Strack came up and told Iginia that he was being shipped out just as an excuse not to see her anymore. They had argued about the postwar future. Eight men shipped out this morning to the infantry. One was

Lou Lopatin, and another was Metz who made a fast visit to see Santa in jail before he took off. I hear they wouldn't let him into her jail cell until he brandished a pistol. He didn't tell her he was drafted to the infantry. A sorry ending.

March 31, 1945

I had several decks of cards to get rid of, and Angelina had a pair of shoes she just bought that were damaged, and she wanted them fixed. We stopped at a secondhand store to browse around. They had the only four or five watches I have seen in Siena, besides dresses, shoes, old boots, and other necessities. From the corner of my eye, I saw Strack whiz by on one of his escapades. He had a civilian's derby and cane and couldn't help mimicking comedian Charlie Chaplin. Even without the baggy pants and big shoes, he captured the comedian's jerky walk and hat-tipping routine. He's a born ham when he's not complaining about air corps chicken. Whenever he goes by, everybody watches. He gets a big hand. It was chicken tonight, and I brought some jam home, which always goes over big with Angelina and friends at Erminia's.

April 1, 1945

Easter Sunday but there is no parade. They do have several other customs though. The first is that you must visit seven churches and pray in all of them. The last is the duty to forgive your enemies, personally, and ask for similar forgiveness.

There should be some promotions coming out tomorrow, but I have no expectations. At chow time, I found Angelina over at supply with Yolanda. They were going to eat Easter dinner with Signora Betti, a previous landlady, and her enormous family. I took a few pictures of us on the road outside of the barracks and left as they met Signora Betti on the way. Signora Betti's grandson, Roberto, did not have the money to buy a gift for her. He wrote a note to that effect asking to be excused and left it under her plate wishing her a very happy Easter. The signora and several others broke into tears and became very sentimental.

April 2, 1945

We move our clocks ahead one hour today, but by mistake I moved mine back an hour and therefore I arrived two hours late for work. Of course nobody believed my alibi. I wouldn't either. However, Morgan, now a major, didn't know about it. He would have laughed it off, I'm sure. Promotions came out today, and Miller made corporal. Some others who were promoted offered drinks on the house and were giving out cigars. I made nothing, but I don't really care. Sussman expected sergeant stripes, but he didn't make it either.

April 3, 1945

Our teaching professor is still away on a vacation and will return tomorrow. Our PX rations tomorrow will consist of two Italian beers and one American beer from now on. It has become so warm that we are beginning to open up the windows, in spite of the flies.

April 4, 1945

Sussman, Miller, and I went to the PX in the morning and waited in line observing the townspeople as they plodded, walked, or skipped by. One old tramp had the line in stitches when he pulled out a pocket watch the size of an alarm clock. He was a pathetic sight really with an eye malady that caused him to remain teared and bleary eyed. His main interest was cigarettes and cigarette butts in any shape, size, or condition. Another more refined-looking little old codger stood around with an Austrian white clay meerschaum pipe in his toothless mouth. He shook uncontrollably at times, wanted a light, but seemed afraid to ask. Sussman came to his rescue and even gave him a book of matches. The little guy smiled his thanks and tottered away. Among the rations I got are a pair of wool-lined white leather house slippers, which I presented to Angelina. Her eyes glowed. She was delighted at the sight of them. The old lady and Iginia oohhed and ahhed over them and were jealous. When they heard the price was only two bucks, they squealed.

April 5, 1945

Paid the rent promptly today with a thousand lira note ($10). We were undecided about going to the dance tonight but finally did. Every time we go, I'm sorry. Too many fellows think it's a time not only to let their hair down but also their pants. They also get into the most ridiculous arguments at the bar. The straw that broke the camel's back for me was at the bar. Yolanda was there with her Bill and so was Charlie Pescher our chief cook but a bit stinko who was poking some guy in the chest with an arrogant sneer. "You are getting too big for that mustache of yours, Sergeant," he says unprovoked and adds that the other guy is "overpretentious." The other guy, hands on hips, rather tritely says "Is zatso?" tilting his head at a jaunty, provocative angle. "Don't you come in here bullshitting me," continues Charlie, his alcohol showing. "You know your place, and I know mine" (whatever that means). Charlie then changes his attack, probably because the other guy with the questionable mustache hasn't come up with any insult strong enough to provoke some fisticuffs. "Yes, sir," he says, "you're getting too big for your pants!" By the way, this other guy isn't even a sergeant, but good-old Charlie calls everybody a sergeant when he's peeved. This has the effect that it's about time the other guy got tough considering that some of his friends were watching and it didn't reflect very well for him to be taking all that guff. "You think you're big enough to take them off?" he dares while leaning forward and pointing at his pants, perhaps trying to scare Charlie out of the idea. Charlie isn't fazed at all. "Just come on behind this bar and we'll see." Now they are beginning to feel each other's hot breath, and this is the time when friends of both protagonists intervene and pin them back. "Take it easy," says one of Charlie's friends while patting him like a pet dog. Charlie is whimpering to get back into the fray, and I figure that it's time to get the hell out of there, and out we went.

April 7, 1945

After dinner, we took a walk. It was drizzling, and Angelina found and bought some live eels. They are a favorite Italian dish. After that we returned to the house and went to an Italian movie. I understood about 50 percent of the dialogue, and Angelina explained the rest.

April 8, 1945

Walt and VanDervelde went to church this morning, and I reset our special plastic-covered war map. Very interesting these days. I mistakenly predict the end to be sometime in July 1945. The landlady is behind somewhat in her changing of the linens. Angelina says it should have been yesterday and must talk to her. She had a bellyache and a little constipation. Some laxative pills didn't seem to do any good. Strack came over this evening saying that he was going to Rome tomorrow on Red Cross business and to get rid of a little merchandise. Nice weather these days. In the morning, most people are going to the stores, and workshops are busy operating. I say workshops because some stores are constructed so that the entire front opens up, and the inside of one is like a foundry or a blacksmith's shop. Another builds metal-lined coffins. One coffin sticks out into the street and people superstitiously shy away from it.

The rising sun blinds my eyes and helps to wake me up. The last of the charts are being drawn up today, and I also take the time out to write a little. I was surprised to receive a letter from my cousin Leon of a very literary family. It brings back old memories. I think I should like to begin writing to him again. Years ago we wrote bizarre comical short stories together, laughing ourselves silly in the process.

April 11, 1945

I expected the boss back today, but he never came. After lunch I was the only one present in the Italian class, and we had a very intensive lesson. The professor says I'm making very good progress. I had gone through the trouble of writing a letter for him that the censor wouldn't permit. The army post office channels are not to be used for civilian purposes. I therefore told the professor to try his own post office, which might possibly permit passage of civilian mail. This evening we had a little run-in with the landlady. She doesn't feel like changing Angelina's bedsheets every two weeks, now to be three weeks. I declared that would be impossible and why didn't she say so when I paid the rent in advance; then I might have looked for another place. She said after hemming and hawing that soap was expensive and the bedsheets would wear out from so much washing.

We expected to take a walk into the countryside, but it was cloudy about noontime when I brought chow over, so I decided to take some other afternoon off. Again I was the only student with Professor Fiore today, and we stayed two hours. Angelina said that the landlady gave her one bedsheet for the time being. I didn't see what I could do about it, so I'll let it go for now. Conditions still seem to be amicable.

April 13, 1945

We received the very shocking news that President Roosevelt had died yesterday. It's hard to picture the United States without that handsome smile. My mother shamelessly admitted to loving him. It is a shame. I suppose there will be well-earned eulogies spoken over him. The war news is very good—fifty-four miles from Berlin.

April 14, 1945

Fog crept in this morning. I thought it would ruin my afternoon off. Morgan agreed to a switch in days off between Miller and me. He'll take Saturday, and I'll take Friday. This way I won't miss my Italian lesson. Finally, toward noon, the fog crept back to wherever it came from. At the house, Signora Gianni, the owner of Angelina's room, had two visitors from the country—farmers who were once old neighbors of hers when she lived in their vicinity. They brought a liter of olive oil among other edibles, and they had a meal together. Angelina was invited but had to go to the tailor for a measuring up of her blouse, so I went back to the office for my Italian lesson and told her to meet me out front at two. She didn't show, so I went back to the house to find that she had gone out with Yolanda. Over at Yolanda's, Yolanda said that she'd gone to the school thinking I was there. I couldn't find her at the barracks and lay down for a few minutes in my bed. I awoke at four fifteen. Bill saw me and said she was over at supply. Finally, I found her. We had a little argument about keeping appointments. She apologized, "I'm sorry, *amore mio*." A big hug and kiss smoothed it all. "Don't do that again. I worry about you." I tried to be serious. She made a face and defiantly stuck out her tongue. "Let's go upstairs." I smirked. She took my hand and led the way.

April 15, 1945

Today is a day of mourning for President Roosevelt. Yesterday, and the day before, all the movies in town were closed, and the flags at half staff. The war news is excellent, and we can expect an end any day now. The boss is in Florence today visiting his uncle. Miller took off early to go to church. After chow, I stayed out until about 3:00 p.m. We went to the *moderno* theater where an Italian movie played. I understood a good deal of it. I silently thanked my teacher.

April 16, 1945

Morgan looked over the daily activity summary and asked us to make a few corrections before it was sent to the 322nd Service Group for photographing. He suddenly insisted on our coming in on time even though things were winding down.

April 17, 1945

This evening I found Angelina over at the supply office with Yolanda. Angelina had a new "bangs over the forehead" hairdo done at the beauty parlor. I accompanied her back to the house with food at about 7:30 p.m. Angelina admitted that she didn't like her new hairdo and would probably change it tomorrow. It didn't look so bad to me, but naturally men don't know about such things.

April 18, 1945

PX day again but this time I go down alone. Sussman is at the dentist, and Miller wants to wait until later. There were the usual other things this afternoon. Angelina had her hair changed before I came up in the afternoon. She loved the copper plate I had bought for her. I asked Morgan about my taking my five days off starting tomorrow. He agreed.

April 19, 1945

My watch had stopped, and the time fooled me. I came late for lunch and ate with the kitchen help. All I had were some dried C rations, lousy dehydrated mashed potatoes, some oily string beans, and a piece of rich-looking pie that fell on the floor before I could even taste it. I wasn't very hungry anyway. This was one of those days that you just write off and forget as quickly as possible. After dinner we took binoculars and camera and walked to where the outskirts of town meet the countryside. It was a fifteen-minute walk down steep grades and along streets that gradually changed from flat closely knit stones to a gravely looseness and then to ordinary dirt. We passed evidence of an underground sewer system that an ancient King Charles of France once said was more beautiful than the upper regions of Siena, a strange comparison. The water was very clear. At the bottom was an array of everything from pots to old cans. The big cathedral that Miller and I once visited was about a hundred feet directly above us. Some Italian soldiers had a camp nearby, and some boys were beating on a drum in a nearby alley. As we proceeded a little further ahead toward the out-of-town area, we came upon an open air establishment surrounded by walls but no roof, and consisted of a large number of wash tubs for civilians to do their laundry.

We then started a steep climb toward the church above us and after stopping a few times along the way emerged on a short stretch of road leading up to the church. The sun was very hot, so Angelina divested herself of the jacket under which was a dress once made from two military shirts. It gave her quite a military appearance. Around the edge of the road that we had just come from and which fringed one side of the cathedral, we stopped and snapped a few pictures of ourselves and the jam-packed dwellings of Siena proper, just over the valley. It gives the impression that there is no room for streets, only adjoining rooftops of all elevations crushed together in a kaleidoscopic mélange. The Piazza del Duomo Cathedral, the horizontally striped cathedral, at the highest point jutted out above everything else. We turned back to town by a different and a flatter easier route. Then we stopped at a bar for some vermouth and found Strack with his glass in hand as he toasted unseen voluptuous wenches who frequent our dances. At about eleven, we left for home sweet home where Angelina was safely deposited, and Strack pranced off into the wings of his imaginary stage taking bows all the way to his sleeping quarters, always the ham.

During all our gyrations in the outskirts of Siena, Angelina was bubbly, happy, and infused in me a deeper attachment than I had ever felt. Only the dread of our future parting blighted an otherwise blissful day.

April 20, 1945

It's the second day of my vacation. After dinner we decided to take another walk to a different location. Angelina had previously gone with Adrianna two or three times out into the country with chicken in a covered basket. We decided to go that way. Because of the heat, I wore my blouse and Angelina her white skirt and blouse. We didn't know exactly where we'd wind up, but I was hoping we'd come across a field or something and get a little sleep in the sun. After a few minutes on the long downgrade, we arrived at a dirt road surrounded and lined by farmland, but there was no place to get some rest, and we felt tired. We passed a tuberculosis hospital with a convenient cemetery across the road. Farms were small and intensely cultivated. They seemed to have everything growing in the same place intermingled together. A couple of kids shouted for some chewing gum. On the way back, we took a right turn at the forked road and came upon, of all things, the main iron filigree entrance gate to another cemetery. We entered after a little hesitation, intrigued by the novelty of the place. The section we were in was filled about the year 1860, and the walks all had graves beneath them, so crowded was it. They were neatly kept, and the marble-encapsulated graves in the middle were slightly above ground. There were a usually high percentage of children's graves with pictures and flowers. Many of the richer families had vaults in mausoleums that circled the graveyard.

We returned up the hot, winding dusty road and came upon a museum of old Siena art that attracted many people. There were guards in every room. These ancient artworks are priceless. Many are painted with gold leaf. After a tasty lunch of potato salad, hard-boiled eggs, and hamburgers, we decided to go to a legitimate playhouse; but the play had started a long time before. So we combined a little bit of business with a little bit of pleasure and visited Signora Betti instead. All the kids came out and carried on with all kinds of pranks. I played some on their ancient piano. Either I or the piano needed a tune-up.

April 21, 1945

After chow, we went out and walked over to the nearby Piazza del Duomo location. The white and black horizontally striped cathedral and its massive pillars were built around the year 1300, typical of ancient Tuscan art. Huge hymnal books are kept in an ornate library room. A museum across the courtyard had a vast array of ancient paintings and religious articles. There was plenty of gold in the form of crosses, flowers, cups, and even as thread in the archbishop's robes on display.

April 23, 1945

At lunchtime, Epter, Angelina, and I started out to visit a pipe factory about a mile outside of town. Siena is noted for its superior briar-smoking pipes. It was warm, and the passing trucks created clouds of dust. Far below through an open courtyard, we could see the railroad station that had been bombed into oblivion. The electric power plant nearby was also blasted away, and some workmen were clearing things for reconstruction. The road stretched out ahead of us for quite a long distance. After not finding the pipe factory where it should have been, we lost interest and decided to turn back and sit somewhere.

Right now while I'm writing, in the house baby chicks are running all over the kitchen floor; and Mino the son is running after them, placing them back in a basket. Angelina is beating up an egg. She is suddenly hungry.

April 26, 1945

There is very little work, I'm happy to report. I complimented Angelina who had fixed her hair in an improved straight new way today. Sussman is excited about his marriage approval, which is coming in any day. He's really sweating it out. Miller and I hope to go to his wedding.

April 27, 1945

It's PX day. The WACs were waiting back in line too, but when the doors opened, they boldly plowed right in ahead of us. I knew one of the salesgirls there, and she sold me a bottle of nail polish on the QT for Angelina.

April 28, 1945

With inspection this morning, I arose promptly to clean up my place in the barracks. We have to rearrange our room somewhat to accommodate some new mosquito nets. All our beds are covered with them. Wartime prisoners sweep up and mop after we arrange everything. At the office, Miller is away, and I am working on a big "Victory" sign for the officer's mess hall with letters two feet high. This evening there is a squadron club meeting at seven. Before going, I bring chow over to the house. I meet Angelina and Adrianna outside. They are awaiting some religious procession that is to come by. I believe it is Saint Catherine's Day, patron saint of Siena. She has a rather strange story attached to herself. She was born in Siena about 1350 and became famous and lived in Rome. When she died, a controversy arose as to what city should have her body. Luckily for the litigants, but not for Saint Catherine, a solution resulted in her decapitation. Siena got the head and Rome the body, and everyone was happy. Therefore, the object of this forthcoming procession was to observe the ritual of parading the head, enclosed and preserved under glass, through the main city streets. I decided to wait awhile, but it was fast approaching the 7:00 p.m. time for the meeting.

We walked over to Piazza del Duomo Cathedral, which was the point of beginning for the parade. They are to pick up the head and then return here after the parade. We four waited on the broad white steps leading up to the church. It was quite crowded. The first aldermen came through the huge doors and down the steps, making a left turn there and then continuing down to the main street. They consisted of an honorary escort (contributed by the fire department) who wore special black and gold metal helmets. After them, various seminary students and priests emerged to give it a religious atmosphere. Then there were many of the laity who followed. Suddenly in a burst of color and trumpeting emerged six men dressed in the old colorful medieval costumes of their ancestors. Long, thin silver trumpets were raised in one hand and blown in a harmonious fanfare for what followed them. No less than the archbishop himself, dressed richly and elaborately, and with an attendant holding the raised hem of his robe twenty feet behind—he emerged piously surrounded by his outspread entourage. He blessed the crowds with raised hand, and they stooped and performed genuflects as he passed them. In that very moment, the true spirit of Italy showed itself embedded in their vast religious tradition. After the archbishop, there followed more antique, beautifully and bizarrely costumed men representing the different sections of the city and carrying banners matching their costumes. Then came the nuns who served in the children's orphan asylum. Twenty minutes elapsed for all to pass while the last of the populace fell in behind and slowly faded away in the distance.

April 29, 1945

I finished up that "Victory" sign and brought it down to Major Landry. "Nice work, Milt" was his compliment. I told Angelina that *For Whom the Bell Tolls* was playing at the Rex Theater where no civilians were allowed in. She didn't mind at all my going without her. Anyway, there was a dance for the civilians, and she would be going there with Signora Betti's pregnant daughter and husband. She was heavy but still likes to dance. When I returned accompanied by Epter and a friend, I went up to the house even though it was late to see if Angelina got home okay. They were still up, and she had been home for some time. I raved as much as I could in Italian about the movie. Angelina always praises my speaking ability when I am enthused or when we have an argument.

My friend Sussman got the news that his marriage to Sarah had the brasses' rare approval. He expects to leave for Rome tomorrow. Tonight we had a bingo session, and Angelina won a bottle of cognac, which was converted into five dollars by one of the men. We spent about five dollars more playing and never won. Strack won a wristwatch, Sussman won ten bucks, and I think we'll begin playing these games a little more often. A heavy payday craps game commenced immediately after the bingo, and a dense crowd pressed hard around a specially reinforced craps table. We left after a drink of white wine served by Rapper, our erstwhile bartender for the night.

May 1, 1945

Today for the first time since Mussolini came into power, the communists' May Day holiday is holding forth. I've seen many flags displayed with the royal family insignia covered, but very few people. There was no Italian class today because of the holiday. All the stores and movies are closed too. I didn't see it, but there was a huge crowd in the Piazza del Campo, the large village square. After all, it was the first May Day (really a labor day) celebrated in twenty-two years; and coupled with the good news coming in from up north, it was a real holiday. This evening they played some cards, and I practised my Italian out of my grammar book. Mino seems excited about the idea that he hopes to go to America after the war. He's young. He is studying to be a surveyor and has been asking me all about living in the United States. When I told him that surveyors made out well, that clinched it more than ever. He took my address and phone number.

May 2, 1945

The PX ration was pretty good today. Maybe somebody got wind of our complaints at the squadron meeting. Angelina had a sore throat. Our doctor was not around, but he would gladly look her over tomorrow. At the house everybody was next door listening to a radio report that the Germans in Italy have quit and that Berlin is taken. Great news!

I heated some water to fill an empty wine bottle to serve as a hot water bag for Angelina's throat.

May 3, 1945

Still pretty cold today. Now that the Germans in Italy have quit, the streetlights are scheduled to go on after five years of darkness that will finally end tonight. This evening before going to the dance, we visited some new friends who needed a few things. Their home was somewhat different from the average. These people are rather well-to-do. The father is a bank clerk. They served wine and cognac of a very fine quality, with some cookies. They were very hospitable, and we talked of the unknown future that had suddenly burst upon them. We left bidding them a very cordial good night. At the dance one half-drunk had been dancing with a young blonde girl, a singer for the orchestra. He wouldn't allow her to dance with anybody else, and she couldn't shake him. He was quickly booted out by a bouncer. Dr. Black was at the dance and was glad to make an appointment to examine Angelina tomorrow morning.

May 4, 1945

We went to the dispensary, but Angelina waited outside while I went in first because sometimes a few naked guys are standing around. After the examination, he painted her throat and said she'd have to return every day, probably for a week at least. She was not to smoke. Then to the mess hall for lunch. Angelina waited while I ate. I had soup, and I brought her two bowls of it. Sussman comes running in to stop the show with an announcement that all the Germans have capitulated. Welcome news! Wild cheering followed.

Chapter XXI

NEWS HEADLINE: ***April 28, 1945*—Mussolini Is Captured and Hanged by Italian Partisans**

May 5, 1945

Everybody is on edge with the war drawing to an imminent close. The relief of long-held tensions comes slowly. The Germans are surrendering en masse now. There must be wild celebrations back home. This afternoon authentic rumors begin cropping up that the war was really over and that surrender agreements had been signed for all German forces. This evening we had to hand in our knives and guns and were restricted to the barracks to avoid dangerous celebrations. Everybody was celebrating but us! The civilians were packing the Piazza del Campo listening to a happy mayor. Angelina came around to the barracks with Signora Betti and her little niece. It was a beautiful and memorable day. Crying was common. Friend and foe alike are happy it's over. Now we will have to pick up the pieces. I contacted Rapper to take my guard duty tonight because I had a bad cold. He readily agreed. At the house we found the neighbors exuberant with praise and prayerful "Madonna Mia" and "Grazie al Dio" and crossing themselves. What a night. Some guy was running up and down the street all night beating a drum in a triumphant march all by himself. No passes are allowed temporarily; therefore, we can't go to attend Sussman's wedding as we had hoped, if the date is not changed.

May 9, 1945

This morning we fall out in uniform and were surprised to march to the Twelfth Air Force service command theater for a showing of *Two Down and One to Go*. It was called off, however, so we marched around the block showing off to the civilians who stuck sleepy heads out of their windows and smiled. A big celebration program was scheduled for the GIs and civilians alike at the town stadium. All kinds of races, tugs of war, greased pig chases, etc. In the evening, a festive outdoor dance was scheduled. Miller, Angelina, and I walked over. We sat on the grass for a while and then took to the grandstand. The event started an hour late. Major General Gubbins judged the tug of war. General Manning didn't show up. Yesterday in a little speech to us, he said we might have a chance to go home before going to the China-Burma-India arena. That was a great morale booster. This evening the dance was a huge success. At first the civilians were a little backward about participating and merely stood around in great numbers. Later on you couldn't get them off the floor. The spirit of elation was truly indescribable. Strangers hugged and kissed, sang and danced to suddenly formed trios of musicians. The public was overwhelmed as if beholding a miracle. About 10:00 p.m., we walked away while the celebrating continued.

May 10, 1945

The holiday spirit is strong and still in the air. We don't have much heart in our work and are hoping that this is the last report we have to make. The bartender wouldn't take any money for a couple of vermouths because I made a price list sign for him, which is hanging on the wall behind him.

May 11, 1945

The military movie *Two Down and One to Go* arrived, and our attendance was mandatory. It explained the point system of military discharge priority, with a possible redeployment of our forces to the Pacific area. It seems that the guy who has three kids is the winner. It does not always take into account the relief of a man from the biting rigors of war, but the financial responsibility of child dependents is given special consideration. While that was important, there is not enough consideration for the frontline men over rear echelon men, which to me should be the very essence of the discharge plan. Almost anybody can get a battle star, representing mere presence in a defined battle zone, and a basis for discharge, by the number earned.

May 12, 1945

Since our rifles have been turned in, inspection does not pose such a problem now. The unit censorship has ceased, and we may now write uncensored letters.

May 13, 1945

My cold is still quite bad, and I can't even smell gasoline. Food is absolutely tasteless, sometimes fortunately.

May 16, 1945

Today is my brother Mike's birthday. "Happy Birthday." I scribble into the void.

May 17, 1945

Just horsing around the office today. I had my private lesson with Professor Fiore. I've been translating magazine articles into Italian. I'm proud of the accomplishment, and it's the hardest to do of all written exercises. The professor also explained the tradition behind the present day palio, the ancient flamboyant risky horse races for which only Siena is known. People come from everywhere to see them on July 2. I hope to be here long enough to see them.

May 18, 1945

Last night Angelina arranged with Yolanda to go to Florence. So Angelina got up early and left at seven thirty in the morning. Sussman's wife came up yesterday by bus all dusty and bedraggled from the journey. Angelina's trip back was very bumpy, and she threw up on the way. She hadn't had time to eat. She did buy a gift for me to send home. It was a leather playing card case. Florence is well known for its leather crafts. She was very tired and lay down for a nap and fell fast asleep for the night. My brother Mike and Bee's package of shoes arrived, and Angelina was thrilled over them. The red sandals will need stretching. Guard duty starts again for some reason in front of the orderly room building. This evening we spent time with some neighbors who had a beautiful little terrace adjoining their apartment. We stayed there late; Angelina playing cards with several people. I was helping the young daughter do her English homework, giving me great satisfaction.

May 20, 1945

Received a package from Mom and Pop today. Too bad the olives lost their liquid and were spoiled. Major Morgan wasn't around today, so we relaxed and napped in the afternoon. In the evening, Strack came over but much more subdued and less plaintive. We miss his former comics and long underwear. "What's wrong, Frank?" I asked. In his somber mood, he responded slowly, "You know, with a war on, I didn't mind making a comic fool of myself, hoping to be a diversion for the younger homesick guys who really didn't know the consequences of what they faced. I didn't know it all either, but my older years and life experiences gave me a more serious perspective. I didn't mind cavorting around and acting silly. Frankly, it was fun and a relief for me too. Now that it is all over, you see the real me. It was all worth it if we had a few laughs."

I couldn't believe the benign flip-flop nature of the man before me, and I could not help admiring him. In my opinion, his resilient nature and concern for others will always serve him well and show again when necessary. Then returning to the mundane subject of cognac which I had sold him, he thought a moment. "I never got it back to the room—didn't even remember paying you for it." I gladly returned his five bucks. This evening Strack got the news that he was going home tomorrow. He is just past forty years old, and he thinks it's time for him. He had just promised Iginia that he'd marry her and take her and her daughter Adrianna to America as soon as possible. Strack had no immediate plans for the boy or the grandmother. He was very much in a quandary. At any rate, his leaving is definite. I saw Strack later and counseled him to think carefully about his promises to the family.

May 25, 1945

Got up early this morning to help Strack pack up. At 6:30 a.m., I found him dead to the world. I shook him, and I noticed that he had his clothes on. He finally got up happy with his departure. He gifted me a pile of stuff he couldn't take with him. I gave him twenty bucks as a token of my goodwill. I sure hated to see him off though. He took my address and telephone number. He left early amid showers of good-byes and handshakes from all who knew him well.

May 26, 1945

We looked around this afternoon for a secondhand furniture store. I wanted to get rid of Strack's stuff, but we found none. This evening we visited Tine, a tailor friend, and we spent a sociable evening together. Angelina, Adrianna, and friend have hired bicycles for a jaunt tomorrow to visit a farmer uncle of Adrianna, and they will spend the day there.

May 27, 1945

The girls got together early and cycled off this morning. I went to the office while Walt and Sussman took off. Walt was going on a trip to nearby Volterra, known for its alabaster artwork and sculpturing. I sure wanted to go. I learned Major Morgan was to be out all day, I believe, so I took off and met Walt and Sussman at the barracks in front of the truck. It was undecided for a while whether I should go because there would be no draftsmen in the office. However, as it was Sunday, a lot of men were in church; no officer could exactly tell who was supposed to be in. Walt and I and about seven others went with us. We had Spam sandwiches and water with us and our cameras. Volterra is a small city, known for its fine alabaster workshops. That's about all they have been doing for the last hundred years. It is situated about thirty-five miles north of Siena, high in the hills. The trip was really somewhat rough, but beautiful blossoming scenery abounded everywhere. As soon as the truck reached the edge of town, a group of kids hitched on for what we later learned was the object of leading us to certain alabaster shops where they were employed. A few even spoke some English.

The kids were helpful and directed us all around town, even to a barber shop where some young boy shaved me. Our guides patiently waited for us, and we were finally led to their place of business. We saw how alabaster was carved into beautiful curios and little boxes that were exceptionally well done. In town we watched the people gathered in the public square who were joyfully gabbing away with almost everybody. The more I see of public squares, the more I think they would be a very nice addition back in the USA. It makes friends of strangers. Inside the lobby of city hall, which was all stone, were escutcheons, names and dates of historic leaders, who had been in power, artfully tacked to the walls. Etruscans settled in the place about the year 1100, and it hasn't changed much except for electric wires and some automobiles. We had the opportunity for visiting a national penitentiary here. It is built inside an old fortress several hundred years old. It looked more solid than Fort Knox. A sign advised that visitors needed a pass from the minister of Justice to enter. Of course we had none. The guard who answered our ring told us to wait. A Spam sandwich gave us entry, and he offered to call the warden. He arrived in a few minutes and was a short man dressed in an army blue uniform complete with hat. He had gray steely eyes and an appearance that made him fit for strict enforcement. He walked us all around the top of the fortress wall. We looked; we listened to his line of patter. He was friendly and gave a good account of the place and himself. He pointed out an ancient tower where a prisoner was once kept for forty-five years in solitary confinement. The window sill showed elbow grooves where he would sit, his chin on the palms of his hands, and gaze out of the window at the free world. After half an hour, we left and went back to our truck. I forgot to mention that on the way up, we passed our three girls on bikes. They had started out late for the farm. We left them in a cloud of dust. When we arrived in town for supper, I brought some food back to Angelina who I'm sure was famished.

May 28, 1945

We were all back in the office today again. Some work was requested for the yearbook that was coming up for the third anniversary dance on June 1. This evening we went to the tailors' again, and a pleasant evening was had by all.

May 29, 1945

The news is encouraging. All of our redeployments and five hundred plane raids are on Japan. Rumors are popping up pretty often now about where we will be shipped. Now certain thoughts begin to consume me. I knew the dreaded time would be coming soon when Angelina and I would have to part. Siena would be the last stop for her since I would be leaving Italy. She has become an inseparable part of me, a love I have never felt before. I want her with me always. I know she feels the same. Her risky travel and dogged determination to follow me was proof. A time separation would really test us, but I was quite sure of myself. Would the rigors of a long separation and the prospect of arranging an arduous Atlantic crossing subdue her? I prayed not. The thought that after leaving she would be beyond my help and protection leaves me uneasy. A powerful objection from my folks was to be expected. How does a young man steel himself for the rigors ahead? Angelina may have asked herself that same question, but she has already answered it by her acts of determination and risk and certainly a strong faith in the happiness that would make the risk all the worthwhile. Failure was not in her makeup, not even a lone ocean crossing. She gave me the strength to follow her lead. Yet I tried not to kid myself. How many well-intentioned parting vows lay broken in the dust of fading memories and the objections of a family who wanted no part of it. The strategy and expense of arranging an ocean voyage could blunt many an amorous young Lochinvar.[12]

June 1, 1945

Today is organization day for the wing, and we had a celebration at the Siena stadium. Everybody is welcome to the sports events and a buffet supper. Angelina loved it, and it made me happy to share it with her. I stocked up on some chicken and potato salad of which there was plenty and brought it back to the house.

June 2, 1945

Yolanda went to Florence this morning in preparation for her trip home and to send off some belongings through an express agency. I suggested that Angelina go with her as a woman traveling alone is dangerous. When Yolanda returned, she first learned that Bill was leaving as soon as tomorrow. She was in a tearful state. She said that Bill tried to arrange an auto for Tuesday. I'd talk to Angelina about them going home together. That night Angelina thought, as I did, that it would be best to go now while I was at least here to help them get ready. Today was also the first of my five or six days off that are due me from the past two months. I heard that Yolanda saw Bill off, much

---

[12] Lochinvar—an amorous knight of King Arthur's time—from the novel *Ivanhoe* by Sir Walter Scott.

to his consternation, and she made a terrible teary scene. We visited her later at her house and tried to comfort her some. Angelina said she's sleep there tonight. We saw the mechanic, named Losi, and his wife the tailor. He suggested that he might find a truck for the girls going to Naples or Sicily at a certain garage he knew.

June 4, 1945

After chow, we decided to see what transportation opportunities there were for the girls. First, I asked at our own motor pool. They knew of nothing going in that direction. Going back to chow, I bumped into Padovich, the motor pool officer. He confirmed also that nothing was going south.

June 6, 1945

This morning Sarah popped into the house with a couple of pounds of sweet cherries. Later, Sussman, Sarah, the girls, and I stopped in a café for some drinks. We sipped and watched the sun sink gracefully behind the darkening horizon. Sarah and Sussman are leaving. I asked the Provost Marshall for passes for them on the courier airplane. He was sorry, but no civilians are allowed. I expected that. We did some more telephoning for passes and got nowhere. We are always referred to someone else.

June 9, 1945

This morning I was preparing to go back to work. However, somebody was asking, "Who wants to go to Florence today?" I figured I might take the crates at least and send that off so the girls wouldn't be tied down with it on the trip. Carl, the driver, consented to take Angelina along too. We loaded everything on at the house and took off at nine in the morning. We had fine weather all the way. I sat in the back keeping an eye on the boxes while Angelina sat up front. We got to Florence and got rid of the baggage first. Florence's famous Ponte Vecchio, the old bridge, is the only bridge the Germans left intact crossing the Arno River. This landmark was lined on both sides with jewelry and curio shops all the way across. We reached the receiving section of the express agency at Piazza Madonna and paid the charges to Catania. After that we returned to the Fifth Army GI restaurant, and I bought chicken dinners for a few lires. I carried out five dinners wrapped up for Angelina because civilians were not permitted inside. Chicken is her favorite dish, and she did it justice.

This evening, Yolanda and I picked up two rabbits, carrying them up the street by the ears. She stopped in front of a wood and charcoal sellers' place and asked a seedy-looking worker inside if he knew how to kill a rabbit. He nodded and took hold of the animals' ears in one hand and the legs in the other and with a couple of swift jerks the neck was broken. It only squealed a little bit. He skinned it, cut it open, and removed its entrails within about five minutes. He removed the skin like you would peel a banana. It was disgusting. Yolanda carried the carcasses into the house, cleaned them up a little further, and dumped them in a bowl of water overnight.

June 10, 1945

Back to work today and did a little drafting this morning. This evening we walked over to a depot to see about that city truck going to Naples tomorrow. We met Gumbelli, a driver, and his wife outside. He said the trip was going and that it would probably leave tomorrow afternoon. They were to come down to the market at about 10:00 a.m. to make sure.

Chapter XXII

June 11, 1945

I guess today will be the last time I see Angelina for a very long time. Maybe . . . never. Although I hate to see her go, it's for the best right now. I know they are probably inquiring about the truck. Soon they showed up with the bad news that the truck had left for Florence and would arrive tomorrow sometime. They were told to come back in the morning. Angelina and I were glad that the trip was called off today. This evening we packed up everything in the house and brought it to Yolanda's place.

June 12, 1945

Well, today was the day. The way it began however made it seem that another delay was inevitable. In the morning they loaded everything in Bepe's cart, and the good man rolled it away. I went to eat and then returned to meet them in the marketplace. They were told that the truck had not returned yet from Florence. I took the afternoon off with a little finagling; and we all went to a café for a place to sit, sip a drink, and pass the last few minutes. About three we returned and found the store where the truck was to show up locked. We walked back to Gombelli's house and found his father in long underwear who was sleeping and awoke to say the truck would surely leave today. We were still there at 6:00 p.m. I figured that the truck must have broken down and we would never get out of Siena tonight. We sat around in the hot fly-filled atmosphere talking. Gombelli didn't know what was holding up the truck. By 8:30 p.m., he and the kids took off for the house, and we sat and sat. At about 10:00 p.m., we walked over to see what was what, and we were told that the driver was coming down directly. We rushed back and got the baggage out in front of the store.

Now it seemed that everything was speeding to a reluctant end. I wished the truck would never arrive, but pretty soon I could hear the roar of the motor and see the bright headlights blinding us as it descended into the market square. It was rather a modern-looking truck and open in the back. Several chains stretched across the truck to keep the sides from bursting apart. Spare tires were in one corner. Into this mess several people and I climbed. Then the baggage was handed up to me, and I placed it as neatly as I could in one out-of-the-way corner. I could see that the trip was going to be rough for them. Then Angelina and Yolanda climbed up and, in the darkness, stumbled around a bit. I warned them to be careful of the chains.

These were our last few romantic minutes together on a pile of junk surrounded by strangers in the dark. I couldn't see the girls' faces, but they were crying, especially Angelina. We said that we wouldn't forget each other and that someday I'd come back to get her. "Don't forget," I said, "because I won't." I kissed Yolanda on the cheek, and then she sat down and left Angelina and me standing up together. We didn't say much. but we understood everything that this parting meant. She only had a little more than three hundred dollars on her, but I intended to send more. She had plenty of unnecessary items she could sell, but I wish I had more money to give her. At least she'll be near Yolanda who intends to help her get a job. Yolanda is well-off and knows several well-to-do people. Just before the truck left, Angelina cried bitterly. "Don't forget me!" were her final words. I have no intention of doing so, I promised. I said I'd write her tomorrow. The driver was ready, and after one last embrace against her teary face, the truck pulled away. I jumped out. I saw her silhouetted against a lamplight, the only one standing in the truck. I knew she was crying. The vehicle turned up an alley and was gone.

June 12, 1945

It was at that moment that I felt so alone that I had to restrain myself from running after it. I was extremely worried about the trip ahead of them. If I could only have done something to make things a little easier, but I was helpless. I felt guilty just the same. A senior citizen who had helped me with the baggage watched me. "The war causes so much," he said in Italian philosophically. "Yes," I answered weakly. "Good night! *Buona note,*" he called as he walked away." I answered, "Buona notte e grazie per aiutaremi" (Good night and thank you for helping me). The words "Prego, prego" (thank you) came out of the darkness, and there I was standing all alone in the blackened market square. I was beside myself with grief, my eyes tearing up. My walk back through town was most depressing. Passing old familiar spots where we both once walked rekindled wonderful memories but also dreary prospects of reminders of our parting. I hope to leave this wonderful town as soon as possible, homeward, to America.

At Vicolo del Verchione, where we had lived, I stopped a moment and looked up at the window of the room she once occupied, but only for a moment because I could not bear it. I imagined seeing Angelina leaning out and throwing me the key to the locked door. I imagined I saw her everywhere, so I hurried back to the barracks, and when I got there, I didn't know what to do with myself. I walked into my room and then walked out into the street. Several GIs were there, but I didn't care about seeing anybody. The only thing that comforted me was my strong resolution to be back someday. That was a very distant comfort at the moment, and yet it was something to cling to. I only hoped I could send money and other necessities to her and that she will keep herself busy in the interim. I met Sussman and told him what had happened. He had been drinking a little and offered me a beer to help me sleep. Talking with him calmed me down, and I began to get a better hold on myself. I finally got to bed on that damned cot without the beer.

June 13, 1945

I awoke early due to my jumpy state. We had a breakfast of fresh eggs that I know Angelina would have enjoyed. I used to bring her some. There was no work back in the office. I moped about quite a bit. I wrote a long letter to Angelina as I had promised. I mailed it at noontime. In the afternoon, I wrote some letters and in the evening started getting some things together to send home, souvenirs, etc. At night I felt completely at a loss as to what to do with myself. Luckily there was a silly movie to watch, which gave me a little relief.

June 14, 1945

Slept a little better than last night. There was not much else to do. The weather continues to be very warm, and the kids below in the courtyard of the Santa Teresa private school make a playful racket all day. My thoughts however are always wandering to Angelina and my worry about her trip. All day I imagine that she'll show up in the most unexpected places and jolt me like an explosive jack-in-the-box. I must go down to the driver's house tonight and find out anything I can about the trip. This evening I skipped our regular dance. I couldn't help hearing the music, and I felt worse than ever. I went to see Mr. Severi, Sylvana's father, and he asked me to come over anytime I wished and visit with his family. He asked if I would like to go to a dance tomorrow night. I thanked him but declined. He understood. He accompanied me back to the barracks, bidding me a compassionate good night. The dance music tortured me as I went to bed, very weary with everything.

Chapter XXIII

NEWS HEADLINE: ***August 6, 1945*—First Atomic Bomb Dropped on Hiroshima, Japan**

June 15, 1945

At the office we were preparing to move, and all work was coming to an end. I went up to the old apartment and stayed awhile. I asked Signora Gianni to let me know if a letter or telegram arrived. Then Mino and I went down to the local post office to inquire about passage of mail between civilians and soldiers in Italy. They seemed to be in a fog, but thought correspondence was not permitted. Later this evening, I visited Angelina's driver to Sicily and brought some chocolate for his family. The trip went smoothly, he said. Here again, everything reminded me of Angelina, and I was not comfortable at all. The old grandfather was listening to the radio as usual while I sat near the table as Signor Losi ate a modest dinner while his baby daughter chased and tortured a defenseless kitten. The same things happen in these homes night after night, and yet they seem quite content. He works from 8:00 a.m. to 8:30 p.m. every day except Sunday but shows none of the symptoms of nervousness or overwork. That's true for many. Maybe it's the two quarts of wine he drinks each day that keeps him going. I leave and say good night, and to Angelina, wherever she is.

June 16, 1945

We've turned in our weapons, and inspection was a formality today. About 3:00 p.m., I took off from the office and brought a few things down to a customer of mine; then I dropped in at Giannis to see if anything had come from Angelina as yet. There was nothing. They were anxious too. About 4:00 p.m., I consummated another transaction with Signor Beppi, the erstwhile and diminutive laboratory assistant—and black marketeer. He always rants and raves about how stingy his farmer customers are. "They are the richest people around here but refuse to pay market prices for anything." "Stop bellyaching, you little runt," I said, knowing he didn't understand. "You're a lucky son of a bitch." At 5:00 p.m. I assumed my duties as charge of quarters and saw that the guards woke each other up instead of my doing it. Everything went well with one exception. The guard out front forgot to wake the next guard up at the headquarters building. The one already on the post called me, complaining because he was not permitted to leave until he was relieved.

June 17, 1945

As a CQ, I blew the whistle as 7:00 a.m. to wake the boys and then went down to eat. Some of the new cooks can prepare powdered eggs remarkably well. Major Morgan told us to start packing our drafting equipment, which consumed the entire morning. The afternoon was quiet, and I wondered what Angelina was doing at the moment.

June 18, 1945

At the office we just sit around the open crates keeping an eye on things. I put a few remaining items in a package for Angelina. About 4:00 p.m., Linzza, our new staff sergeant, told us that we might as well take off, which we promptly did. I went down to the central post office to find out once and for all if civilians could write to soldiers. They said no, but in response to my comeback that some soldiers have been receiving mail from civilians, they shrugged their shoulders. I met Mino on the street. He said no letters or telegrams had come as of yet. Later I meandered around town looking at some of the famous landmarks, indicated now by special signs. At the Siena Cathedral, workmen are removing some wartime protective brick walls from some ancient marble columns out in front. I step inside and gape around the cathedral built of solid marble and was richly ornamented with statuary. I returned to the barracks and met Miller there. After dinner, we walked out of the village gate on Via San Marco into a very hot atmosphere and then proceeded to look for a plot of grass on which to lie down. Below us was stretched out a great panorama of farmland, roads, and a few sparsely separated houses. Farmers with sickles in hand passed us and waved. At Gianni's place, we got our laundry, and I forgot to mention that at lunchtime Mino came over with a telegram. Angelina had a good trip home, and I breathed much easier.

June 20, 1945

Major Morgan came up this morning and asked if we'd like to go to Venice for a day. The plane would be leaving Tuesday morning. A friend and I accepted. Miller had been there before, so he doesn't feel like going. About ten thirty, I took the bundle I had prepared for Angelina over to Gianni's and her son, and I sent it off at the new shipping agency in town. After chow, I typed a letter so that she will be able to read it easily. This evening I concluded a little business with Beppi, and we had a long conversation on the bedraggled state of Italy. He's such a helpful, good little guy. The weather is very warm now, and night falls about 9:30 p.m. these days.

June 22, 1945

One day seems much like the next. When Angelina was here, even if we did nothing, there never seemed to be a dull moment. Now time passes terribly slowly. Still not the slightest hint as to where or when we are moving out. Our own commanding officer won't give us any hint. We've sort of given up guessing, especially since my clairvoyant friend Charley has already been shipped out. He's probably outguessing new friends elsewhere.

June 27, 1945

Today Lizza and I were expecting to go to Venice. We got a lift out to the airport and promptly discovered that we should have put our names on a waiting list. Since the plane was full, they wouldn't take us. So we waited around in the operations room and would take a flight anywhere. We learned that Major Ware was flying to Naples, and we went along anyway. We are to pick up some people in Rome and take them to an unidentified location. We had a beautiful view of Rome from the air and landed soon after.

We arrived at Naples late, discharged the passengers, and returned to Siena. At our barracks, all of the furniture was placed out in the halls. Many civilians were jealously eyeballing it. This evening the previous order about furniture was rescinded, and now we could sell our own furniture instead of the officers doing it for us and collecting the cash. Then the rush started. The halls got as crowded as a Macy's sale day. I handle all the sales in my room. Old women, old men, kids, everybody was carrying stuff on their backs; and it was junk that even a poor American family would throw out as rubbish. During the selling excitement, Mino brought us some bad news in a telegram from Angelina. She was down with malaria. I remembered how she had suffered in Rome last fall. I hoped her aunt would take good care of her. I wrote a letter immediately.

The Piazza del Campo racetrack was all dolled up for the coming horse races with colorful bunting on the balconies. I couldn't concentrate on that now, and there were no flights to Sicily.

June 30, 1945

Two hundred Palio tickets are being reserved for us at a dollar a piece. After work we went down to the piazza to see approval tryouts for the horses. The center of the square was jam-packed with several thousand people besides those standing on balconies and leaning out of windows. There was a great spirit of enthusiasm among the crowds; and when the colorful, gaily bedecked horses and jockeys made their appearance; a terrific cheer went up. The animals pranced about displaying their colors like show horses in the circus. Then they were herded back into the starting box. A second later, after a giant firecracker goes off, they're off. One horse stands pat, and doesn't move at all in spite of the prodding of his jockey. The others get away pretty well and run around the slippery track clockwise three times. The winning horse is besieged by the happy mob together with his jockey in a frenzied uproar. We leave the square entering the crowded streets. Everybody is in a joyous mood.

Sussman, Eptor, and I went to the Bar Lizza to have some soft drinks and sat around watching the people go by. A few other boys joined us at the outdoor coffee table. They all soon left, leaving Epter and myself alone. At the park we watched a dance at the Bar Magno, another small outdoor café that was full of GIs. The male civilians were cautiously afraid to chance an entrance. They stood around and gaped somewhat enviously. On the way back, a man with two kids wore colored hats from different rival *contradas* (boroughs) and showed great rivalry between them. The old man explained that they were born in different contradas, but he wasn't concerned over their differences because they'd be good friends after the race was over. Next we sat down in our reserved seat section to try out the view. It wasn't bad, but the sun blinded us.

While on guard duty tonight, a young man came up and had a friendly conversation with me to break up the monotony. He had some business in the school and spoke to me while waiting for somebody to come out. This fellow had been a hostage and was taken out in the woods to be shot because of an infraction of the Nazi law. He was saved by French troops advancing on the same day, forcing the Germans to beat a hasty retreat. He sweated as he spoke. This evening we again went to witness the second day's qualifying tryouts for the palio. We bought seats for twenty cents and had a pretty good view.

July 1, 1945

At about 3:00 p.m., I visited the Giannis to tell them about a letter I got from Strack. She, Iginia, gave me an affectionate letter in Italian to translate and send it along on my own. About 5:00 p.m., after supper, I went to the third palio tryout this evening. The sky was overcast and threatened rain. The police cleared everybody off the track; the rain started, not too heavy at first, and we all hoped it might blow over soon. Instead it poured, and there was a heavy stampede for the exits. Many little groups huddled under umbrellas and pieces of canvas that some were thoughtful enough to bring. All in all, it was a complete fiasco, and a great deal of dirt was washed down into the sewers and into the square. We waited about half an hour and then left, drenched to the bone.

July 2, 1945

This is palio day. There is plenty written on today's pageant, so I'll be brief. We didn't work today and had plenty of opportunity for observation. Every contrada had its flags strung up, and all the newspaper stands were selling literature and postcards. The weather was somewhat hazy, but our weathermen predicted no rain for today. VanDervelde, Linzza, and I walked downtown in search of some contrada flags to buy as souvenirs. Linzza wore a little paper badge on his shirt with our contrada colors, coincidentally in red, white, and blue. This afternoon at three thirty, our contending horse (adopted only superficially), named Bozetto, and his grooms came up to our barracks. Some *Stars and Stripes* reporters had a grand photo session. Then the horse proceeded to church to be blessed. It was a good omen if the horse relieved himself in the church.

We ate an early supper and then quickly proceeded to the Piazza del Campo. We came just in time because the grandstand allotted to us was fast filling up. Pretty soon it was apparent that there were more tickets sold than there were seats, a common practice in events like this. We were very crowded. I got a front row low seat so that I could jump out and take a few pictures whenever I wished. One of the 302nd boys was slightly drunk, got out of hand, and climbed into the grandstand section reserved for town politicians. When the English MPs came after him, he retreated to one of the four flagpoles attached to the back row. He climbed one of them carrying the French flag and refused to come down, to the howling delight of the forty thousand people in the enclosed track. He waved his ticket gleefully at the dumbfounded MPs, vaunting his right to be in the stands. With dire threats from his commanding officer, they finally got him down just as the events began.

A vast array of gaily bedecked men and horses filled the entire racetrack in their ornate medieval costumes. That took about two hours, and the crowds were enthusiastic as each contrada made his grand entrance. The middle was so packed with people that some used pocket periscopes for a better look. A woman up against the fence posts below the mass of humanity sat breast-feeding her baby. Little kids sat on the concrete posts waving little flags and having a helluva good time. The race itself was over quickly once it got started. Legally the horses can be doped up with anything from vino to TNT, but it makes the start much more difficult because the horses get very nervous at the public's catcalls and whistles. The jockeys take things quite seriously, especially boos from the crowd, and their falling off their unsaddled horses several times during the race didn't add much to their good humor. They even took a few mock swings at the crowd with their riding crops. One irate civilian, upon seeing a jockey's inability to mount a horse, jumped out of the stands, shoved the jockey aside, and in a flash was on the animal's back. In a flash, he was dragged off by the police, despite his vehement protests. La Lupa won the race in spite of whippings from other jockeys as he passed them. Our Bozetto came in seventh. The fans of La Lupa ran down the track after the horse and past the finish line. The whole place was a bedlam of people trying to get out of the square. We finally squeezed out and made our way back to the barracks. Luckily it was rather chilly all afternoon. Otherwise there would have been plenty of fainting. They had stretchers ready for all possibilities.

July 3, 1945

We needed this quiet day, VanDervelde and I went for tea and cake at the English teahouse at about three. In the evening, we took a stroll to the park and had some tamarindas at the bar.

July 4, 1945

We had our special program. It was a beer party. Some of the boys brought some fireworks. I don't know where they got them. In the morning, Epter and I walked down to the Campo and saw the merchandise carts set up on Wednesday only. They reminded me of the old pushcarts on the poor New York East Side many years ago. Always bargaining and more bargaining. At last we learned where our next station is to be—namely Nuremburg, Germany. A plane was sent up today but was forced safely back over the Alps due to bad weather. That was the advance echelon.

July 5, 1945

We are finally falling into a very lackadaisical work routine where we come and go pretty much as we please. I haven't seen Major Morgan for about ten days now. We take many days. I got a letter yesterday from Angelina. She really made me feel pretty bad. Things are very hard in Sicily, and she doesn't like it down there anymore. She has been in bed with malaria for eight days. I sure wish I could see her and help her. I'll be sending her some money soon. I've already written a letter to go.

July 6, 1945

It's quite cool these days, very unusual for this time of year. This evening a few other boys and I went out for a walk and a few soft drinks at the Lizza bar. Most of the boys hang around to watch the girls go by because the bar is situated directly on the route to the park. After supper, I sat on the steps in front of the school and watched a gang of kids playing around. The little girls are very cute; their shiny faces appear more so in contrast to their tattered clothing. Their handmade dolls of sticks and rags are hugged and fondled. None is bashful except the very little ones. I see one soldier, who allows a lot of kids to crawl all over his jeep, suddenly grab one troublemaker and slap his behind. The kid, about twelve, pretended to be in pain and then beat it, only to begin laughing. Then the GI took after him down the street, never caught him, and returned tired and empty-handed. Pretty soon that little curly-haired boy leered over the backseat at him, and it began all over again. That's the way it is almost every evening, so I turn in and see a couple of the boys are drinking beer and eating little salami sandwiches they had made up in town. I try one, and it tastes very good—drink some water, gaze at Angelina's picture, and go to sleep.

July 9, 1945

Played bingo tonight and won a quart of illicit whiskey and a case of beer, which I traded for cash.

July 10, 1945

Our interest is on the trip to Venice tomorrow, which we hope comes off this time. VanDervelde is taking his movie camera this time.

July 11, 1945

We started for the airport at 7:30 a.m. and were early for the promised trip to Venice and The road was so dusty. In the back half of the open vehicle, we were completely covered with a heavy layer of it by the time we arrived at Malignano, our place of departure. We flew past Florence and Bologna. We arrived at the Venice airport at about nine thirty in the morning and took a short bus ride to the dock where we got on a barge operated by the English. They brought us to the Saint Marco's Square across the lagoon. Immediately upon landing, we were amazed by the photographic opportunities of statuary along the waterfront. A sidewalk photographer snapped us and said we could get it at two this afternoon. We took many photos around Saint Marco's Square with its famous pigeons and clock tower. We climbed to the top and had a fine view of the canals and homes from there. A loudmouth shill accosted us and led us to a store where they really sell some fine glassware. I sufficed with a glass elephant to send to my mother. Then we had dinner at the Fifth Army restaurant in a fine attractive building. Dinner consisted of cold cuts and hard-boiled eggs. The service however is what we like best at these meals, very genteel.

A gondola ride up the grand canal while our gondolier explained everything to us was delightful. It seems that every famous person in European history had lived in one of the old palaces that line the ancient canals. Marco Polo, Giuseppe Verdi, Douglas Fairbanks, Napoleon, and kings and dukes. We passed under the Bridge of Sighs[13] on the way around and the big Rialto Bridge, the largest of the canal. The famous palace of the Doges (Dukes) was our next stop right on the Saint Marco's Square. An English-speaking guide took five of us around and was quite informative. Venice was an aristocratic democracy in its day, he explained. He showed us the courtrooms, the Bridge of Sighs, and the old prison on the other side of the canal. Lord Byron once volunteered to sleep in one of these prison cells to get some inspiration for his poem "Childe Harold." It was windowless and dingy. Then we dashed back and took the civilian ferry. It made one stop on the way then headed for the Lido section. An electric bus took us to the airport. All in all, Venice was thriving in its business and had plenty of goods except food. They have delightful cafés and shops that ring Saint Marco's immense square and on most of the small canals that serve as the open air sewer system of Venice. Kids swim in it nevertheless. From the air, the city appears to be built on rafts. We left early evening and flew to Siena without mishap.

July 12, 1945

Today marks one month since Angelina has gone. Time creeps. How many more will pass until we see each other again? It is a year now that I used to fly back to Catania to visit her, and it seems like

[13] Enclosed bridge in Venice that held a final view a convict would have on his way to prison.

only yesterday—no flights there for several months. A trip to Milan has been announced, and the list of thirteen was filled in a few minutes. Luckily, a friend put our four names down, so we're all ready for tomorrow.

July 13, 1945

Up at the crack of 6:30 a.m. and I woke a few others. After a breakfast of fresh eggs, we rode to the airport. I got a seat in the cab avoiding the dust this time. We took off with a few officers who were to remain in Milan. The Milan airport and its fine condition amazed us. Here there were no rubble piles, no collapsed hangars, no airplane junk piles. All it needed was a paint job to appear as good as new. This was something new indeed. In the administration building was a restaurant bar and a PX type store where some unrationed items were sold. We had a free snack, picked up a free *Stars and Stripes* newspaper, and waited around until the airport bus rode up at 10:00 a.m. A fifteen-minute ride took us near the American Red Cross club, and from there we studied our mimeograph maps and written matter for points of interest while the hot sun beat down on us. We walked along Buenos Aires Boulevard, a beautiful tree-bespeckled area, toward the railroad station. Our camera shutters click all the way. The train station was a beautiful ivory-tiled building scarred only slightly by bombs. Inside we got permission to go to the train platform without tickets for some pictures. Some of the trainmen explained various things to us and pointed out the "little palace" where the former king would get off every time he would have the occasion to come to Milan. Then we proceeded to Laredo where Mussolini's body had hung along with his mistress Clara Petacci. Civilians watched us and cheerfully assisted with some informative details. Then it was about time to go to the Fifth Army day leave restaurant where we had an elegantly served meal. The free streetcar ride to the restaurant gave us ample opportunity to look at the town. The first thing one notices is that it is alive with people and traffic. There's a hustle and bustle about it that is very untypical of southern Italy. The people are open and involved. The streetcars are clean, and the people are well dressed. There are many wide boulevards and squares and fountains. There is a feeling of great open spaces and modernity, with a future.

After chow, we visited the Duomo Cathedral, a great big hunk of ornate sculptor and spires. Inside it is typical of the ancient cathedrals with its great pillars and huge stained glass windows that were breathtaking in their splendorous colors and artistry. From the cathedral, we went to the church of Maria delle Grazie where, in a partly wrecked-side wing of a rectory, we saw Da Vinci's *Last Supper*. It was faded and washed out and difficult to study. It must have been a beauty though, but it will be restored. A streetcar ride and a short walk brought us back to our starting point, the American Red Cross, while an all-girl orchestra played for us. Since we had time before catching the bus, we joined others on the park grass, just like the old Prospect Park days in Brooklyn. This city pleased and impressed me very much. At the airport, the crew chief announced that a tire would have to be changed before takeoff. Luckily the English always have odd parts on hand, and while the change was being made, we had supper in the administration building as guests of the Royal Air Force. The scotch and soda reserves supply was well appreciated by the time we flew back to Siena at dusk.

July 14, 1945

Epter was off this afternoon, and he suggested that we take a ride into the country to visit some old former friends of his. Farmers are well-off. Epter's friends were always earthy-type people. We went out into the fields to watch the farmhands. Women work just as well as the men on top of the thresher pitching wheat bundles into the machine. One or two little girls in big straw bonnets like their elders ran around carrying wine to the parched laborers. The threshers were moving around in a swift breeze and covered us all with little particles of straw and dust. We returned soon and made ready for our return trip on bicycles, which was the way we came. On the way back, we had our usual ups and downs, and the last up was pretty steep. Luckily a GI vehicle passed and gave us a lift. We were utterly exhausted from the traveling and had to rush to make supper on time.

July 17, 1945

Received a letter from Angelina today. She wants to come back to Sienna because Catania is very, very poorly off and depressing. I went down to see Gianni and asked if Angelina could come back to stay with them. Naturally that's a lot to ask of people in times like these, but I said that I'd take care of the expenses until whenever. They agreed to help her out somehow.

July 21, 1945

This evening Van and I walked down to the park and had some strawberry drinks at the Lizza bar. One officer among them was Major Howard of the A-1 section. They were sitting at the entrance. Everybody else says "good evening." He sneers and asks me, "Where's your hat, soldier?" It had been in my back pocket although I should have had it on. He remained unchanged when I whipped it out and put it on. "Keep it on all the time," he ordered nastily.

July 25, 1945

We made a trip to Venice today and had a very busy day. We climbed the tower of the famous bell clock where two iron men alternately beat out the time, each holding an iron sledge hammer, built in 1497 and still in fine condition. We revisited the Doge's Palace and rerode the gondolas, always with a peaceful serenade from our singing gondolier.

July 26, 1945

Our new outdoor bar and dance floor has opened up and is a real improvement. The girls are as classy as we had hoped for, very friendly, and they loved to dance. I carefully joined in. I rationalized that Angelina would have cautiously approved, but with great limitations, to which I needed no special prodding.

July 29, 1945

This evening Epter and I took a walk downtown to the park and listened to some music and sat on a bench for a while pondering some thoughtful questions. Jerome Epter was more of an introvert and always thought before he spoke or answered a question, and when he did, he seemed to be preparing a speech. "Epter, what will you be doing when this is over?" I asked. Those questions always rattled in the labyrinth of my mind. His brain was probably involved in some other matter, and he didn't answer until I repeated the question. He stroked his chin for a good ten seconds looking for the right word. "Really,

I wish I knew. I'm unqualified for anything special, but just like the last war, there should be a flood of opportunities when it's over." He frowned thoughtfully and continued, "I'd like to attend college to be ready, perhaps a philosophy and literary field with a leaning toward religion. Religion has always been a comfort to me, you know. And maybe some charity work." His gaze wandered off. "What do you think?" he asked.

"I expected something like that, Epter, but I think you are actually too young to think of giving up the advantages of a moneymaking job, at least without trying it. You know money is the oil that makes the machinery run smoother. Granted, it's not a cure-all, but there's little you can do without it. It's true, there will always be others who have more than I, but that's no reason to drop my ambition. We've got to make the most of whatever possibilities there are. Will you be doing that?" I asked rhetorically and continuing, "Yes, the world owes as much to our great thinkers as to our great builders, who have removed much of life's drudgeries with great inventions and advances in medicine." Epter smiles. "You put it very nicely yourself, Milt, but there is even more to it. Yes, the world owes as much to the thinkers as to the doers, and I'd like to be even a small part of that thinker elite group. I think it behooves us all to try to leave this troubled earth even the tiniest bit better than how we found it. Those thinkers and doers did it. Don't we owe them even some small debt of gratitude? I would like to repay my portion." I felt transcended by this eloquence and forthrightness.

"Epter," I said, "you really do think, and you've put it much more nicely than I did. I believe someday I will be reading about you, Epter. As for me, I come from a family of successful house builders. We are more of the mercenary type, and I will probably join in even though I have a college degree in business administration. All successful builders have big egos, which I shamelessly believe goes with the territory. We expect big housing demand for returning veterans everywhere, and we will be ready." A period of silent assimilation followed.

Back at the barracks club bar, the girls were dancing with each other because some of the men were tipsy. Miller joined us, and we formed a little clique in the corner, but I seldom have danced since

Angelina left. A letter from her told me that things are a little better now. I certainly hope so.

July 30, 1945

Rumors are flying thick and fast, but actually nobody knows where or when we are all going. One rumor is that we will leave Europe for the Philippines. A trip to Nice has been cancelled, probably due to the pending move. At the evening dance, finer femininity prevailed. Since we don't offer any more free food and drink, most of the old folks and kids stay away.

July 31, 1945

Payday—and we wait for the "nickels and dimes" to start rolling. At 10:00 p.m., I was suddenly ordered to guard duty because the regular guard couldn't be found. At 2:00 a.m., I tried to wake this guy who returned very late. He refused to get up to take his post. I shook him and bounced him and whatnot but he only squirmed. I called the CQ who, having had previous entanglements with this fellow, carried a glass of water over and threw it in his face. Burson, the name of this character, jumped up swinging saying he didn't want to go on guard duty and complained about a bad leg, which had a bandage. However, his whole attitude was "get the hell away and stop bothering me." The CQ received a blow from Burson, which was deftly returned. He was turned in, in the morning, for punishment.

August 2, 1945

Started off the day on the wrong foot when Major Howard asked me why I had not worked on the calendar job he once gave me. I reminded him that he had found already-printed calendars somewhere and had dropped the project. He denied it. He asked me my rank, and I told him PFC. Then he had the nerve to ask if I had any aspirations for advancement, meaning that if I continued my irresponsibility I couldn't expect the divine gift of a corporalcy. I wanted to tell him off, but I thought better of it. I finished fifteen calendars for the major. When we returned, I met some of the young high school and university boys talking to the sentry at the squadron orderly room, worrying about Italy's entry into a never-experienced democracy. Beppe joined us and began telling dirty jokes in Italian. I reciprocated with one just to test out my ability. It went over with a good laugh. "Beppi, are you laughing at the joke, or my Italian?" "Both," he said, slapping my back, good-naturedly.

August 3, 1945

I signed up for a trip to Nice on the sixth of August, took a shower, and got my laundry at Gianni's. Iginia is very upset over not hearing from Frank Strack who was back in the USA. I told her that none of us have been receiving mail from the States lately.

August 6, 1945

We got to Nice safe and sound and immediately made arrangements for a boat ride up and down the French coast. We stopped in at a former tourist agency that now catered to GIs and spoke to a couple of young English-speaking girls. Their sexy French accent was very becoming, and they were extremely friendly, ready to make conversation. After a little difficulty about making meal arrangements, we were sent to a little restaurant especially for one-day visitors like us. Restaurant Tivoli it was called. Then we went to the Hotel Ruhl for our bus to the anchorage and got aboard a small launch, about fifty of us. We then started our one-and-a-half-hour trip to the tunes of an accordionist and a clarinet player, which reminded me of the old ferry boat days on the Hudson River. We hugged the shoreline and passed some interesting cliff-hugging homes and other stony structures. Blasted open pillboxes lay silent on prominences that jetted out into the sea. There were few beach spots for swimming because of the sheer drop of the cliffs. Then we went into a bay and stopped at a little town called Villefranche. Our pilot said that we had fifteen minutes to look around, but it was a petty ploy just to get us off at a local bar for closer to half an hour. Then we continued up the coast toward Monte Carlo, never reaching it but turning back and reaching the dock in time for the bus, which took us to the airport.

Back at the airport was an American soldier who wanted to get to the Milan vicinity to see his sick mother. In an effort to get to Milan from Marseilles, he wrangled a seven-day pass from the CO and came to Nice by train. At the airport he hoped to get a lift direct to Milan but decided to go with us to Siena as we were scheduled. "I'll ask the pilot. You'll have to show him your pass." He was very happy when the pilot checked him out and came aboard. When we got back to Siena, I took him downstairs with us to eat a late supper. He practically kissed us as he boarded our courier plane to Milan the next day.

August 8, 1945

I discovered that our trip to Cairo would be postponed temporarily because of pending action on our outfit status. Our airplanes are not leaving for the present. Got a letter from Angelina. All's well.

August 10, 1945

Finished up a letter to Angelina today. It seems that the end of the Pacific War is at hand. Complete peace was at hand.

Chapter XXIV

NEWS HEADLINE: ***August 14, 1945*—Japanese Agree to Unconditional Surrender**

August 12, 1945

At noon a bomb shell landed in my lap in the form of a telegram from Angelina. She's coming back to Siena. I sure will be glad to see her. It seems unbelievable, and now that the trip to Cairo has been rescheduled, I will not go since she is on her way.

August 13, 1945

I hope that she is traveling safely, but I'm always worried even though travel restrictions are gone. In the evening, a piano was brought down for the dance, which I played from 6:00 to 8:00 p.m. It was nice to get back into the swing of it again. At eight I left, since the orchestra had not yet arrived. Miller was on guard duty tonight, and we kept him company for a while on his "beat."

August 14, 1945

When I came off guard duty, I heard Dion yelling in the hallway that the Japs have accepted surrender terms—yahoo!

August 15, 1945

I wrote a few letters while sitting on my cot, and Major Ware came in calling "At ease." He was looking for a couple of his contrada flags from the palio that had just been stolen, and policemen had seen one being carried into our barracks. He glanced around and left in a few seconds after not finding it—a humiliating experience for us. I saw Gianni this evening about our old room when Angelina gets back. It looks like I'm out of luck because some traveling salesman has it. Maybe we can make a deal with him, but doubt it.

August 16, 1945

Palio day again in Siena. This time there is a greater crowd. Many Allied soldiers knew about it and came in from other cities. The streets were jammed. At about 5:00 p.m., Epter and I weren't too hot about paying a buck for a seat as we had already seen it once. Good-old dependable Epter had met an elderly man who had agreed to take him up to an apartment with a window facing on the square. This window had a few gradually rising stadium-type benches behind it so that four rows of people could observe. The man had a tragic story to tell. During the German occupation, he took a trip to Milan. When he returned, he was horrified to find his wife and two daughters kidnapped from the house. The elder daughter was engaged to an Italian officer who tried tracing them. Nothing was ever heard from them again. Now there is a committee investigating all such disappearances, and he showed us some photos that he was preparing to give them. He had hopes, although three months had passed and no word. There is little chance of them being alive. Now all alone he tries not to dwell on his misfortune. Some vermouth braced us all.

Epter and I walked around the market square. All sorts of sights—watermelons being sold by the slice, a poor old man evidently eyeing a piece but unable to spend the fifteen lira for it, women wheeling their carriages or carrying their babies, trucks and produce baskets here and there in front of the door for protection during the race trials—all awaiting for it to start. At the sound of a low starting explosion, all became tense and quiet. Exception—a woman began running around in circles crying hysterically. At first I thought that someone she knew was a jockey and might have gotten hurt, but it was just a plain emotional outburst. La Civetta ("Owl") soon won, and the word was flashed rapidly to the outside crowds. We walked back and watched the Tartuga contrada putting its horse away in a stable. The jockey was hopelessly explaining to his angry constituents why he lost. We walked back through the crowded streets and went up to see the Giannis hoping but not finding Angelina as yet. Then Mino took me where I found a room for Angelina. It might be ready the next day or the day after tomorrow. Mino accepted a cigarette, and we separated.

August 17, 1945

I was sitting in the office typing a letter to Strack when one of the Italian cleaning men said that some civilian was asking for me outside. I guessed right away that it was my Angelina, so I dashed out, and there she was with Mino. We kissed and hurried to Gianni's house and were warmly greeted. Angelina had arrived earlier and slept with the old lady for a few hours, spruced up, and then came to call me. She was looking pretty well and had a new dress on and didn't look as worn-out as she had after her trip to Lido last year. The poor kid has certainly been traveling. We talked and talked awhile, and then I went to eat dinner and brought back something for her. Gianni arranged for her to eat there. About 3:00 p.m., I went to see if the room was ready. It was, and I told the landlady that we'd be back about 5:00 p.m. We went to visit old friends. It was nice to see them all again, especially with Angelina. We returned to the new room and stayed awhile before returning to get Angelina's things. The room has a beautiful view over the surrounding countryside and is the highest spot in Siena.

August 18, 1945

I went to work this morning, and Angelina said she'd be over at Giannis at lunchtime. We ate with the family, and I returned to the office.

August 19, 1945

The contrada (borough) of Acquila in which Gianni lives has its horse downstairs in a barnlike room under the building facing onto the street. All the boys and interested parties are keeping an eye on the horse and seeing to it that it is kept well groomed. However, many are discouraged because it is quite certain that this puny horse will not keep up with the rest. Nevertheless, their true spirit is hardly dampened because the unexpected has always been known to happen in that crazy race. Every man and boy is sporting the yellow and blue colors in the forms of kerchiefs, ties, and flowers. Acquila is a "poor" contrada relatively speaking and has not the ability to buy off the sure winners like the contrada of Torre, for instance. Torre is the richest contrada, and when they do win, it is always claimed they bribed some of the better entries. Yes, there is nothing on the books preventing bribery or for that matter any other skullduggery to win. So the citizens merely shrug their shoulders when they hear about deals under the table. We watched the parade as it went down the street to the piazza just as a few drops of rain began to fall. We were on our way down to the piazza when it began to pour and sought shelter in one of the long tunnel-like archways leading into the square. Great windy gusts of rain however sprayed us and the crowd that had gathered. It was over in twenty minutes, and we walked back very damp to the old house. The palio had been called off. It cleared up altogether soon, and we visited Signora Betti for the evening. The kids asked me to play the piano for them, and I was happy to oblige. What a household, very crowded and practically all women, kids, and babies. Never a dull moment. We all left, and they went to dance at the Dopo Lavoro where we left them.

August 20, 1945

Angelina spent some time taking things out of her valise and straightening her clothing out. "Let's go to the park," she suggested. We walked there, sat for a while on a sunny bench, talking and looking at each other. After supper, we prepared for the palio and watched the passing parade once more as we had yesterday. Then the grandmother, Iginia, Adriana, Angelina, and I walked down to the piazza amidst throngs of people. In a few minutes, we overflowed into the center of the square. Adriana suggested a spot where we might see quite well and headed there. It was as near to the fence that separates the racing area as we could reach and high enough for a good view.

The parade and flag-tossing spectacle began and lasted for about an hour. Then the fun began. The horses lined up for the start twice, and both times the break was called off because of some foul on the part of one of the horses. Those that were in the lead on each occasion were mad, and tension began to mount. One horse was disqualified. The third start was all right, and the race narrowed down immediately to two horses neck to neck. Bruco and Drago's jockeys beat each other mercilessly with their little whips; and finally Bruco had to drop out of the race, running up a side street and into some people as he did so. Drago ran on to victory. However, that was not the end by any means. The first sign of trouble was noted when Drago's jockey dismounted and was immediately pounced upon by some irate members of the Bruco group who gave him a good pummeling before the carabinieri came to his rescue. They carried him off quickly into the communal palace, closing the heavy door behind them. Then the public took to fighting amongst themselves in front of the palace, but mostly with the carabinieri. At first, no one knew why the tumult arose. Things happened so fast. It seems that Bruco had paid Drago to lose the race, and Drago double-crossed him. The Bruco group was all set for a big holiday supper too.

A group of young hoodlums of Bruco paraded up to the judge's stand demanding the palio win banner trophy, which was naturally refused. They insisted, and as the Drago jockey was afraid to venture forth to claim the banner as he was supposed to, the situation became very tense. The carabinieri tried to disperse the gang from beneath the judge's box but could do little. One flourished a pistol, and the crowd retreated in wild disorder for a few moments, but they soon returned. This time they began to climb up into the judge's box. By some unknown means, the judges had all disappeared, leaving the police to handle the situation. One lone carabinieri stood before the banner in defiance, with a rifle across his chest, daring the few who had come into the box to try to steal it. He looked ready to bash in the first one that moved. They retreated slowly. The spectators were in a frenzy, and most of them were rooting for Drago. One or two people had been carried out in covered stretchers from the excitement. I was only hoping that the spectators in this crowded area did not take to fighting amongst themselves; otherwise, there would have been a real slaughter with many trampled upon. The situation was at a standstill for a few minutes, and many thought that Bruco would go away, but one smart guy went up into an apartment adjacent to the judge's box. He dashed out onto the balcony and with a quick thrust pushed the banner on its pole out of the judge's box and into the crowd below. Then all bedlam broke loose. It was quickly torn to shreds so that the Drago men wouldn't get it and pieces, of it were carried away by the victorious Bruco men. They smashed the black and white striped palio pole and waved it disrespectfully at the crowd. That was the end of it temporarily, but tonight there will probably be several broken heads as the feud is carried into the contrada's backstreets.

The unconscionable results of the palio race caused me to wonder as to the readiness of the general public for the acceptance of democratic elections and levelheaded approach so necessary for a future government to function. Of course it is understandable in this very close parochial climate of pride and competition that tempers can easily clash into chaos. Let us hope such energies will be properly directed on a national scale when the time comes.

August 21, 1945

Today we learned that a woman and child were killed when the Bruco horse ran into the crowd yesterday. New restrictions will be imposed on the race from now on. A sad funeral entourage crept down the street to the cemetery the next day.

August 24, 1945

This morning the landlady jacked up the rent to one dollar a day. I told her that it was impossible and that I'll find another place, which I did. When we returned to the house this evening, I told the landlady, and she was very surprised that I had acted so quickly and agreed to cancel the raise. I was glad that Angelina wouldn't have to move again.

August 26, 1945

At lunchtime, I learned that I and six others are to go up as advanced detail to Wiesbaden, Germany. We are to leave tomorrow morning at 7:30 a.m. by plane. I especially didn't want to leave Angelina now. At least she had been here ten days before I left. When I returned to Giannis after chow, I told them the bad news, and Angelina cried. "It was worth the trip even for this short time," she sobbed. Angelina and I took a walk in the park, but we didn't say much. Another sad parting was looming, probably the last.

CHAPTER XXV

NEWS HEADLINE: ***November 20, 1945*****—Nuremberg War Crimes Trial Begins**

August 27, 1945

Saying good-bye to Angelina was quite rough, and she cried and sobbed a great deal, and I made her promise not to come down to the barracks to see me off in the morning because of the terrible scene she might make, even though I promised to return. It was not much comfort. Nevertheless, much as I hated to, I tore myself away and left for camp. Early morning I leave for the airport, bag and baggage. The trip up was uneventful except for one sharp explosion we felt somewhere over Austria. The pilot later said it felt like flack that fell short. Everything in the plane bounced. The pilot, at the time, thought that it might have been a blowout, so without telling us, he landed on a nearby airport runway at Frankfurt, where they would test the wheels. He immediately took off again after not finding any problem and flew to Wiesbaden, our original destination. There was no damage whatsoever. A truck picked us up, and in five minutes we were at our new barracks, which was a former German peacetime barracks, in spite of a damaged condition, something like what we had found at Lido di Roma. We have five buildings, but one is still occupied as of yet. Two men are assigned to sleep in five of them just to keep an eye on things. We picked out clean rooms and parked there. The weather is quite cool.

August 28, 2012

We were issued PX cards today. All of the lieutenant colonels and their crew had us carrying in desks and furniture around and in the headquarters building, and we were tired by suppertime. German civilians are working here now, repairing the sabotaged electrical and plumbing systems.

Private Zwirn who came down here with us speaks some German. I can get along in German just enough, and I don't feel much like fraternizing much anyway. I went into town this evening. Zwirn drove us into town and left us at the Red Cross. People here give you the fish eye and only young kids and eager fräuleins associate with GIs. I noticed an aged couple peering at us through their shuttered window. There is a good deal of wreckage, and I imagine, poverty although people are far better dressed than in Italy. The younger boys stand around in groups smoking and sporting rather long hairdos and furtive glances. We got lost once or twice heading back to the Red Cross to catch a ride back to camp. Several of us walked to Erbenheim about half a mile down the road in darkness. We saw nothing but some moonlit, silhouetted skeletal remains of buildings. The boys were looking for a little beer but found none. There were plenty of fräuleins on bicycles talking and walking with GIs all the way. On the way back, we watched the engineers at the airport working by electric light, pouring concrete on the new six-thousand-foot runways.

August 31, 1945

At ten forty-five, we were looking for some drafting equipment that had been mislaid, and the major thought it was at another airport. My first motor trip in Germany to this other airport was pleasant. The countryside had long spread-out hills, green and cool looking even in the sun. The roads are in very good condition. Bicycle travelers dot the roads, and wayside hikers rest in the grass nearby. Everybody is carrying some kind of knapsack, and a few times I saw what must have been whole families trudging with loaded backpacks back toward Wiesbaden. One smiling woman waved to us in the hopes of getting a ride. Tonight I work on some signs.

September 1, 1945

We are eating with the 302nd now, and I am on KP duty. The eating is only temporary, and so is the KP, I hope. There was a cancelled meeting this morning because Major Ware didn't show up. I continued working all morning on the signs and then left for lunch. I had my hair cut for a dime and went back to work. We now have a barber and a tailor on the premises. At about 2:30 p.m., I knocked off after Major Morgan left. I searched and found a bedstead for my bedspring. A list came out stating the number of occupants in our room was six. We only planned four, but Schermerhorn seems to want to get in with us, but we were against it, although we didn't tell him. He can't seem to take a hint.

September 3, 1945

Van and I found some old 1904 telephones that were in an old building, and we bunked them in his darkroom. Van is a collector. After dinner, the Siena plane got in; and the boys, that's Miller, Snearing, and Epter, flopped into our rooms temporarily.

The Germans are terribly embittered with their fate. There is a feeling of disbelief, coldness, and despair among them. Not so much in relations with us, but among themselves. They are understandably a rather sad-looking populace with nothing of the good nature of the Italians. They had just lost a terrible war, a futile war. Kids always got our sympathy, candy, chocolate, and gum. We worked all afternoon, ate supper, and we just sat around the big table in our room and did whatever we wished, but we could not help wondering how one man could cause such havoc and dupe his countrymen into the preposterous belief of racial superiority and invincibility. Is it possible that enough of the public wished it to be true and didn't care who fell by the wayside?

September 9, 1945

Another cloudy and rainy morning. I picked up my *Stars and Stripes* in the special service office. I worked alone this morning. Everybody wants signs of some kind, and they are running in every five minutes. I put their order on the bottom of the pile and tell them to wait. The building is to be painted, and we are ordered to have our walls cleaned of all soot and dust in readiness. They hope to get displaced persons, known as DPs to do it. Miller and I went to the ARC for a hot shower and a movie. Epter came in later, and we listened to part of a concert and left.

September 10, 1945

It's drizzling this morning. After chow, I took over with the cleaning of our room. We have to have our walls rubbed clean of soot and dirt so that they may be painted soon. It just so happens that both DPs are Polish, and one speaks Italian. Through our conversation, I mentioned my mother's brother, Uncle Joe, to him; and strangely enough, the one who didn't speak Italian had seen him in Baranowicze, Poland, in 1941. I described as much as I could to him through the interpreter. He feels sure that he knows my uncle's bookstore, wife, and two children. He says those two were put on the same and only train with him, but he never saw them again, explaining that they might have escaped when the train broke down at different times. I gave him my uncle's address, and this fellow says he will try to find somebody who lived in Baranowicze who might know more. I hope to hear more tomorrow. During all this, we shoveled and scraped the caked powder off the floor. It was a difficult job. Miller and Epter returned, and we mopped out and wiped everything down with wet rags. Van handed out a lot of candy and stuff that he received from home and was originally intended for the kids back in Siena. Epter and Miller played a drawn-out and quiet game of checkers.

September 11, 1945

Miller keeps working on signs. I picked up a few books from Special Services. We went to the Red Cross tonight, heard a concert by the Wiesbaden Symphony Orchestra, and we stuffed ourselves with doughnuts and Coca-Cola. Miller and I took off at about two thirty and went to town. There was a park around the American Red Cross that we really saw for the first time. There was plenty of fraternizing going on there. Miller and Epter were playing checkers again. A new detail has started today. Last night, a furious general saw someone lower the American flag, stuff it into a sack, and throw it inside the building. Therefore, starting tonight, a special color guard will take the flag down at 5:00 p.m. and put it up at seven every day in the morning. The three-man detail lasts for a week, and then it is rotated. Miller and

I and another person are the first crew, and we put on a stiff military performance for the benefit of the brass who had ordered it.

September 15, 1945

Up at the crack of 6:30 a.m. to get ready for our color guard detail. At five minutes to seven, we walked out and, with not a soul watching us in the misty morning, raised the flag in all the ceremony that we could muster considering the uninspiring surroundings. For all we knew, the general might be secretly peering down from a window. Heaven help us if we are caught off guard fooling around. Rain again today and it was generally dreary all day. I brought a radio from headquarters and hooked it up. We hear American broadcasts and German broadcasts.

September 16, 1945

Our working hours have now been changed from 8:00 to 8:30 a.m., but the flag goes up at the same time, so we have to get up at six forty-five anyway.

September 21, 1945

This was our last morning of color guard, and we heaved a sigh of relief as we hoisted the flag for the last time. However, little did we know that we had pulled the ace of all military boners. At about 10:00 a.m., our sergeant of the guard came rushing in carrying our two pistols and belts. "Quick! Come out!" he said, "The flag is upside down!" It was incredible but true as we looked up. Luckily there was no wind, and only a particularly observant person would have noticed it, but it was directly in front of the general's office. We dashed out in formation and lowered the flag hastily, got it back, and disappeared from the scene as quickly as possible. That was the last we heard of it, and we sweated awhile expecting a fuming general to throw us to the lions.

September 22, 1945

News as to discharge systems holds top priority on gossip these days. Everybody asks, "How many points do you have?"

September 24, 1945

I decided to help Mulholland in getting the squadron laundry ready. He got six German girls to do the washing, and they were happy to get the work. I spent the rest of the morning playing the piano next to the mess hall.

October 1, 1945

Sweating out a new "go home" list. We seventy pointers don't expect to be on it.

October 5, 1945

A long-awaited letter from Angelina came today and an attractive picture of herself. She is getting along well, it seems, for the time being.

October 9, 1945

Yesterday Van told me he was going to take out a motion picture projector permit and asked if I would be interested in doing the same. It was through a request of the Special Services. I agreed, and this morning I picked up a pamphlet on the sound projector. We will have a tryout in a Manheim Signal Corps laboratory. A Lieutenant Marburger of Special Services accompanied us. We then proceeded on the spacious Autobahn Highway, pride of Hitler's road system, to the outskirts of Manheim. There the Signal Corps asked us many questions about the operation of the projector. We nodded yes to everything because we had handled similar equipment. He made out permits for us, and we picked up two new projectors and screens. We put on a movie show tonight at the Ninety-seventh ADS. I operated the projector, and Van watched. The audience applauded, which made us feel kinship with the movie characters' performance.

October 10, 1945

This afternoon Lieutenant Marburger asked me if I'd like to show a movie over at the general's house. I couldn't very well refuse, and I loved the chance to see his home on an island in the middle of the winding Rhine River. He said it was all right for Van to go along too. We made an appointment so that the general's driver could pick us up at six fifteen. We were to eat supper there too. At about 5:30 p.m.,

Sergeant Derry, the general's driver, showed up at the barracks in a jeep for us. He said he had to get back early and that he'd like us to leave now. We were disappointed that he didn't call in a plush staff car. The motorboat anchorage was twelve miles away along the Rhine River. Derry parked the car in a garage, and we walked down to the little dock alongside of which was moored a motorboat of about thirty feet in length. Some men were refueling it, and we boarded it carrying the film case. The Rhine is wide at this point and calm. The house lights from across the river show as we approached and details became much clearer. A large type of craft was moored at a dock as we pulled in. Two MPs were stationed there. Up a gravel walk we approached the house just as a few officers came out escorting two women. They said they'd be back later for supper and asked what picture was to be shown. I responded and saluted.

We entered the steam-heated vestibule, very large and decorated like a conservatory. The general was inside but not in view when we came in. The home was magnificent and formerly the "hideaway" of a countess with a Nazi bigshot—three stories and a basement with a total of thirty-seven rooms. It was furnished conservatively with many good paintings and antiques on display. Nothing was out of place. Persian carpets covered the finest imported wood floors. It had a feeling of being ripe and mellow, something like an English baronial home. Two enlisted men showed us to the drawing room in which there were two grand pianos. We went into the dining room to test out the setting for the projector, and I found the dining table beautifully set with five tall candles. Finger bowls with floating flower petals in them caught my eye. I was thinking how nice to be a general. Van and I were testing the sound system when we discovered the amplifier was not working. The general suddenly showed up in the doorway and said, "Good evening," to which we replied in upright unison, "Good evening, sir." I had seen him a few times at headquarters, but I observed him better here at close quarters. He must be fifty and without the accompanying pompous, overdignified airs some are said to have. He plunged right in and tried to help us fix the thing, but it was futile. Then he left to eat, and so did we, separately downstairs. The caretakers served us a bite. Their quarters were very adequate. After supper, the other four officers joined us and asked if we had eaten and were a little disappointed that there would be no showing tonight. There was one young colonel, two lieutenant colonels, and a major. Just those five men lived in this thirty-seven room house with sixteen civilians to help. I sat in that luxurious drawing room, mesmerized by those beautiful pianos that probably nobody used and the rare books that probably nobody read. Going from our hovel-like barracks was like a time warp shift to this Shangri-la on the Rhine. I hoped I wouldn't have to take much more of this cycling between rags to riches. It was great going but depressing coming back. Our return trip on that beautiful, winding tree-lined river and the full moon was really spectacular.

October 19, 1945

Returned at 2:00 p.m. with Dave to Mr. Bauman's house and found him heavily dressed in an overcoat in his living room. The drafting equipment had not arrived as yet, and I was beginning to lose confidence in him. We had a long discussion on world politics over a few cigarettes and a bottle of champagne, which he kindly poured for us. We drank almost profusely, maybe because it was a good-old German custom never to leave a bottle unfinished. He works for the CID as an interpreter, speaking very good English. He was not a party member, he boasted, being formerly a hotel manager in Stuttgart. He told us many stories of his travels and with his connection in the hotel business. He was most congenial, friendly, and had an infectious smile that would have produced a natural liking in anyone he met. His laugh was contagious and remained quite levelheaded even though he lost everything he had in Stuttgart. This house belonged to the first man we met here in our first visit. When the CID moved Bauman in, they told the owner that he had to share the house and didn't want him to get sore about it; otherwise, he would be evicted. We stopped at the Red Cross for a snack and got a lift home in a staff car with some of the boys in the Stat section.

October 20, 1945

Nothing new except that we will probably be leaving early in November, but to where?

October 21, 1945

It was misty, and many of the boys who intended to go on the scheduled boat ride up the Rhine didn't go. Those who did go, fourteen of them, had a serious accident. On the return trip, the truck turned over, and many were badly injured. All fourteen went to the hospital. Schermerhorn was one of the seriously injured.

October 22, 1945

Went to town at about 10:00 a.m. The people are as busy as ever shopping and going about their business. This afternoon I went in again after buying PX rations and looked around for any items that I could send Angelina in case I accumulated any cash.

October 24, 1945

Morale isn't very good these days because of the delays in military discharging. I suspect that some available ships are being used for commercial trade purposes. Officers are friendly and informal now that the war is over.

October 25, 1945

Dave and I went to see Bauman this afternoon, but he had no drafting sets as yet. He ushered us into a new room of his home and brought out a bottle of Schnapps, which almost knocked me off my chair. He toasted the memory of each old friend with a drink. Bauman likes to recall World War I and the incredible inflation period that followed and how his hotel employees had to be paid every day because they never would have been able to carry so much paper at the end of the week.

October 26, 1945

The processing of our records finally began yesterday for possible discharge, but no announcements are made. I spent all afternoon waiting around and in the meantime sent a few packages off to Angelina.

October 29, 1945

This afternoon I went into town and bought myself a collection of postage stamps to rid myself of some of my German money. This evening Van and I went out to the general's house again and showed a movie for him and his staff. We had no problems as we did last time. Some of the servants gathered in the dining room to watch also.

November 3, 1945

A second chalazion is developing on my lower right eyelid. The doctor prescribed heat for as long and as hot as I could stand.

November 4, 1945

I continued the treatment all morning. In the afternoon, Van, Epter, and I took our cameras including one 16 mm movie camera and went to visit Mainz. That city and Nuremburg are the two most bombed-out cities. It was a frightful sight. Hardly a building was left intact, and rarely an inhabited one was found. Mostly there was rubble and piles of it neatly pushed away from the streets so that people could walk. Narrow gauged train tracks lined many streets to carry dump carts of rubble away. It was cloudy today, and the drabness of the sky blended in with the mangled steel and stone to form a distressing picture of cold loneliness and deserted wasteland. Through the narrow streets we wended our way with always the same view before us—pieces of broken architecture jutting up like fractured bones out of torn flesh. Few people are around but are well dressed. Children romp on the rock piles and the rusted iron rubble carts and are apparently as content as kids on a sandpile. These innocent victims can turn anything into a playground. We walked back over the "highest, widest, longest U.S. engineered bridge" in the world as the signs on either end boasted. It is a remarkable piece of construction built entirely on the ruins of the old one that was bombed into the river below. American MPs guard one end, and French police on the Mainz side guard their end. All civilians must have permission to cross. We waited on the American side while an MP found us a lift going to Wiesbaden.

November 6, 1945

I decided to go into town with whatever German money I had left and buy something. There was very little to buy as I already knew.

November 7, 1945

Today the men thirty-five years and older, if any, left on their first leg to the States. The good news was that all sixty and seventy pointers are to leave Monday came through. I sent a box of mail and other incidentals home for safekeeping and began packing and throwing out what junk I could. I knew my departure would be soon.

November 11, 1945

My birthday—twenty-seven years old. I received cards from the family. That's two birthdays spent overseas. Miller, Epter, and I packed all day and accomplished little. I finally ended up with two barracks bags going home. At least we're well motivated.

November 12, 1945

Up bright and early and stumble around getting down to breakfast. About 8:00 a.m., we carry our bags downstairs into one of a few trucks. We say good-bye to Van and got a lift to the old motor pool for transportation. Then on to Frankfurt where we found the old, familiar smelly forty and eights railroad cars waiting for us. Our destination was a small village on the outskirts of Paris. It happened to be a sixty-man car for eighteen men, and we were therefore not as crowded as on our Casablanca to Tunis trip in similar cars. Stomping around the cars brought back memories of almost two years ago when the first half of this round trip was just beginning for many of us. Some of the same boys who came into Casablanca are on this train. One is wearing a jaunty fez and another sporting a battered top hat pierced by a fancy stickpin. Another, tipsy, was pushing them around in a cart. At about 1:00 p.m. we shoved off to Mainz twenty miles away. Progress was slow. The sun set, and we unrolled our bedding. I brought along the mattress and made myself somewhat more comfortable than on my first trip. We still slept fully clothed, however, due to the cold. We had K rations for food instead of C rations, which is an improvement. Progress was agonizingly slow with numerous unaccountable stops all along the way. A coal stove installed by some moonlight requisitioning prevented frostbite.

November 13, 1945

Sleeping could have been better. The jolting was very bad. At about 8:00 a.m., I awoke, and we were standing still. We hadn't moved for six hours. We passed the day snoozing and looking out onto the misty scenery. Our train was split into two parts, the seventy-five pointers and over, and the seventy or less pointers, on our way to Poix, our destination.

November 14, 1945

The black market continued with the GIs getting rid of their excess goodies. My French was awful. When we hit Amiens, we only had twelve miles or so to go to Poix. It was dark when we arrived, and trucks took us quickly to camp. Getting into the muddy camp at night was bad, and tents were hard to find. My two barracks bags were dragged along, mostly in the mud, with my haversack hanging around my neck.

November 15, 1945

At 9:00 a.m., we had our records processed. Our point scores were rechecked, and we sweated it out while they did it. That came off all right. The latrine situation is quite a frosty one, out in the open. The twenty-fifth of December would be the day of our ship's sailing.

November 16, 1945

Up early but it was too cold to go to breakfast. The mud thaws out about noon then gets nicely slushy. Our shoes and pants are always covered with it. This morning I walked to Poix and showered at a GI post and looked around town. It was typical of small French villages. Dirt streets, little shops and cafés, children wearing culottes, ducks and geese waddling about in the street oblivious to human and horse traffic. Quiet blanketed all.

November 17, 1945

Here and there I bump into a stray friendly Frenchman who always has a happy "Bonjour" to offer. There were flocks of geese all over. I worry over Angelina now that I won't get her letters for a long time. She does know I'm leaving for home.

November 20, 1945

We are going to Marseilles for embarkation. That's another rotten trip in those rattletrap stinking forty and eights. Due to unexplained delays, each passing day is telling on our patience. Yet I know our officers are doing all they can. After all, we're literally all in the same boat.

November 25, 1945

Started packing this evening and throwing out junk again.

November 26, 1945

Got up at 5:00 a.m. and it was a very cold morning. We dragged all our bags outside the tent, and about 5:30 a.m. we started tearing down the tent, pushing the wooden sides in and taking out the stove. At 6:00 a.m., we returned to the area to find many warming bonfires blazing away. We all gathered around the fire, piling on boxes and broken chairs. When we were roasted on one side, we turned around like a pig on a spit for the other. We went by truck to the Poix railroad station and, after we boarded a car and got comfortably settled, were told we were in the wrong car. In town, the bakery refused to sell any bread to the GIs because of a shortage, so we found a little girl, gave her some money, and she bought me a loaf of bread. I gave her some gum for her kindness. We pulled out of the station at about 1:30 p.m. Progress was better than our previous trip. At least we had cots.

November 27, 1945

I slept in my coveralls, which I had been wearing since Saturday. We headed south through the Rhone Valley. It gets dark early now, but candlelights brightened us up.

November 28, 1945

Made good time today and we hope to be in Marseilles tonight. Finally, Marseilles while still in daylight. The air was filled with music coming from the PA system. The stove was kept going, and later I cooked up a mess of "requisitioned" meat and noodles from our supply car.

November 29, 1945

It was 5:30 a.m. when the trucks called for us. We got everything out of the train and built bonfires to keep warm at our final stop. The camp is enormous at about fifty-five thousand men in all; and everything, including streets, areas, and buildings are systematically numbered. We delayed taking showers because water was in short supply, and there were hundreds of guys waiting. After dinner, we shaved in some hot water made over a tiny stove. There are sixteen men in these large tents. The camp reminds me of the one in Casablanca, not too attractive. German POWs do most of the work, and food is good.

November 30, 1945

We had a formation at nine in the morning and more speeches and handed in our francs for currency exchange. We signed customs statements, and I wrote letters to my mother and to Angelina.

December 1, 1945

A movie called *It's Your America* especially meant for us redeployees to build up morale and confidence. Nothing new as to shipping but an outfit that came with us has been alerted already and should leave today.

December 2, 1945

First hot rumor came today with news that a French liner would take us on Wednesday. God, let it be true! There was a roll call at 9:00 a.m., and when we had all assembled, we were told that our baggage would be inspected. I had to give up a small movie camera used in fighter aircrafts.

December 3, 1945

Epter came over today, happy with the whole world. It was great to see him again. We promised to meet in Brooklyn and parted with a manly embrace.

December 4, 1945

This morning we were told definitely that we were sailing Wednesday or Thursday on the *SS Frederick Lykes*, a U.S. transport. I sent a cablegram home and to Angelina with the news of our departure. The weather has been clear lately but very windy. I'm hoping for a smooth voyage as a welcome back to America.

December 5, 1945

Moving out was again confirmed at morning formation. We are all restricted to the area.

December 6, 1945

Everything was returned to us, baggage and pistols and souvenirs. Had an extra snack at 10:00 a.m.—melted cheese and bread was handed out to us. At eleven, everything was cleaned out of our tents and enough items to open a PX were thrown out in the trash barrels. They meant to travel light this time because where we were going those goodies and more could be plentiful and bought without a ration card. Two hundred of us loaded onto big trucks, and we joined a much larger convoy of men—creeping slowly over the tricky narrow roads down toward the port fifteen miles away into the low flat port area. We boarded the ship rather quickly at 1:15 p.m. It was very different from the boarding at Hampton Roads in Virginia. There was no fanfare or music, but I never noticed. The Red Cross girls gave out travel bag kits as we walked up the gangplank. We were quickly assigned bunks, and our luggage came a few minutes later. *Adieu la belle, France*!

It was problem enough to get myself in among the ventilating pipes and girders to say nothing of throwing or carrying that blasted barracks bag, so I just stayed down hoping none of the lieutenants around would mind. Lieutenant Johnson was my compartment chief, and he saw my predicament. He jokingly ordered that if I wasn't up there in the bunk immediately, he'd toss me and the baggage up together. He grabbed my bag while I climbed up and squeezed it in. It was beginning to get as crowded up there as a Marx brothers stateroom comedy movie. Tugs pulled us out by 3:30 p.m. into the channel. I was down below and so didn't have an opportunity to toss a personal farewell to the European theater of operations.

At 4:00 p.m. we were tossing around like a cork on the water, but I didn't feel bad until I stood up. I grabbed my life preserver, and up I went with another fellow to get chow. As soon as I hit the deck, it was dark. I got very sick and grabbed the first thing that came into sight while I barfed. It happened to be a greased steel cable on one of the derricks. I wasn't in a position to be observant at the time and hardly felt the grease on my hands. The wind was very bad, and we rocked from side to side at a dangerous angle. Everything was rolling over the deck including the guys in the mess line, a large number of whom would have gone over the side had the railing not stopped them when they all piled up during one of the ship's more severe lurches. My friend propped me up between two little shelters, and I lay over a covered winch for a while out of the spray and the wind. I began to feel a little better, but the others who were stalwart enough to chance the mess line finally got the assistance of a long safety rope put up by the crew. All around me, I could feel fellow sufferers groaning and spitting. Nobody curses, they just pray for the ship to stop rolling even for just a minute. I was one of them.

I chanced going below after being out more than four hours. I loosened as much clothing as possible so that I could undress quickly and get into bed. As I climbed up, I found that all the stuff I laid out on the air duct had fallen down to the floor. I avoided a box full of vomit as I descended to look for my stuff, which was all over the place. I squirmed my way into bed after collecting my things and lay there in my clothes the whole night with a hot ventilator blowing on my face. Come what may, nothing could dampen my vision of the New York harbor arrival.

December 7, 1945

The morning found the sea to be calm and the sun to brighten things up. The public address system made an announcement about Gibraltar to be passed sometime tomorrow. They played music and mentioned something about the ship newspaper soon to be issued. I felt fine as I waited on the stretched chow line for breakfast. These lines take about half an hour to go through, and the line itself takes all sorts of turns and twists, and strangely going upstairs and down, finally reaching the mess hall where we must present a chow ticket for punching—no complaints.

December 9, 1945

The north coast of Africa appeared to our left as we passed through the Mediterranean funnel leading to Gibraltar; then the shadowy outline of Gibraltar appeared on the horizon. At eleven, everybody on the right side caused us to list slightly. It appears as an island at first because the huge rock is connected to the mainland by a flat isthmus and is heavily armed. We pulled into the harbor for refueling, which gave us plenty of opportunity to study the harbor and the vicinity. Soon, from apparently nowhere, little boats came out to meet us. Yes, they were selling stuff or at least that is what they intended. They waved a few big Spanish scarves, perfume, and liquor. However, they were just things to be bought as souvenirs from Gibraltar. Liquor was bought by many, but an announcement was made saying that all liquor found would be thrown overboard.

Once or twice, the ship started up its engines to maneuver into the harbor, and the little boats ran for cover. They soon returned again, feisty as ever, and business resumed. A tanker pulled up alongside and began pumping oil into us on the starboard side. The port side was dotted with little boats. Somebody on the highest deck turned a fire hose on them to drive this "illegal trading" away. Many got drenched when they threw themselves over their dry goods as a protective measure. It didn't last long, and they soon returned. At about four thirty, the trading ceased, and the little boats turned away for their mile sail back to shore. All during the trading, money was sent down first, and goods came up second. The tanker left us, and a few minutes later we left. The rock was all lit up. It was a colorful sight, like an apparition in the blackness. I stayed on deck until about ten thirty because the night was calm and only a light breeze wafted over the bay as we headed out to sea.

December 10, 1945

This morning the ship was riding over high swells, and stomachs rose and fell with each one. The bow and the stern seesawed while the mid-ship was the quietest section. I felt pretty well nevertheless and missed no meals. At noon, the ship's report told us that we had about three thousand miles to go.

December 11, 1945

The ship is taking the reduced swells calmly. Breakfast and spirits are great. High hopes and calm seas are on the dessert list.

December 13, 1945

They tried an outdoor movie tonight by hoisting a screen between two masts. Everybody stood, and although it was crowded, it was welcomed. I had seen the picture, so I left and stood on the fantail. Some guy there cornered me with stories of what he did before the war and about his relatives, mentioning all by name as if I personally knew them. I was caught up with his good humor and before I knew it found myself doing the very same thing.

December 14, 1945

After breakfast, I try to sit on a port side and let the food settle before it decides to do its own thing. The benches are always full, so I lean over the railing with many others, not to barf, but to enjoy the very warm sun playing on the gentle swells. When I sit, I read a detective story.

December 19, 1945

We made good speed when the sea became very smooth. In the morning, we ran into a bad storm that rocked us badly. The sweating was almost over. We knew we'd be in port by morning come what may. Four days longer than our expectations. We were to rise at 3:30 a.m. with an early breakfast. The full effect of our glorious homecoming was just beginning to creep into our sleepy souls.

December 20, 1945

Our last night out at sea was uneventful but smoother than usual because our speed had been reduced. At 4:30 a.m., we saw the first lighthouses, and an hour later the low flickering lights of land. It was ice-cold, and we only stayed out a few minutes at a time. Then we saw other ships and more lights. Dawn exploded, and we were home. We approached very slowly, a dock painted in red, white, and blue with a big "Welcome Home—Well Done" banner. Some tiny figures were visible on the pier. "Women!" shouted one. A brass band came out to play "Hail, Hail, The Gang's All here." There weren't many greeters besides the dockhands, but they waved to us cheerily as we sidled in. The starboard rail was jammed by us as our attention was focused down to three or four welcoming, prancing WACs smiling like magazine-cover models. They carried papers and rosters in preparation for our debarking. That was about 11:00 a.m. We were last to debark. Nothing could stop us now. At 1:15 p.m., the long-awaited call for the 705th to debark came. That was us. It was not long in answering, and a few minutes later with heavy loads on our backs, but lighthearted, we hurried down the gangplank to touch the promised land.

POSTSCRIPT

Roll Call on the dock—quick customs inspection—fast train to Fort Dix, New Jersey—short talk on reenlisting—honorable discharge and bus back to Manhattan.

The rhythm and rumble of the subway to Church Avenue, Brooklyn, was a glorious victory march on the road to home, family, and to whatever the future would bring.

My little Angelina? Happy ending. She had the guts to make the toughest, longest, and most important voyage of her life to the United States. I never doubted her determination. We lived happily together for sixty-three years until God needed a feisty, loving sidekick and called her. But that's another story.

SYNOPSIS

World War II was upon us. Survival on both sides was paramount, sometimes disregarding simple humaneness. We were strongly influenced by how the civilians faced the many shortages and upheavals of their former lives. To the contrary, ensuring a fountain of plenty for the soldiers' existence was the military PX "minishopping center." I and others must confess to abusing the privileges afforded by the generous handout it made available. Cigarettes, chocolate, chewing gum, coffee, sugar, and other basic elements (no alcohol) provided cash for us. None of these basic necessities were available to civilians. As a result, intensive small-scale black marketeering was inevitable. Survival demanded it.

For our customers, it made life tolerable. For us it gave access to much of life's guilty pleasures—what we missed most, good food, some fun, liquor, and female companionship. Yes, they were the basic human drives, but understandably and undeniably still human; not the time for self-critiquing, or so we thought.

Some of my adventures finally led me to my future Sicilian wife, who taught me the true meaning of steadfast affection. Her laborious travels following my movements through war torn Italy convinced me and finally led to her joining me in New York.

Visions of home were never far. "There is no place like home" never had truer meaning.

Thanks,
Milton Pashcow

Edwards Brothers Malloy
Thorofare, NJ USA
July 26, 2013